IMAGES
of Rail

THE GREAT NORTHERN RAILWAY IN MARIAS PASS

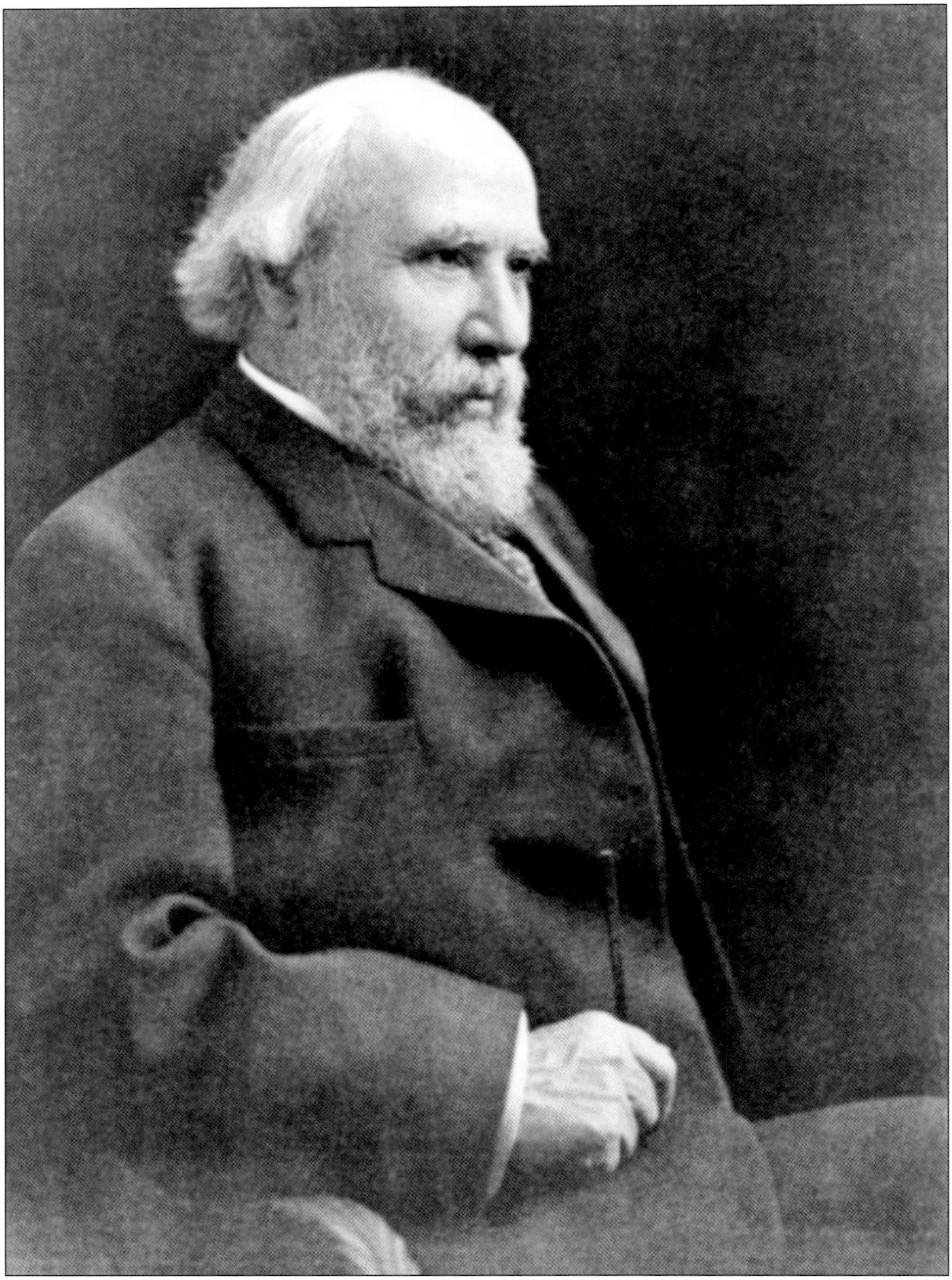

James "Jim" Jerome Hill, also known as the "Empire Builder," was the driving force behind the formation of the Great Northern Railway. (Author's collection.)

On the Cover: The Great Northern Railway was instrumental in promoting Glacier National Park. Montana's Rocky Mountain Front provided a perfect backdrop for the 1955 version of the eastbound streamlined mid-century *Empire Builder* at Rising Wolf. (Great Northern Railway.)

IMAGES
of Rail

THE GREAT NORTHERN RAILWAY IN MARIAS PASS

Dale W. Jones

ARCADIA
PUBLISHING

ISBN 978-1-4671-2519-2

Published by Arcadia Publishing
Charleston, South Carolina

Printed in the United States of America

Library of Congress Control Number: 2017933997

For all general information, please contact Arcadia Publishing:
Telephone 843-853-2070
Fax 843-853-0044
E-mail sales@arcadiapublishing.com
For customer service and orders:
Toll-Free 1-888-313-2665

Visit us on the Internet at www.arcadiapublishing.com

To all railroad workers who have battled Marias Pass in winter cold, summer heat, and spring flood keeping Jim Hill's dream alive.

Contents

Acknowledgments

Many historians admit that after years of researching a subject, the names of some individuals who contributed details to the final story may have been forgotten. First, I need to acknowledge the efforts of volunteers in the various libraries and historical societies I visited, many of whom are operating with limited resources. The passion these folks display for documenting and preserving local history is commendable. Below is a list of the contributors I could remember, and I thank you for your assistance. If I have omitted someone, it was not deliberate.

I want to posthumously thank Dave Emerson, Mike Denuty, Ken Good, Ted Holloway, Dan Perkins, and Doug Snackenberg for the many conversations and railfan excursions we shared together. I am grateful for railroad historian and master model railroad builder Gerald "Jerry" Quinn, who generously allowed me to peruse his extensive collection of Pacific Northwest photographs. A thank-you is owed to Kevin McCready for sharing his vast storehouse of early Northwest Montana newspapers and connecting me with the Ed Krona family and their invaluable 1920s Marias Pass photographs. My appreciation goes to John Langlot and his efforts to convince Harold Absalonson that his father's exceptional winter Marias Pass photographs would provide a personal view of combating dangerous snowslides. Lastly, I thank Charles "Chuck" Hatler, Bob Kelly, Jim Mattson, Cordell Newby, and other members of the Great Northern Railway Historical Society and the Pacific Northwest Rail Archive for their assistance.

My collection of railroad photographs and memorabilia spans 50 years. During that time, I have gathered materials from a variety of sources, including original owners, photographers, online groups, swap meets, and donors who wish to remain anonymous. As the images have circulated from collector to collector, the identities of some photographers may have been lost. If I have used your photograph without proper credit, it was unintentional.

Of course, heartfelt thanks go to my wife, Bonnie, for her unfailing support throughout the years, and lastly, to Stacia Bannerman and the staff at Arcadia Publishing for providing me the opportunity to write this book on my favorite subject—the Great Northern Railway in Marias Pass.

INTRODUCTION

The Rocky Mountains in what would become the state of Montana were a formidable challenge for any railroad seeking a route to the Pacific coast. The Great Northern was not the first railroad to conquer the Northern Rockies. The Northern Pacific Railroad reached the Rocky Mountains in 1882–1883 but could not find a pass lower in elevation than the 5,702-foot Bozeman Pass or the 5,556-foot Continental Divide crossing at Mullan Pass. Our story will follow Great Northern rails from Browning, Montana, through Marias Pass to Whitefish with a side trip to Kalispell-Somers and the lesser-known Haskell Pass. Traveling east from the Flathead Valley through the almost 100 miles of trackage into Marias Pass, the rails snake through narrow canyons, cross the swift Middle Fork of the Flathead River, and twist through numerous snowsheds and tunnels on their way to the Continental Divide at 5,213 feet above sea level. As Rocky Mountain passes go, Marias Pass is one of the lowest crossings in actual elevation of any of the major railroads in North America.

The search for a railroad route through the northwestern Rocky Mountains had been pursued since the 1850s. In March 1853, Secretary of War Jefferson Davis appointed Isaac Stevens (no relation to John F. Stevens of Marias Pass fame), governor of the Washington Territory, to lead a survey party west through the Dakotas, Montana, and Idaho to assess the feasibility of a transcontinental railroad across the northern United States. After six months of exploration, Stevens arrived at Fort Vancouver, Washington, on November 19, 1853. The final version of the survey was published in 1859, but the outbreak of the Civil War in 1861 prevented any railroad expansion at that time.

In 1889, James J. Hill, the power behind the Great Northern Railway, had pushed his line into Central Montana and down through Great Falls to the ore-rich Butte mines. Economic conditions at the time convinced Hill to complete the routing of his railroad to the Pacific. Jim Hill wanted to know if it was possible to cross the Continental Divide at a lower elevation than preceding railroads. In November 1889, Elberdge H. Beckler, chief engineer for the Great Northern, summoned John F. Stevens to Helena, Montana, seeking his aid in determining if there was such a route through the mountains. If a direct route across the Montana Rockies could be located, it would shorten the railway's distance to the Pacific by more than 100 miles.

Questions have been raised and debated for years as to whether John F. Stevens can be credited with the actual discovery of Marias Pass. Many stories, some of which include evil spirits, circulate concerning who found the pass first; some believe that Native Americans did and purposely hid the pass. On closer inspection, history may have been manipulated by a railroad publicity campaign. In an effort to romanticize Stevens's discovery of Marias Pass, the Great Northern Railway's publicity department composed a press release in 1959 describing the finding of Marias Pass:

> His [John Stevens's] small party consisted of a mule team, a driver and a saddle horse, who proceeded for a distance and then refused to continue. Colonel Stevens induced a Flathead Indian to accompany him from that point. They fashioned snowshoes from frames and cowhide for easier movement through the deep snow. Shortly after, the Indian dropped out and made camp, a few miles from the true summit. Colonel Stevens later reported he finally walked directly into what now is known as Marias Pass after a few futile attempts. In order to determine if the pass was the lowest passage between the mountains and the top of the Divide, he continued West until he discovered a creek draining West into the Pacific watershed.

In a letter written years later, Colonel Stevens wrote, "The short days of winter made a rapid move necessary, and after a terrifically hard and exhausting struggle, I managed to get back to the summit where I remained all night . . . It was almost impossible to build and keep a fire going, so I tramped a track about 100 yards in length and walked it back and forth until enough daylight broke to make it safe for travel." Constant motion prevented him from falling asleep and freezing to death, and one advantage of the extreme cold on the summit was that "the mosquitoes didn't bother [him]." Upon returning to the sleeping Indian, he found him half frozen. They made it back to their party and learned the temperature there was 40 degrees below zero. From an aneroid reading he took while in the pass, Stevens knew he had crossed the Continental Divide at the lowest point north of Lordsburg, New Mexico. The Great Northern Railway built through Marias Pass without a tunnel at an elevation that is 350 feet lower than the Northern Pacific route. In 1925, a statue was erected at the discovery site to commemorate Stevens's achievement. On the occasion, and in his usual calm manner, Stevens remarked, "I regarded it at the time as only another engineering experience."

This account might be considered the embryonic text of all other transmutations of the John Stevens story. In the author's research collection, there are dozens of different references using the same words of the above passage. Other accounts of the discovery of the pass state that fellow engineers Elberdge H. Beckler and Charles Haskell or local resident Ed Boyle had located the summit of Marias Pass before John Stevens. There is also the possibility that some other explorer should receive the accolades. Regardless of who was first through Marias Pass, John F. Stevens did in fact document the lowest elevation railroad crossing in Montana, but probably without the bravado bestowed on him in later years.

My interest in the Great Northern Railway began in the 1960s. Montana has always been somewhat of an enigma to me. I tried to visualize trains in Marias Pass at places with intriguing names such as Red Eagle, Blacktail, Rising Wolf, and Triple Divide. I often wondered about the extensive operations at Essex and the massive wooden snowsheds. As the years passed, I lived at Essex and Glacier National Park, which allowed me to visit locations that were once just a dream. The objective of this book is to take the reader on a pictorial journey through Marias Pass on the Great Northern Railway. This mountain railroad is James J. Hill's legacy. Upon retiring in 1912, Hill said, "Most men who have really lived have had, in some shape, their great adventure. This railway is mine."

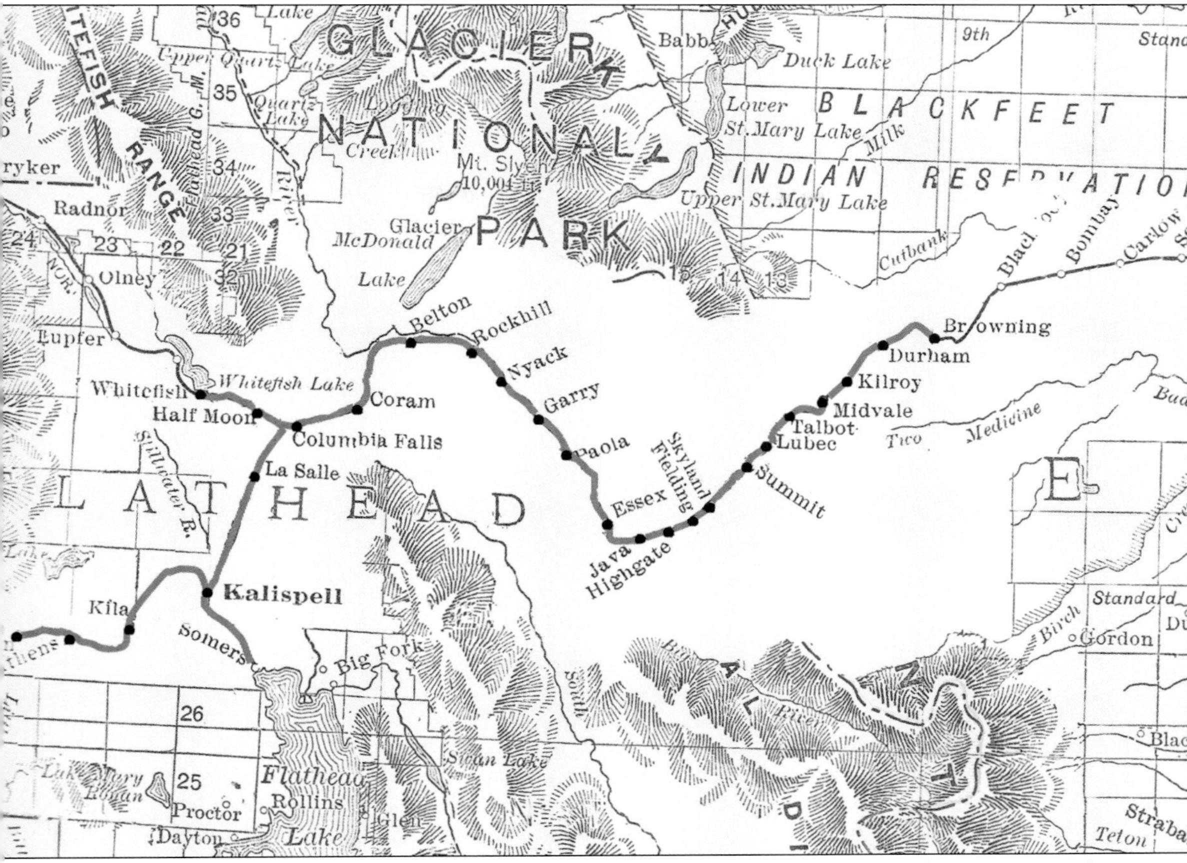

What is now referred to as Marias Pass encompasses an area of diverse geography, scenery, and weather. Following the map east to west, Browning could be considered the entry point of Marias Pass from the prairie. In the 12 miles from Browning to Summit, the railroad approaches the Rocky Mountain Front; from Summit, the route parallels Bear Creek and the Middle Fork of the Flathead River through Essex downgrade to Belton. After leaving Glacier National Park at West Glacier, the vast Flathead Valley opens up at Bad Rock Canyon, providing access to Flathead Lake, Kalispell, and Whitefish. (Author's collection.)

One

Beginnings

History of Marias Pass

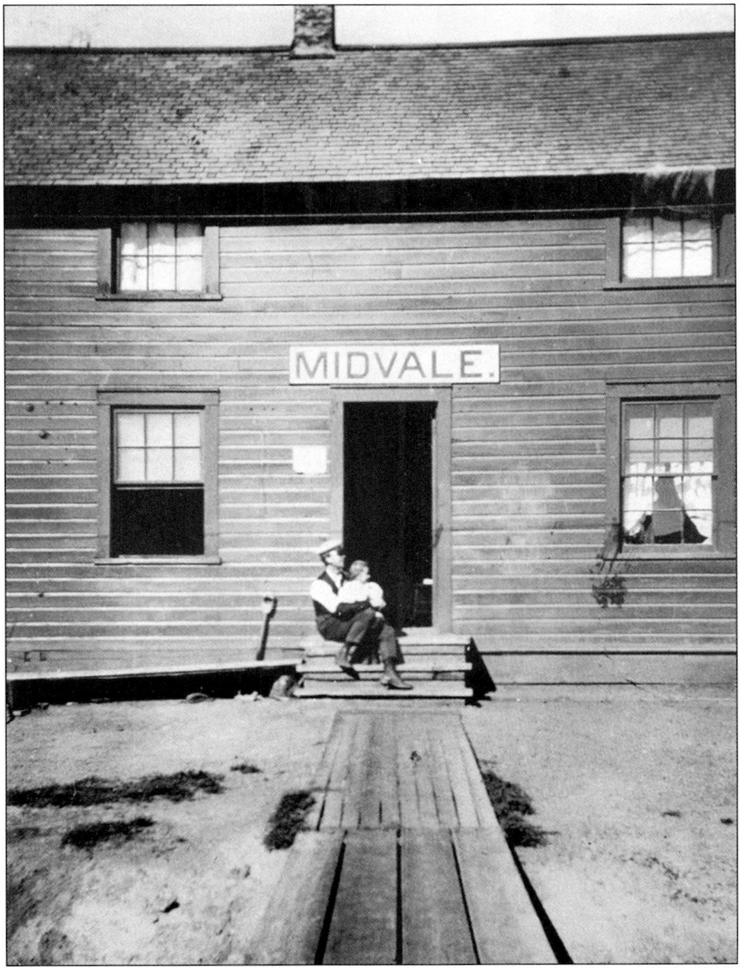

The Great Northern Railway as an operating entity was established in September 1889. Construction of the Pacific Extension began in October 1889 at Pacific Junction, Montana. At this early date, the path through the Rockies had not been selected, but by early 1890, engineers had located a route through Marias Pass and to the Pacific coast. Midvale, later known as Glacier Park, was one of the small towns developed along the Rocky Mountain Front. (Author's collection.)

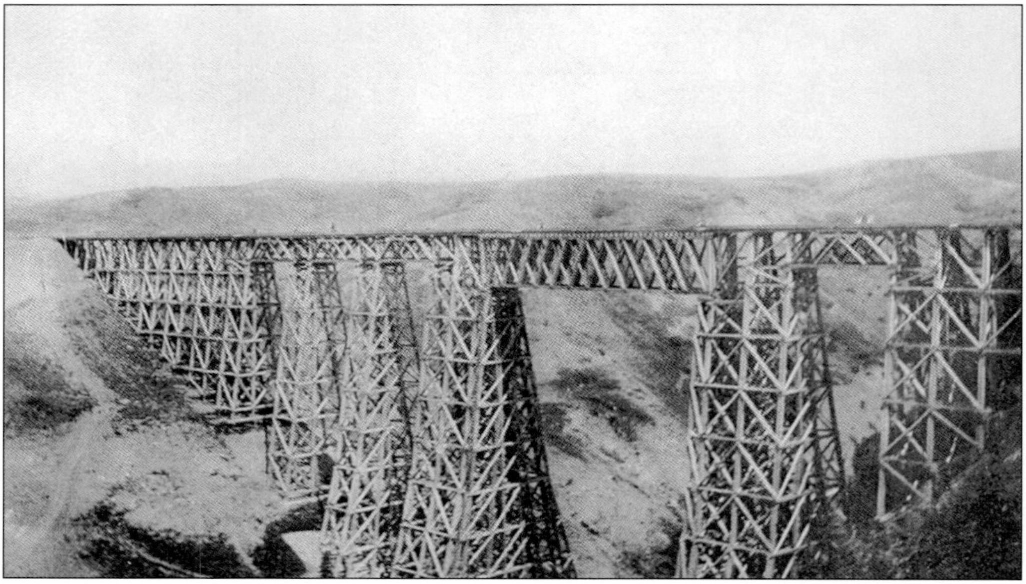

Before beginning the climb into Marias Pass, the crossing of the Two Medicine River at the eastern edge of the Rocky Mountain Front required a spectacular wooden trestle. The 751-foot-long structure was 211 feet from river to rail, appearing from a distance to be built from thousands of board feet of matchsticks. (Author's collection.)

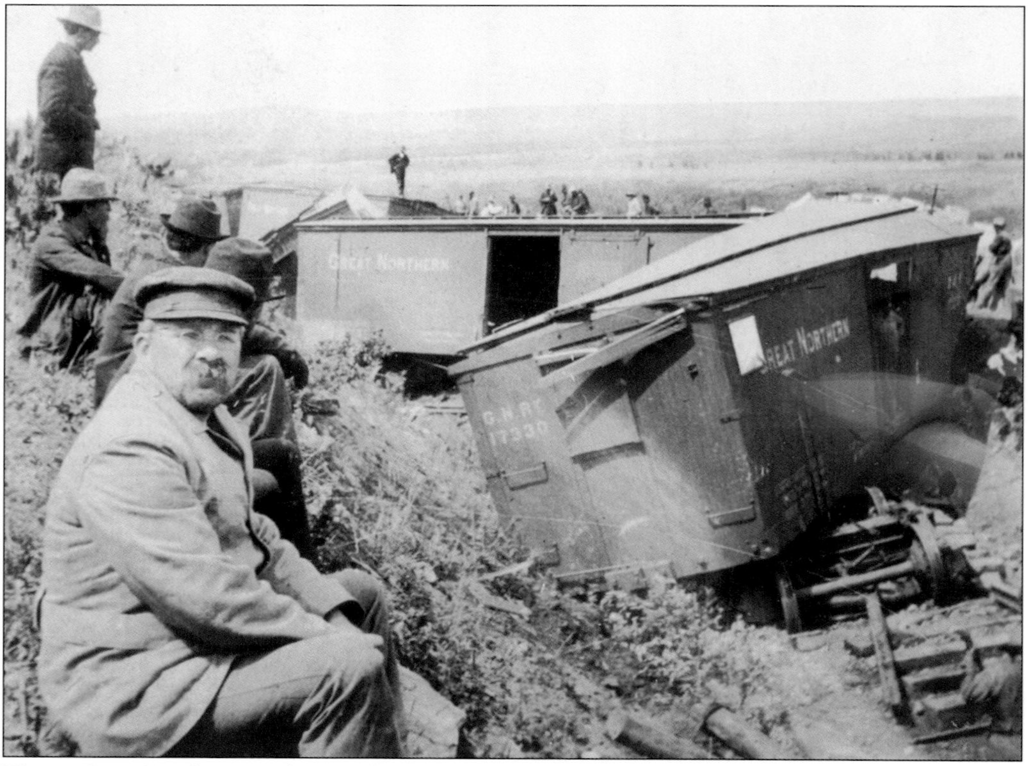

This early 1900s photograph was taken somewhere along the hundreds of miles of Great Northern track in Montana, and though the details of this pileup are lost, it is apparent that the onlookers took advantage of this diversion from the endless prairie sky. (Author's collection.)

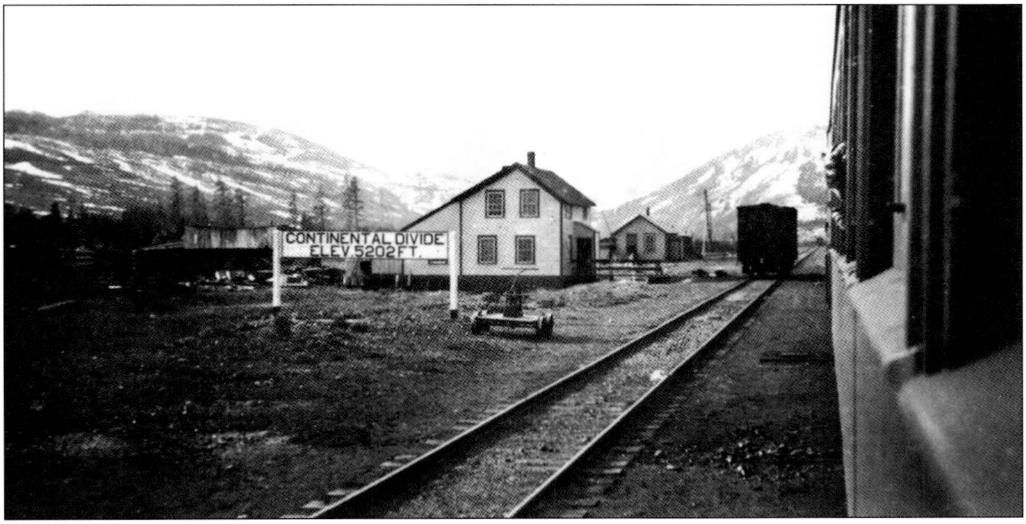

The altitude of Marias Pass is somewhat ambiguous, as there are at least four "official" elevations. This early-20th-century sign along the railroad lists 5,202 feet. Other sources maintain that the elevation is either 5,216 or 5,236 feet; however, the current and widely accepted altitude is 5,213 feet above sea level. (Author's collection.)

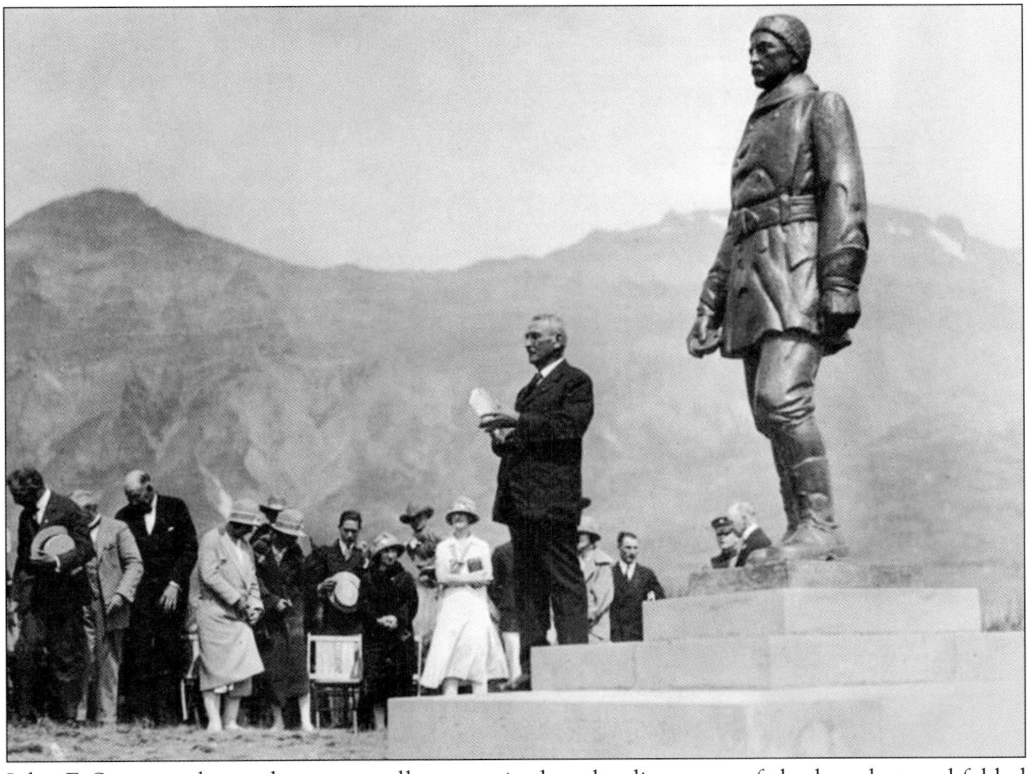

John F. Stevens, the explorer generally recognized as the discoverer of the long-lost and fabled Rocky Mountain crossing, shares his recollection of locating Marias Pass while US Supreme Court associate justice Pierce Butler dedicates the monument erected in his name at Summit on July 21, 1925. The bronze Stevens, located in Theodore Roosevelt Memorial Square along US Highway 2, stands next to a miniature Washington Monument obelisk. (Author's collection.)

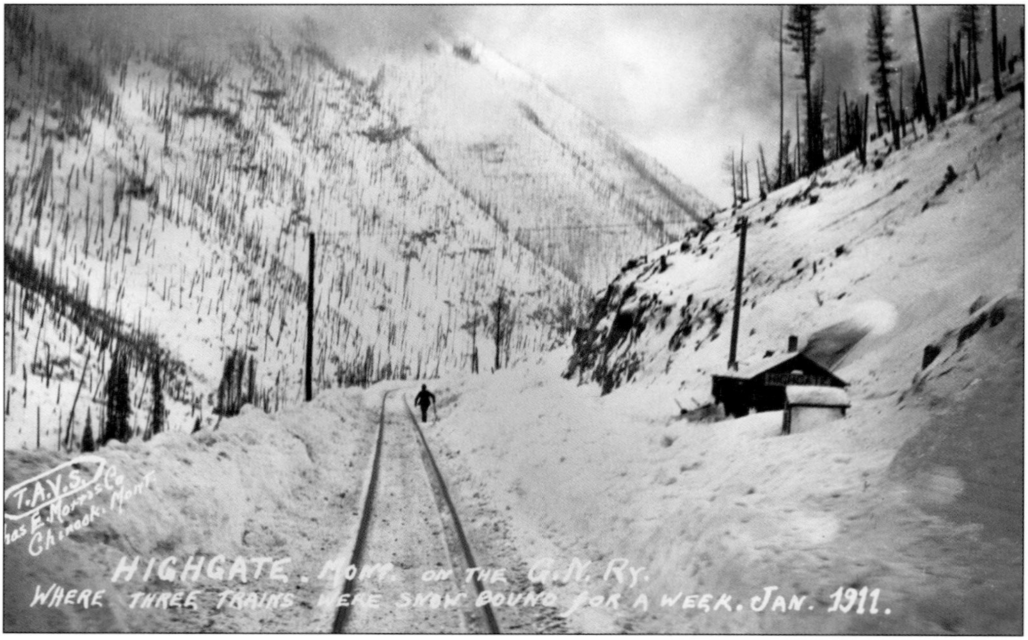

Snow removal has always been a challenge for the Great Northern in Marias Pass. As noted on this postcard, snowslides in the steep-walled valleys along Bear Creek trapped three trains for a week in January 1911 at Highgate. Commencing in 1912–1913, the railroad began building numerous snowsheds to lessen the avalanche danger. (Author's collection.)

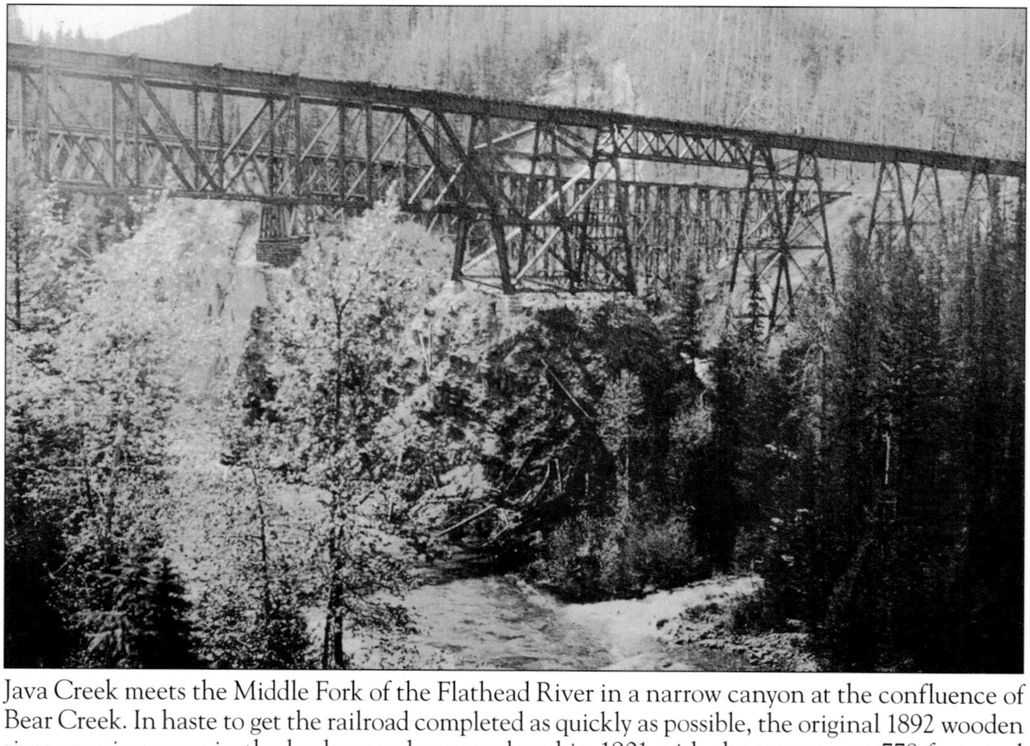

Java Creek meets the Middle Fork of the Flathead River in a narrow canyon at the confluence of Bear Creek. In haste to get the railroad completed as quickly as possible, the original 1892 wooden river crossing, seen in the background, was replaced in 1901 with the permanent 778-foot steel trestle. (Courtesy Jerry Quinn collection.)

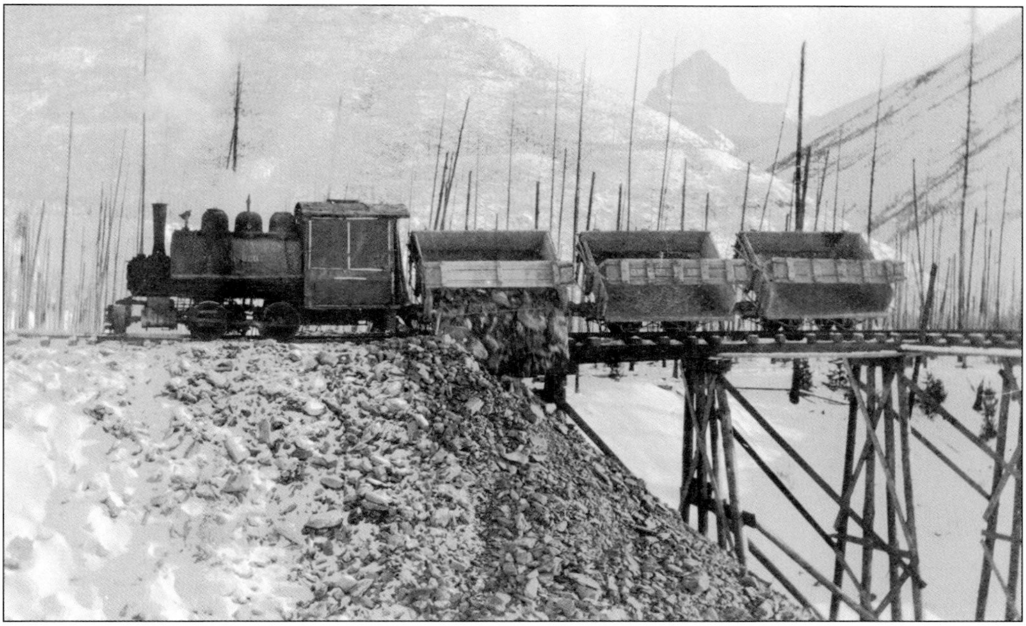

Marias Pass required numerous alignment changes and other improvements for efficiency and safety. The Porter Locomotive Company built thousands of small 0-4-0 dinkey locomotives for light industrial and construction use; note in the image above how Mount St. Nicholas dwarfs the dinkey and three tiny mining cars, which are dumping rock on a temporary trestle to create a new railroad grade. The geology of the mountains in Marias Pass is such that irregular and unstable rock formations required the Great Northern to reinforce tunnels to prevent collapse. As seen below, it took primitive construction equipment and manual labor to complete the concrete lining of Tunnel No. 2 in the early 20th century. (Both, author's collection.)

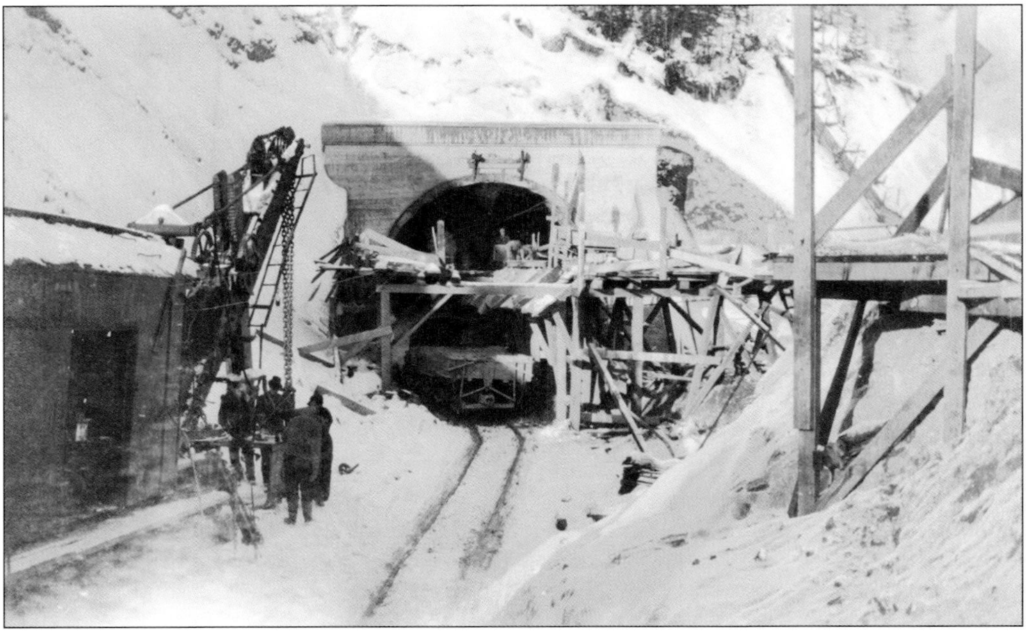

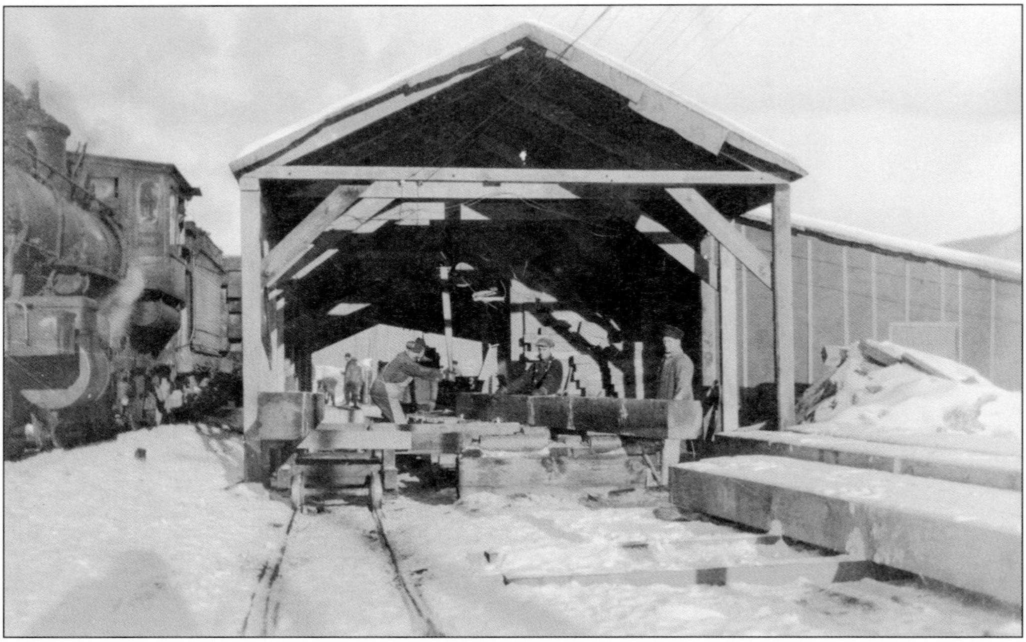

Millions of board feet of lumber from forests along the right-of-way were harvested to build the transcontinental railroads. Pictured is an early-20th-century sawmill, located between Essex and Paola, cutting logs into large timbers for one of the nearby line relocations at Tunnel No. 2 and the Paola-Pinnacle area. (Author's collection.)

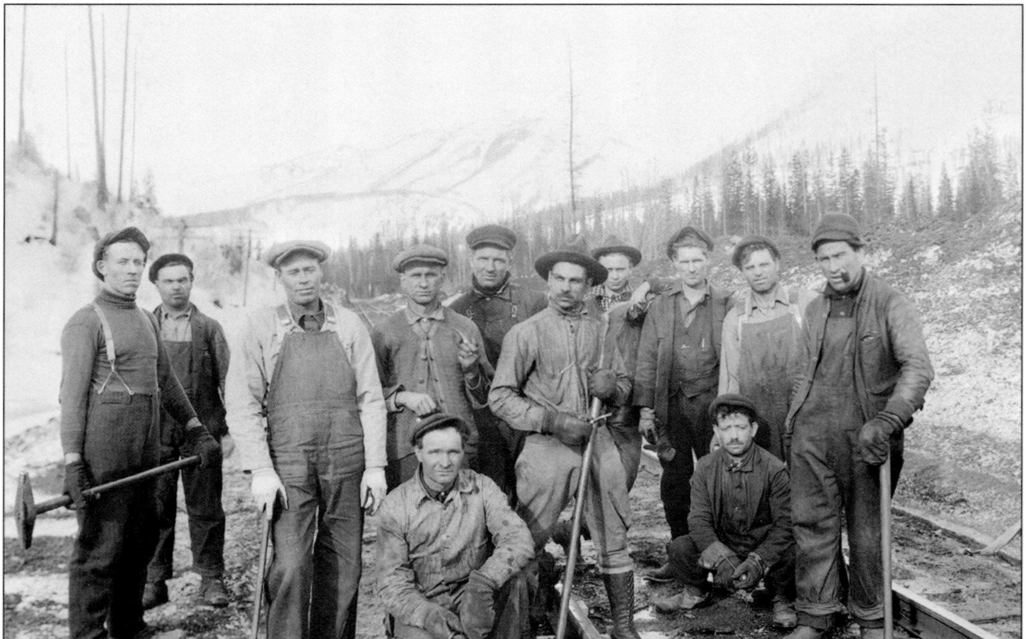

The serious expressions on the faces of these railroad workers reflect the determination needed to endure ever-changing Marias Pass weather and other dangerous conditions, where a false move could kill or maim a man in an instant. These Great Northern employees are standing at the west end of the Essex yard in the early 1900s. (Courtesy Ed Krona collection.)

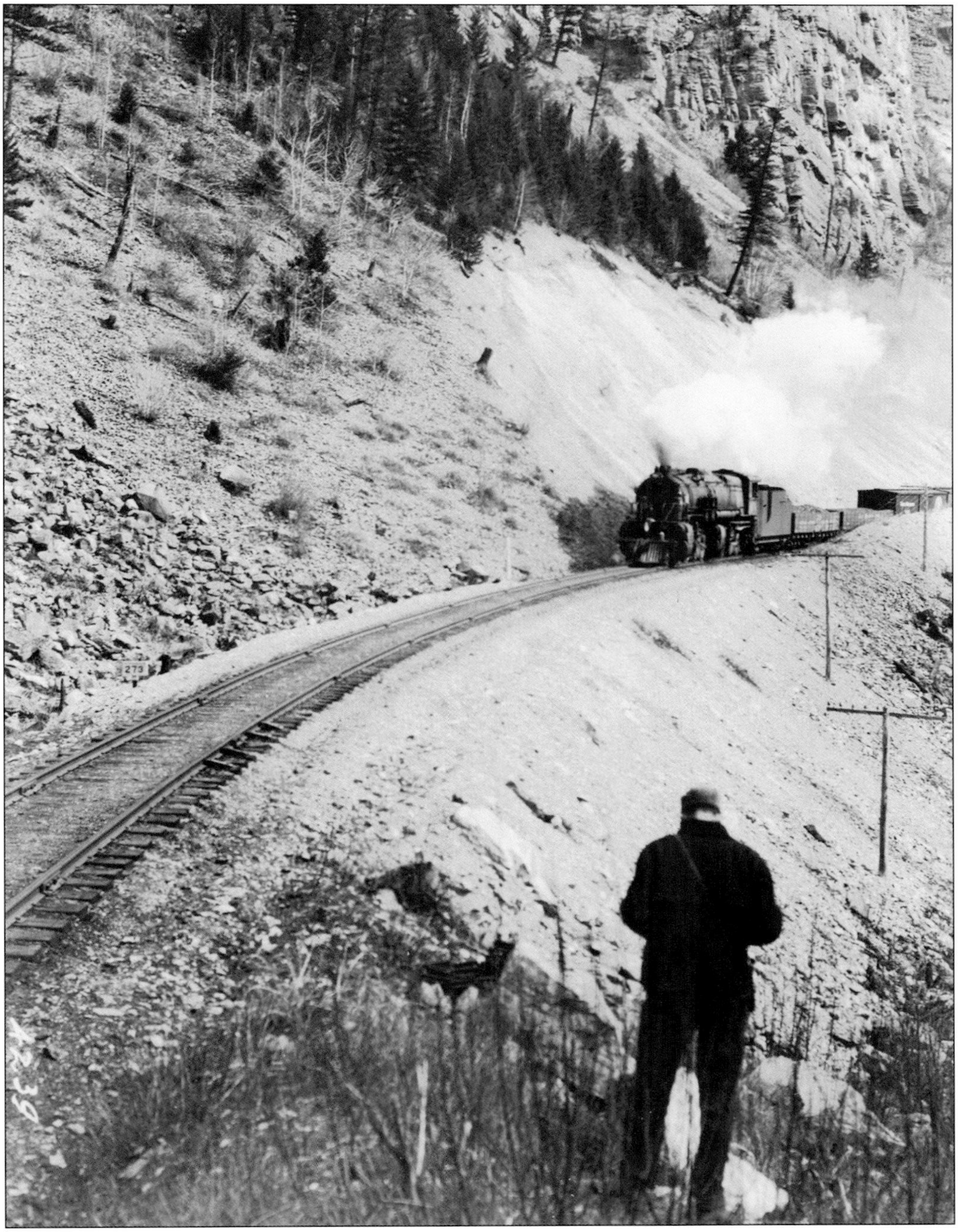

Bad Rock Canyon, located about 2.5 miles east of Columbia Falls on the Flathead River, has long been identified by "bad rock." On the south side of the canyon, an early wagon tote road was routed over many rocky cliffs or "bad rock" above the river. For a brief time in 1892, the steamboat *Oakes* endeavored to reach coalfields on the North Fork of the Flathead before running aground in shallow water near Canyon Creek. In the foreground, a photographer captures an image of a westbound Great Northern Class L 2-6-6-2 articulated along the north side of Bad Rock Canyon, where steep cliffs and falling rock are a constant threat. (Photograph by Ferde Greene from the E.B. Gilliland collection.)

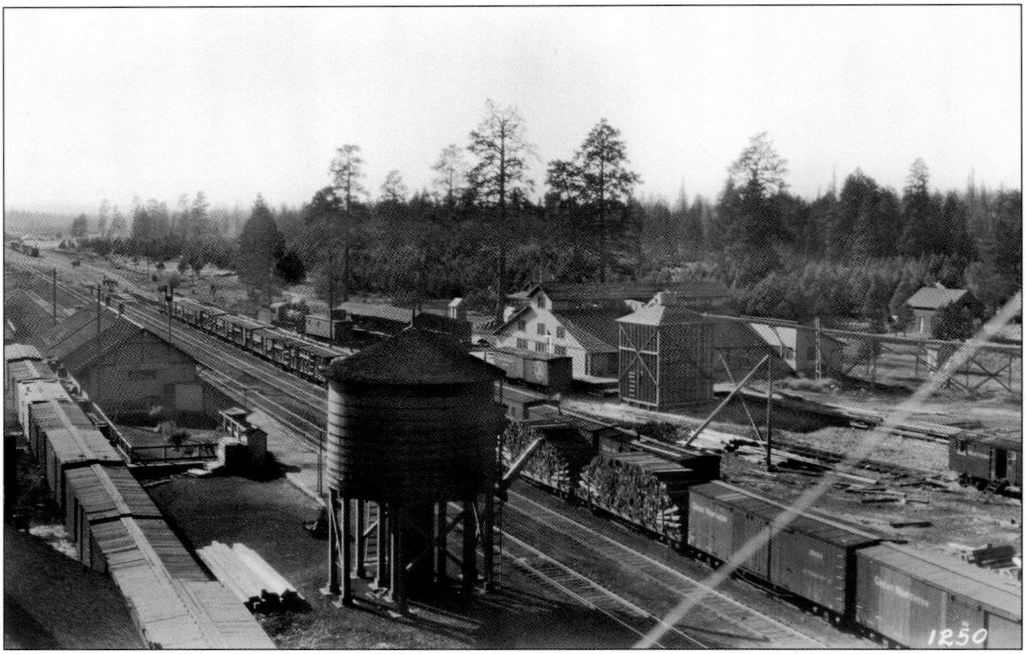

Industries in the Flathead Valley are well represented by the variety of railcars in this photograph. The flatcars in front of the water tower are stacked with crossties headed to the Somers crosstie treatment plant; on the left, stock cars are readied to load sheep that graze in nearby meadows. (Photograph by Ferde Greene from the E.B. Gilliland collection.)

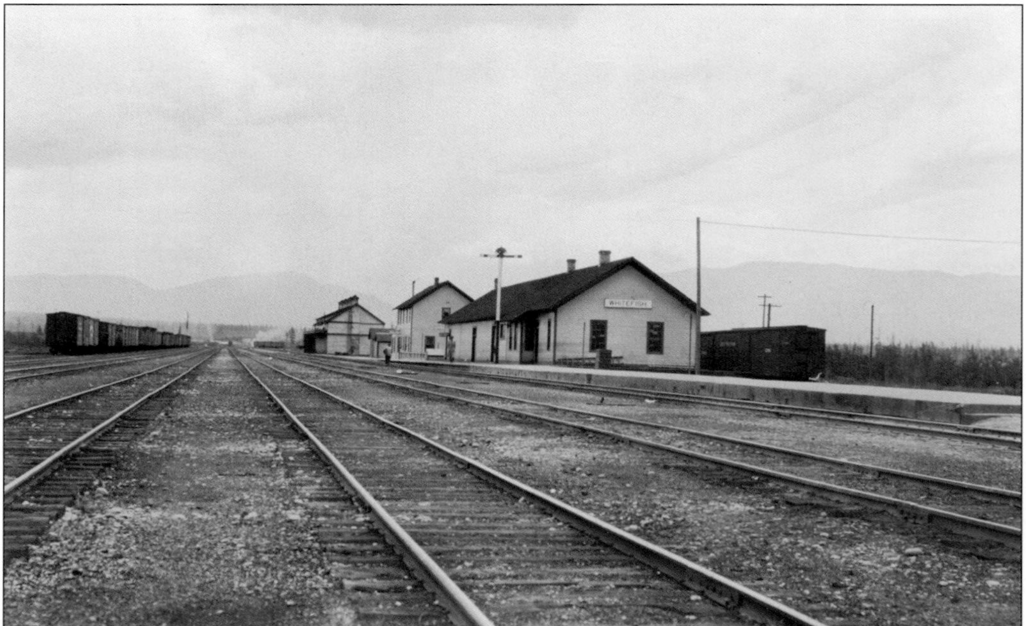

Whitefish was created as a division point on the Great Northern in 1904 when the Haskell Pass line through Kalispell became a liability. The new route along the Kootenai River from Jennings, Montana, looped through Eureka and south to Whitefish, eliminating a long tunnel and steep mountain grades. (Photograph by Ferde Greene from the E.B. Gilliland collection.)

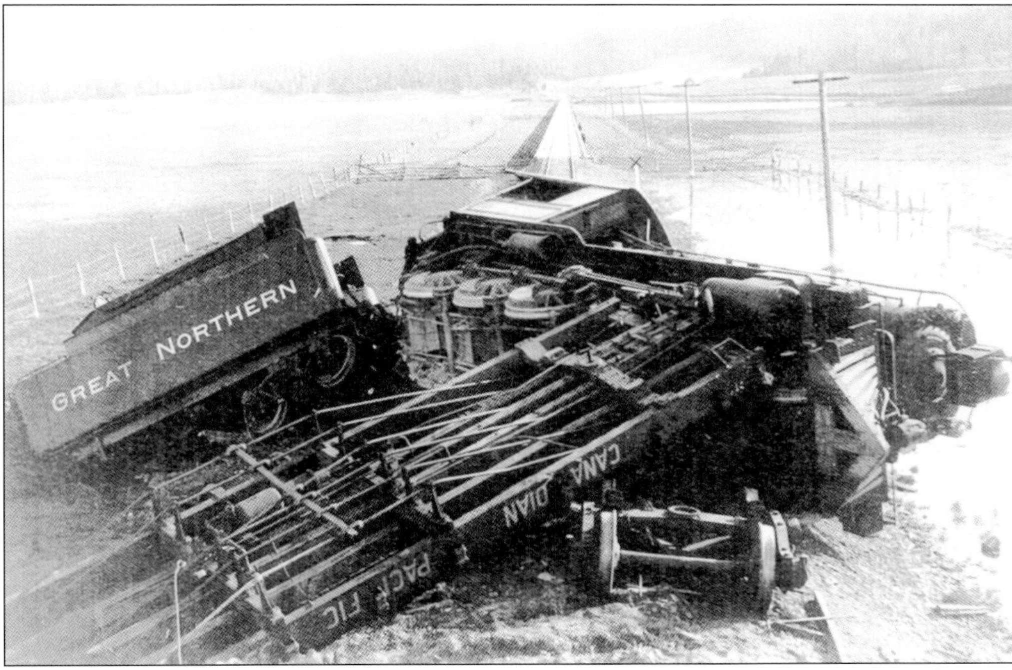

Photographs of trains on the original 1892 Haskell Pass alignment are relatively rare, as the route from Kalispell to Jennings was operational for just over 10 years and was not accessible except by rail. This accident was near Kila on the railroad grade across Smith Lake, a few miles west of Kalispell. (Doug Snackenberg collection.)

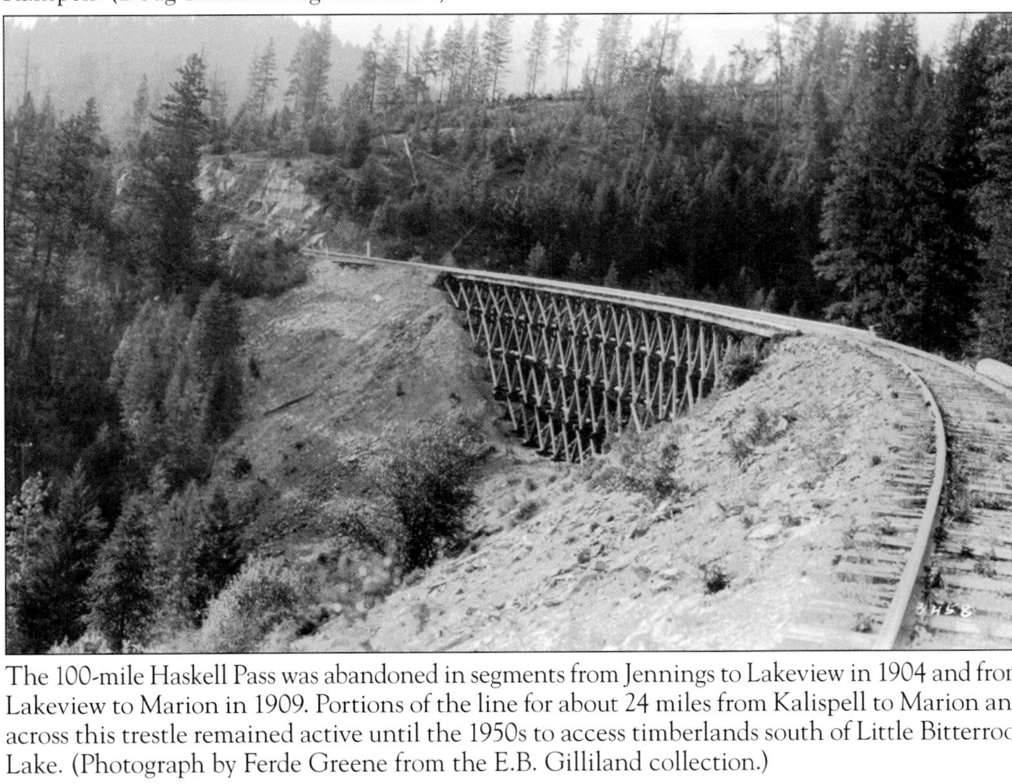

The 100-mile Haskell Pass was abandoned in segments from Jennings to Lakeview in 1904 and from Lakeview to Marion in 1909. Portions of the line for about 24 miles from Kalispell to Marion and across this trestle remained active until the 1950s to access timberlands south of Little Bitterroot Lake. (Photograph by Ferde Greene from the E.B. Gilliland collection.)

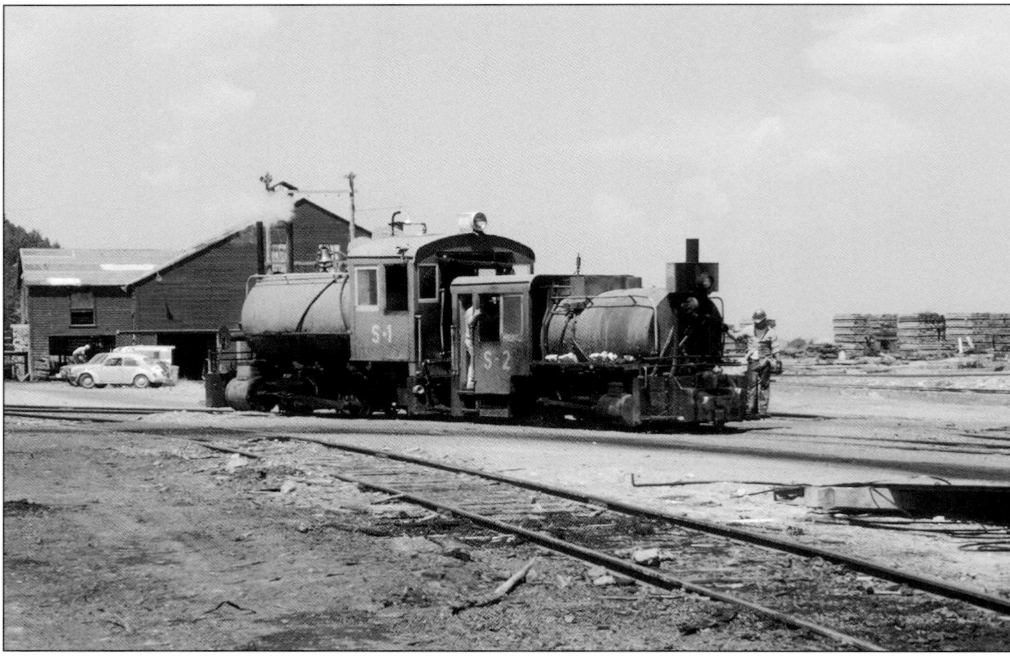

Somers, Montana, at the north end of Flathead Lake, was the site of the Great Northern Railway's primary crosstie treatment facility on Lines West—rail lines west of Havre, Montana. Wooden railroad ties need to be treated with preservatives to prevent rotting from ground moisture. Two interesting 0-4-0 steam locomotives, Nos. S-1 and S-2, built by the Porter Locomotive Company, were used to shuttle railcars until 1986, when the plant was closed. Since there was an ever-present danger of fire, these locomotives were charged with steam from a stationary boiler and were termed "fireless," as no open fire was needed for operation. (Both, courtesy Jerry Quinn collection.)

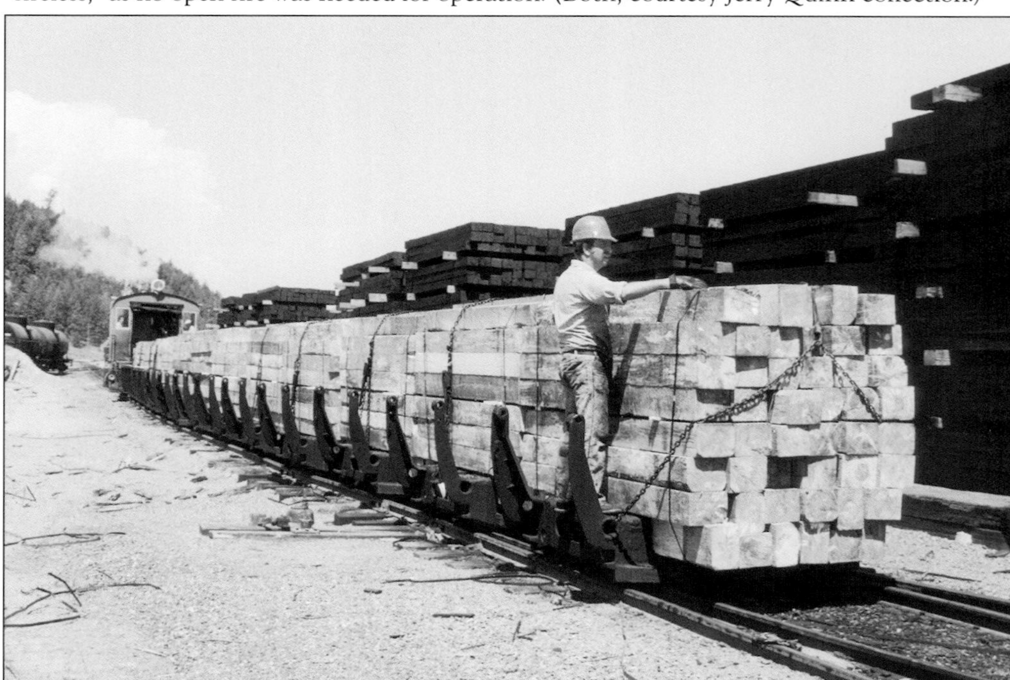

Two

The Pass

A Photographic Collection from Whitefish to Glacier Park

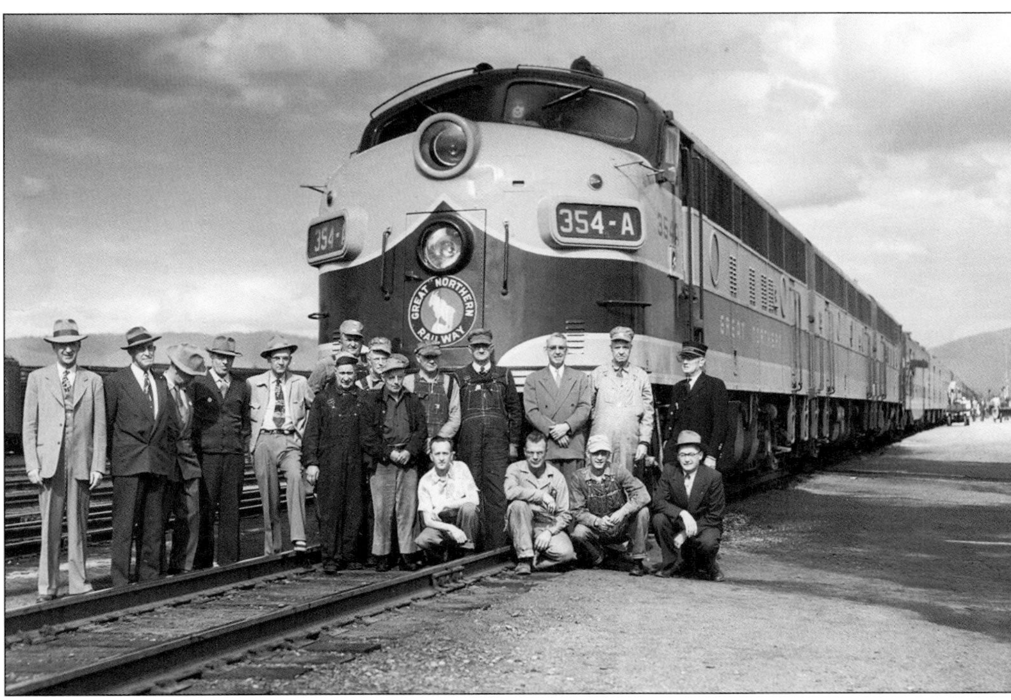

The clothing and uniforms of the employees in this company portrait at Whitefish represent the types of jobs required to operate trains in Marias Pass. On the left, the suits and ties belong to senior division officials; at center, overalls indicate roundhouse and yard workers; and to the right are probably engine crews with passenger train personnel. (Courtesy Ed Krona collection.)

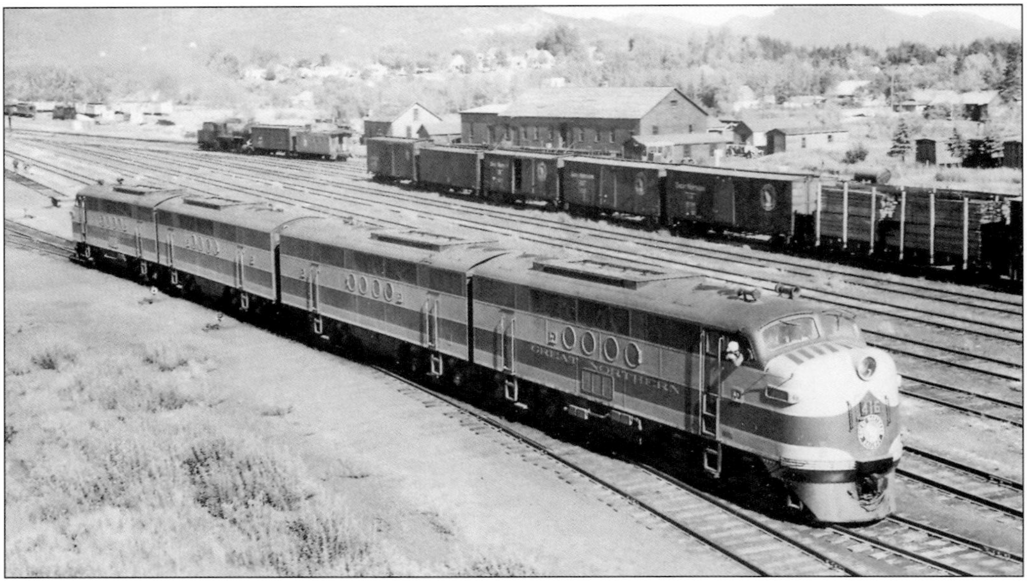

The Electro-Motive Division (EMD) of General Motors Corporation began building its distinctive F-series locomotives in 1940. Pictured at the Great Northern shops in Whitefish shortly after being delivered by the builder in 1944, FT 416 is being readied for service as a helper in Marias Pass. (James Mattson.)

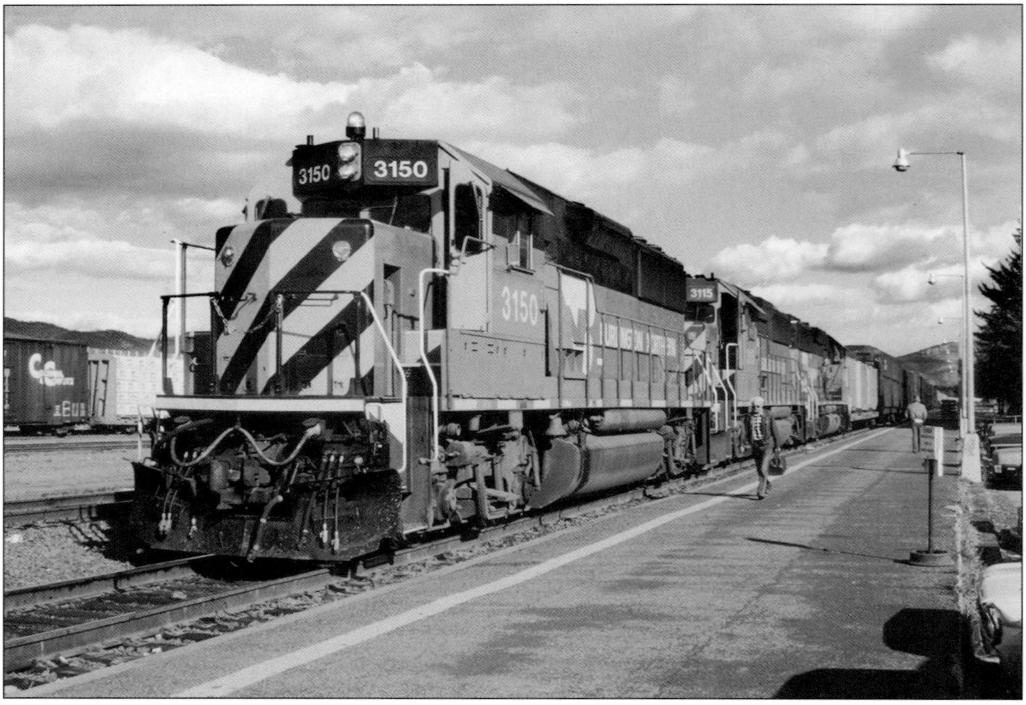

Whitefish became a division point between Troy and Blackfoot after the main line was relocated from Haskell Pass and Kalispell in 1904. Pictured here in 1986, forty years after the photograph above, GP50 ("GP" stands for "General Purpose") 3150 is preparing to depart Whitefish with a westbound Burlington Northern Railroad freight. (Courtesy Jerry Quinn collection.)

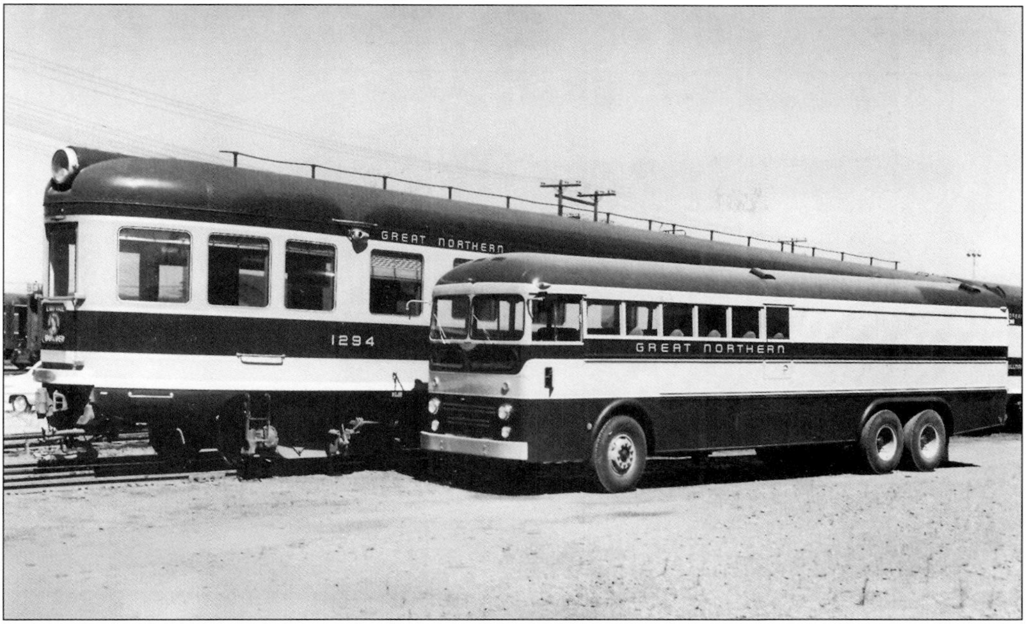

After gas-electric doodlebug service between Columbia Falls and Kalispell ended in the 1950s, to shuttle passengers between Kalispell and Whitefish, the Great Northern had Kenworth Motor Truck Company of Seattle build a one-of-a-kind 39-foot, 21-passenger-and-baggage-compartment combination vehicle, aptly named a "Bruck," for connections with the *Empire Builder* or *Western Star*. (Great Northern Railway.)

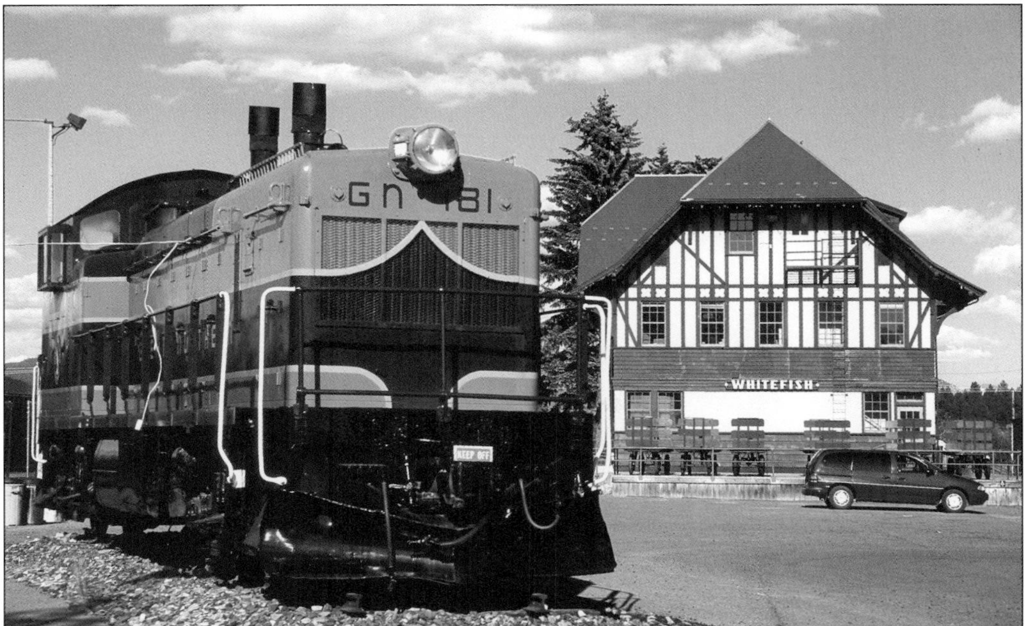

The Great Northern Railway was a pioneer in acquiring diesel locomotives to replace labor-intensive steam engines; an example is this 1942 road-switcher NW-3 181 on display at Whitefish. This locomotive was intended to be a cost-effective alternative to steam power for servicing branchline mixed (both freight and passenger) trains. (Author's collection.)

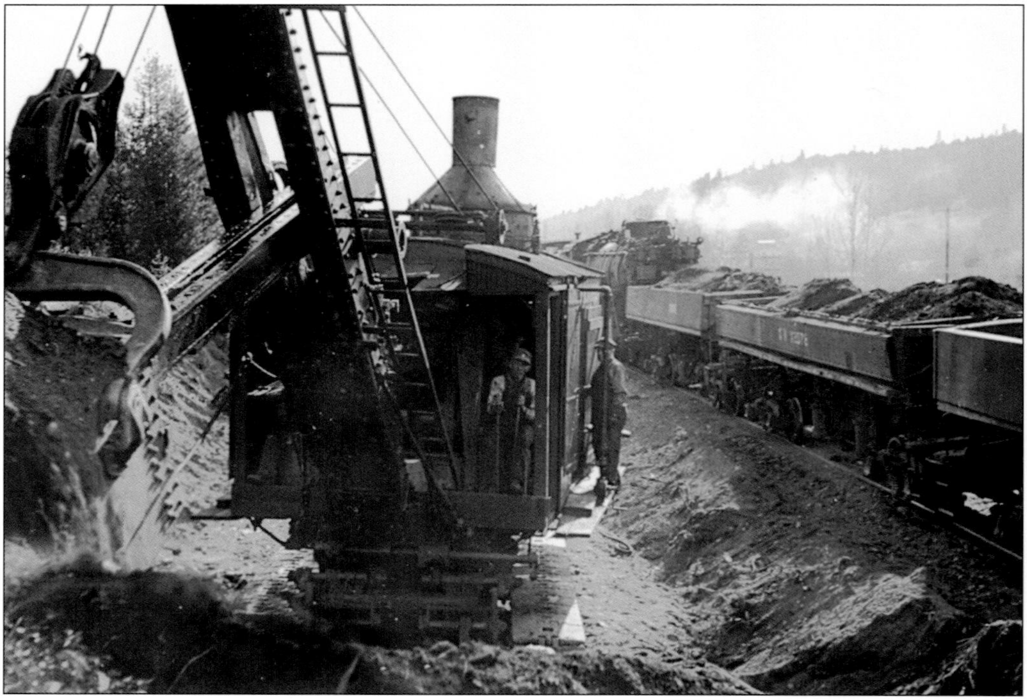

At times, the rail line eastward between Whitefish and Columbia Falls near Half Moon became saturated with seepage from adjacent streams, causing uneven track alignment. Stabilizing the roadbed is critical, so special maintenance-of-way side-dump cars were designed that allowed ballast to be released from either side of the train. These Austin-Western side-dump cars operated on compressed air from the steam locomotive and could drop 20 to 30 tons of fill with each load. (Both, courtesy Ed Krona collection.)

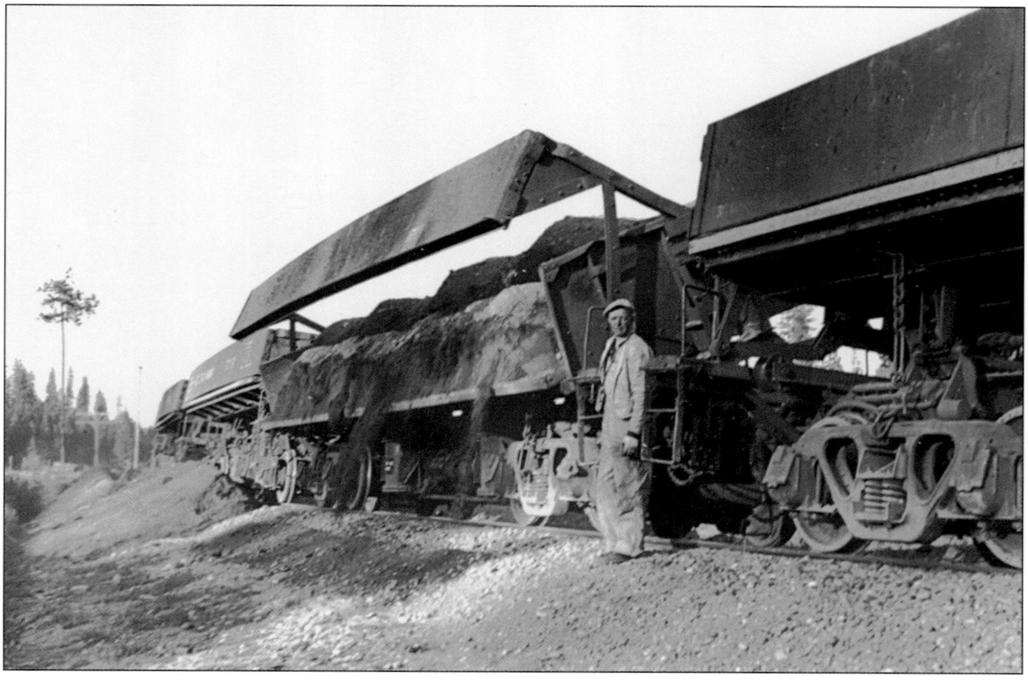

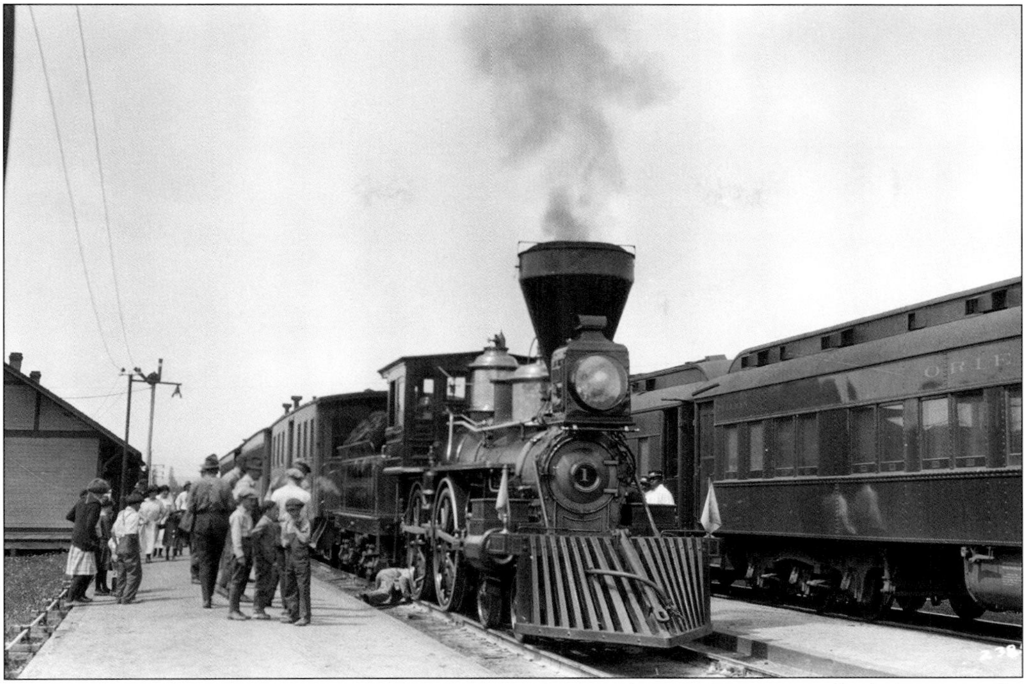

Great Northern Railway 4-4-0 No. 1, *William Crooks*, was the first locomotive built for Jim Hill's original St. Paul & Pacific Railroad in 1861. The locomotive was restored for Hill's 70th birthday in 1908 and was scheduled to be scrapped afterward; when Hill heard about it, he declared, "Not as long as I live." In 1924, the locomotive went on an exhibition tour from Chicago to Seattle, pausing here at Columbia Falls. (Photograph by Ferde Greene from the E.B. Gilliland collection.)

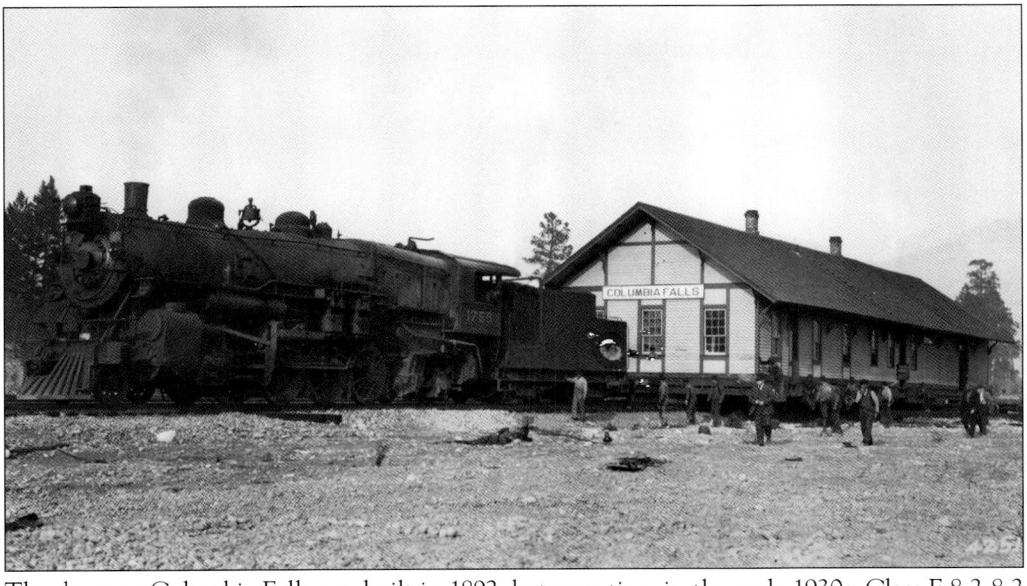

The depot at Columbia Falls was built in 1892, but sometime in the early 1930s, Class F-8 2-8-2 1755 had the job of moving the depot west from its original location to a spot on the north end of Nucleus Avenue; in the 1950s, it appears that the depot was cut in thirds and moved to its current location along US Highway 2 in Columbia Falls. (Photograph by Ferde Greene from the E.B. Gilliland collection.)

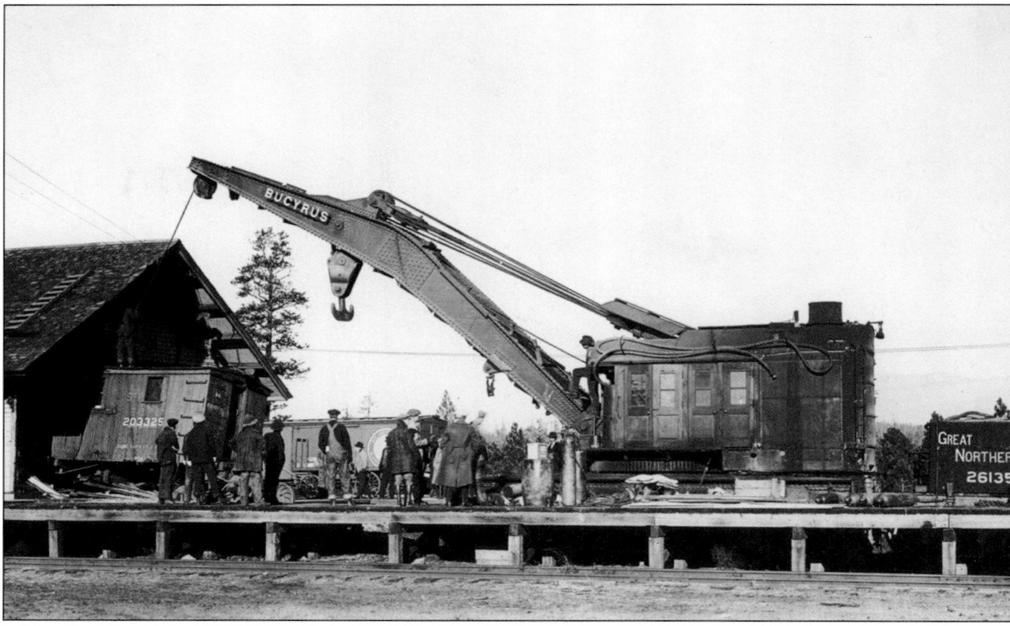

The circumstances of how this boxcar crashed into the Columbia Falls depot are not known, but Great Northern records indicate that the depot was extended in 1918, perhaps because of the severe damage sustained; nevertheless, the event created quite a stir in town. (Courtesy Ed Krona collection.)

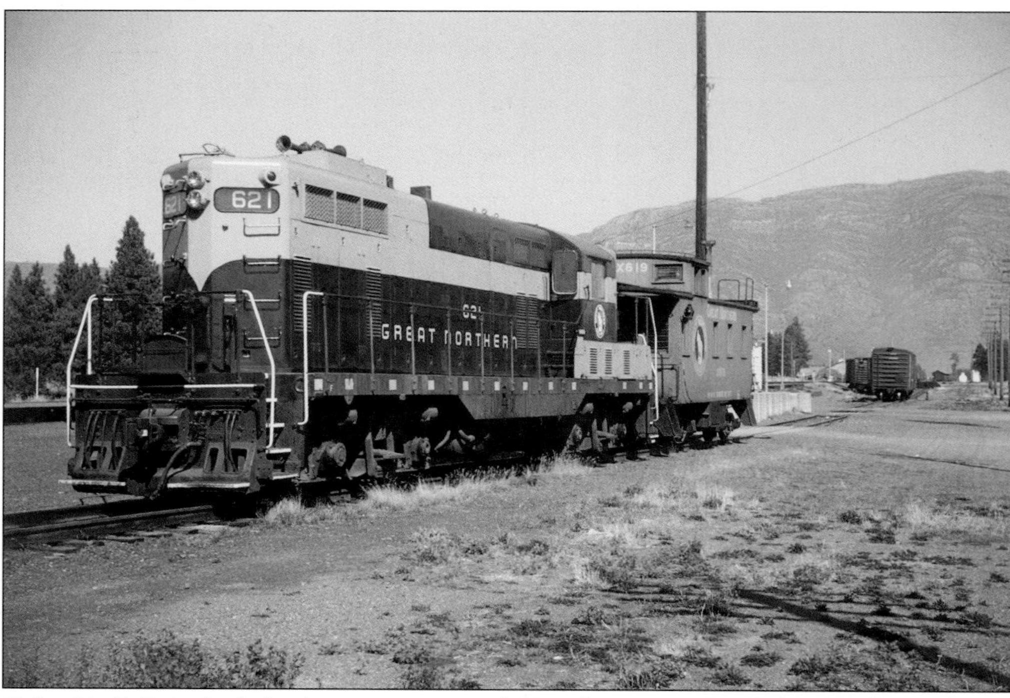

Columbia Falls is the hub of access to many of the industries in the Flathead Valley. The GP-7 621 and wooden caboose X-619 sit behind the 1953 depot ready to transfer cars to the Anaconda Aluminum plant in Conkelley or to switch some of the various businesses on the way south to Kalispell. (Author's collection.)

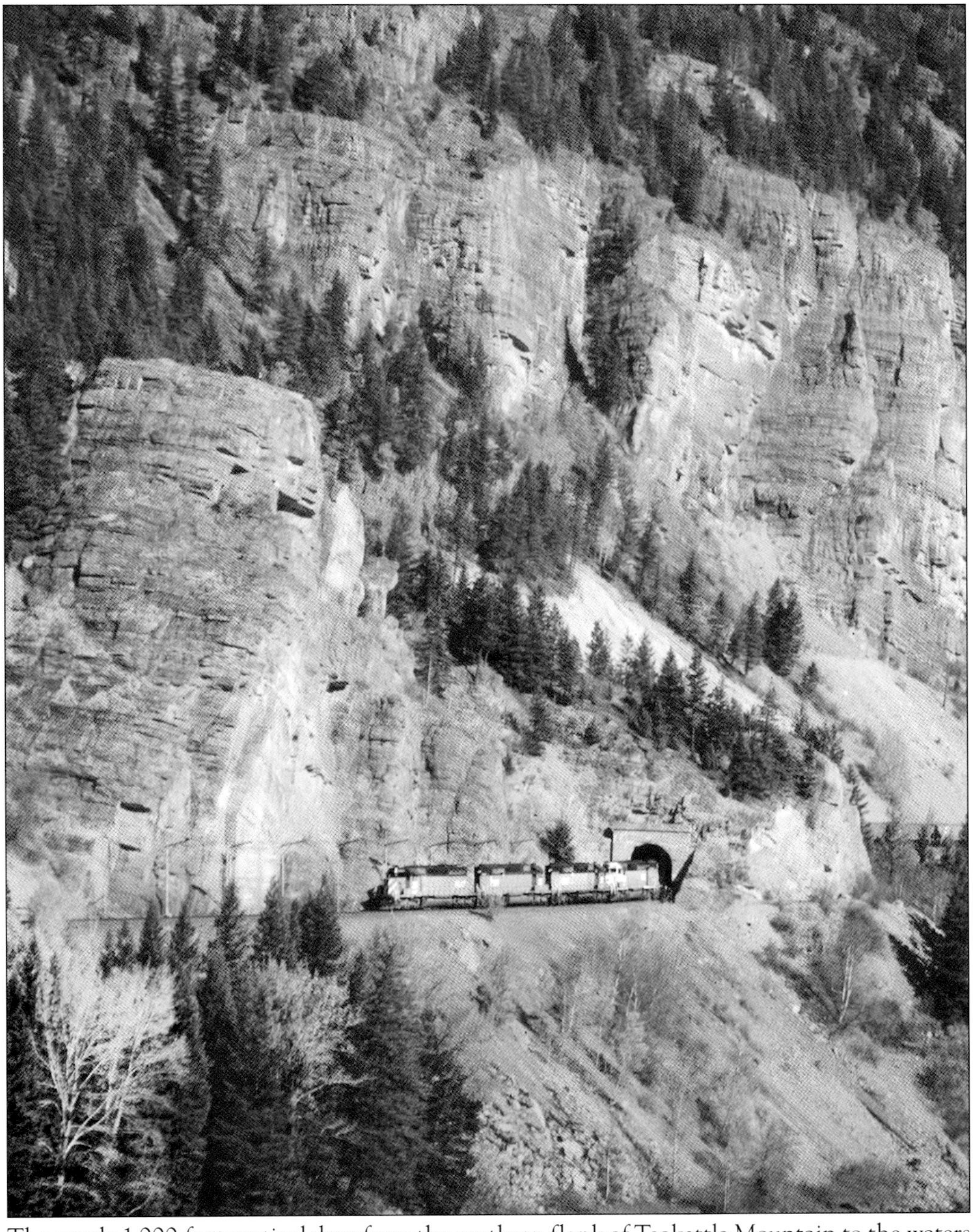

The nearly 1,000-foot vertical drop from the southern flank of Teakettle Mountain to the waters of the Flathead River dwarf a westbound Burlington Northern grain train. It is quite evident from this photograph that the hillside poses a threat to the railroad. Bad Rock Canyon has had three major improvements to increase safety: in 1900, Tunnel No. 5 was built; in 1919, the concrete retaining wall visible today from US Highway 2 was constructed; and in 1928, a right-of-way relocation shifted the tracks away from the canyon walls. On August 16, 1929, a slash fire, named the "Half Moon Fire," started on the west side of Columbia Falls and burned 103,000 acres in just three days. Teakettle Mountain was named "Teakettle" because the trees left in the wake of the fire resembled the shape of a teakettle. (Courtesy Jerry Quinn collection.)

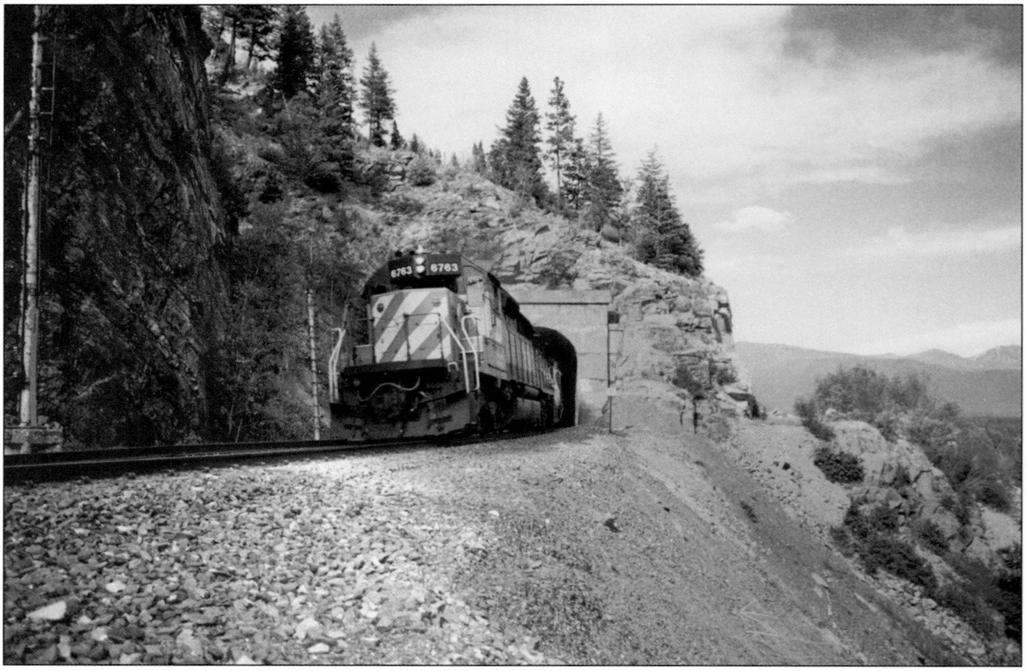

Burlington Northern SD40-2 6763 exits Tunnel No. 5 westbound into Bad Rock Canyon at Milepost No. 1207. Every mile on a railroad requires a unique location identifier for maintenance. The Great Northern started its milepost numbering system from St. Paul, Minnesota; therefore, Tunnel No. 5 is 1,207.6 miles west of St. Paul. (Author's collection.)

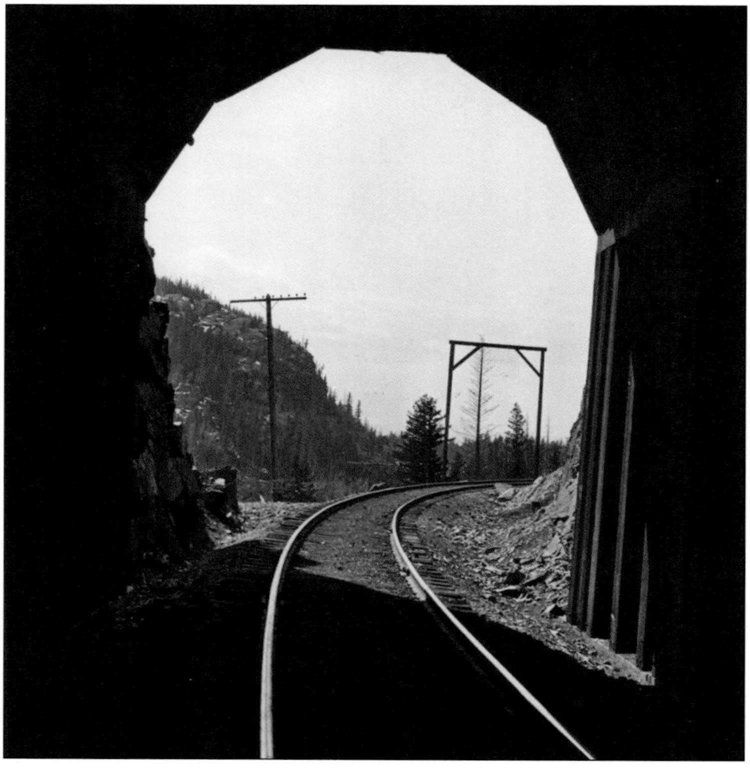

Photographer Ferde Greene documented many early Flathead Valley scenes. This view from the darkness of Tunnel No. 5 opens up into Bad Rock Canyon. In the background is a telltale, a series of ropes suspended over the tracks warning brakemen on top of boxcars that they were approaching a low-clearance obstacle such as a tunnel or a bridge. (Photograph by Ferde Greene from the E.B. Gilliland collection.)

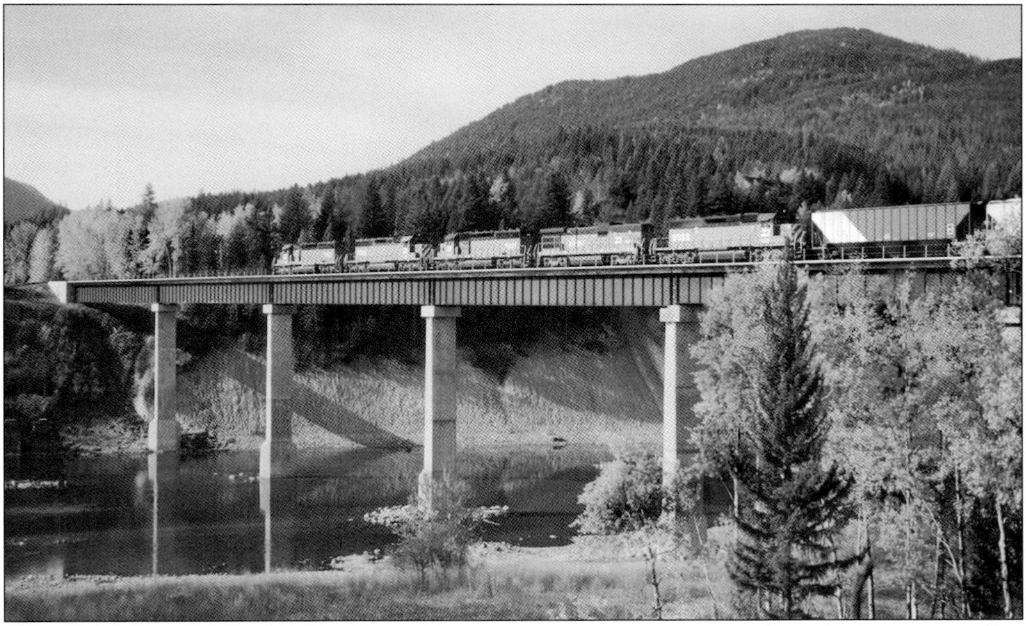

Tragedy struck on November 28, 1891, during construction of the original 929-foot Coram Bridge. Eleven men had just commenced work on the western span when someone accidently dropped a large iron rod that knocked out the falsework, causing a collapse. Three men were killed outright, and three more died later from their injuries. This westbound Burlington Northern freight crosses the North Fork of the Flathead River on the current bridge built in 1986. (Courtesy Jerry Quinn collection.).

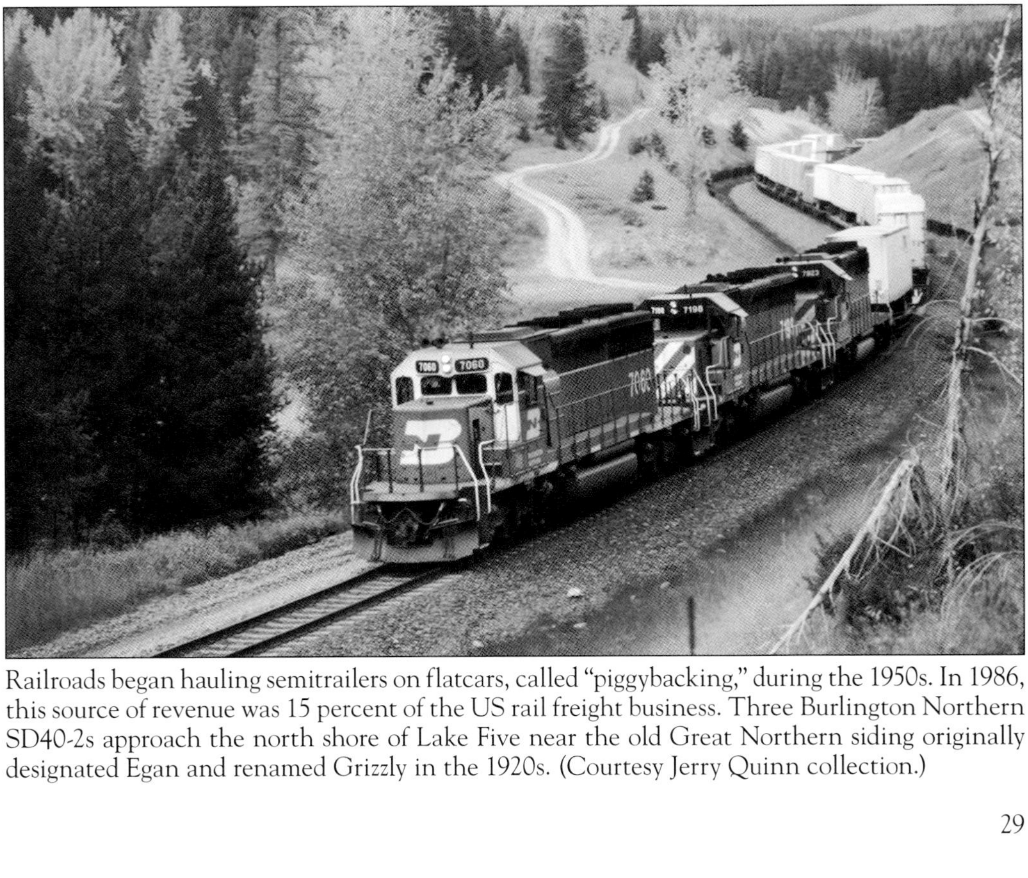

Railroads began hauling semitrailers on flatcars, called "piggybacking," during the 1950s. In 1986, this source of revenue was 15 percent of the US rail freight business. Three Burlington Northern SD40-2s approach the north shore of Lake Five near the old Great Northern siding originally designated Egan and renamed Grizzly in the 1920s. (Courtesy Jerry Quinn collection.)

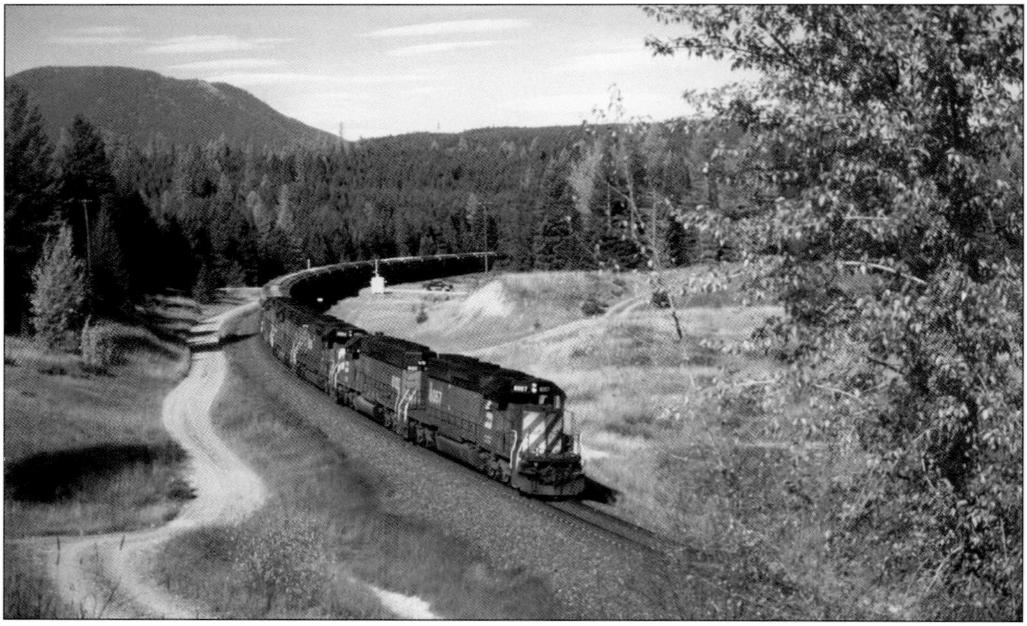

The Burlington Northern Railroad owned 835 SD40-2s. The reliability and versatility of the 3,000-horsepower SD40-2 made it one of the best-selling locomotives in EMD's history and was considered the standard of the industry for several decades after its introduction in January 1972. Five "Dash-2s," as they were nicknamed, glide downgrade on the tableland from Belton to Coram. (Courtesy Jerry Quinn collection.)

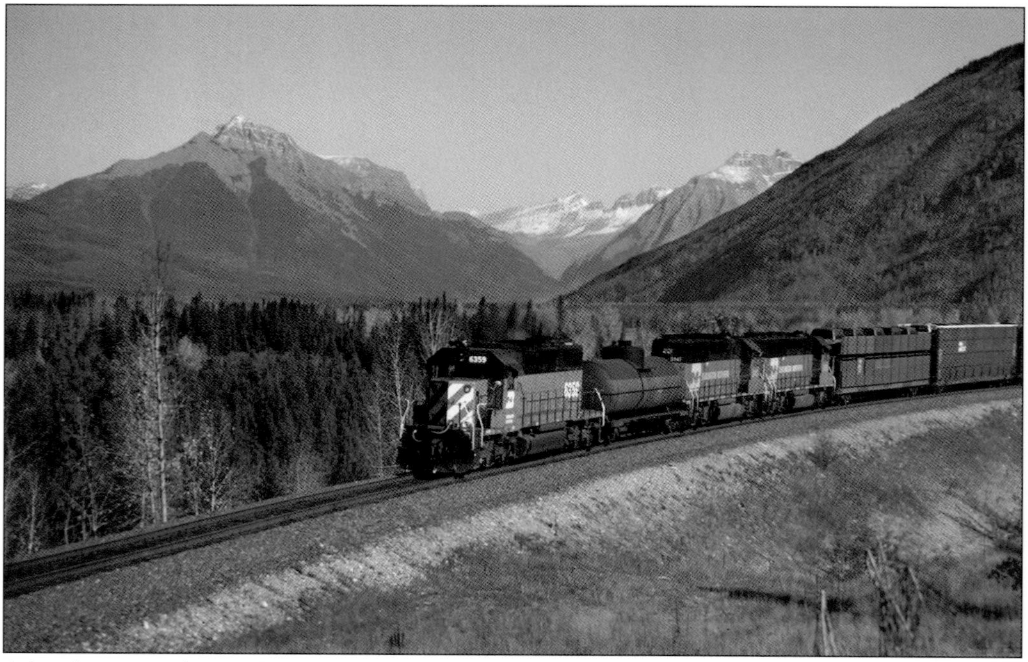

After departing the confines of the Middle Fork of the Flathead River canyon just west of Belton, the view widens out into the Lake McDonald valley. In the mid-1980s, Burlington Northern implemented the use of diesel-fuel tenders on some locomotives, allowing nearly nonstop operation without the need for refueling. (Courtesy Jerry Quinn collection.)

Three

Glacier National Park

Great Northern Railway's Connection

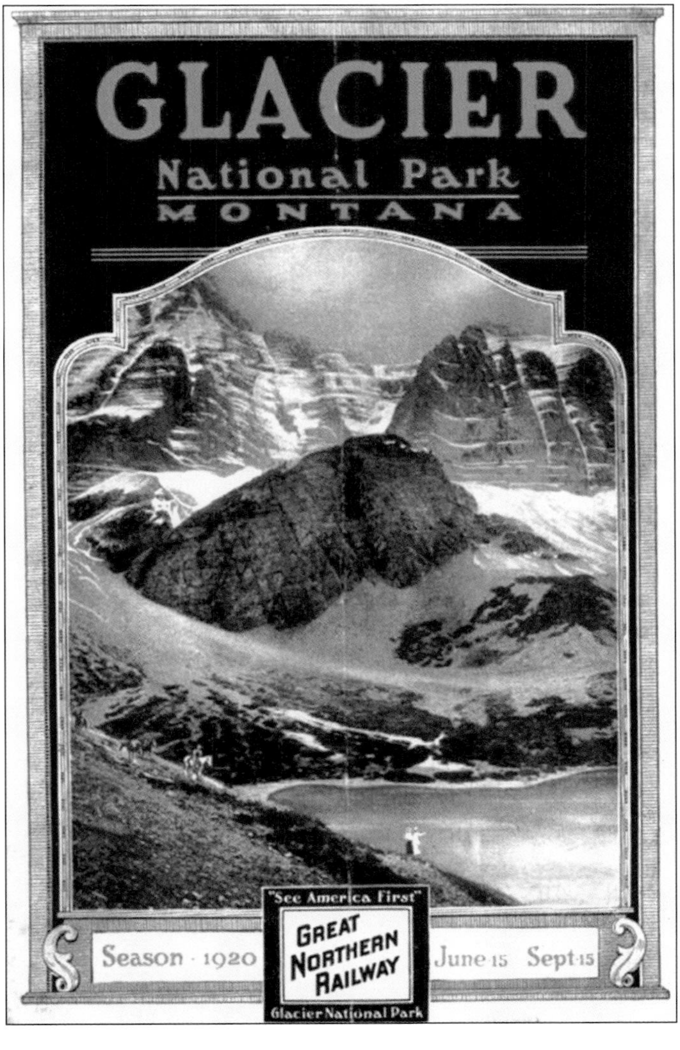

From inception, Glacier National Park's history and the Great Northern Railway's story have been intertwined. In the late 1890s, influential leaders like George Bird Grinnell pushed for preservation of this unique area in Montana; on May 11, 1910, Pres. William Howard Taft signed the bill establishing Glacier as the country's 10th national park. The Great Northern spearheaded the park's development and created the slogan "See America First" to encourage tourism. (Author's collection.)

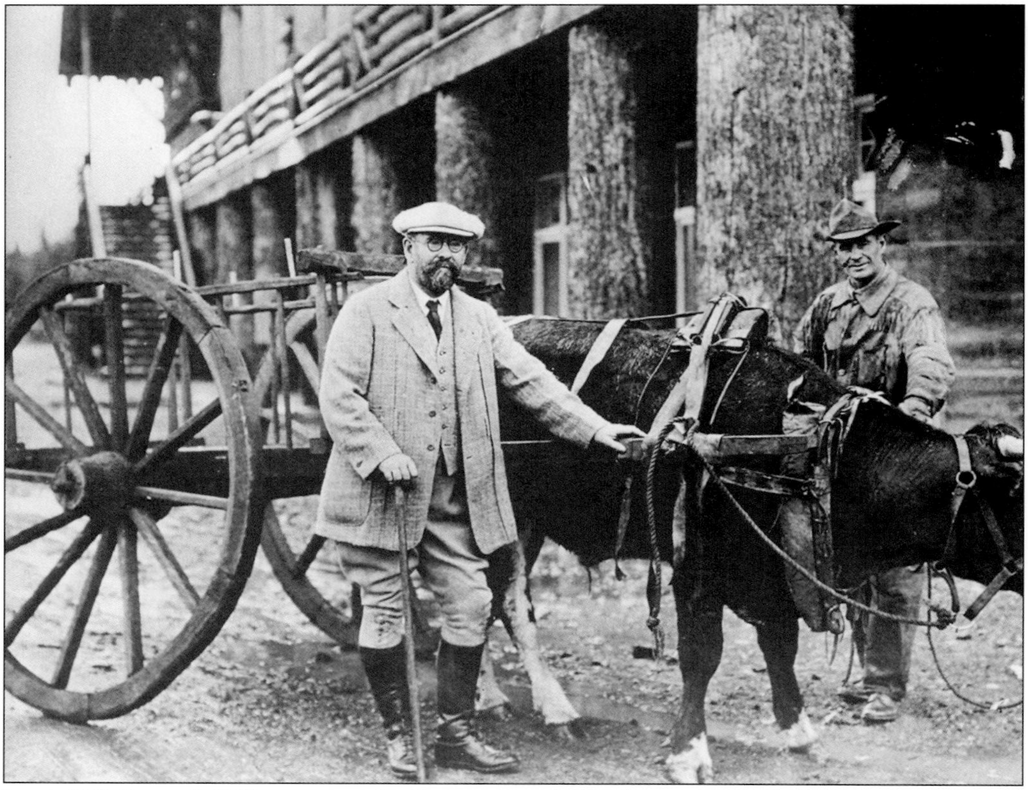

Louis Hill, James J. Hill's son, was the driving force behind promotion of Glacier National Park. Louis Hill stepped down as president of the Great Northern to stimulate interest in the newly formed park. Hill wanted to portray Glacier as "America's Switzerland" and set out plans for the Austrian chalet theme used throughout the park. (Author's collection.)

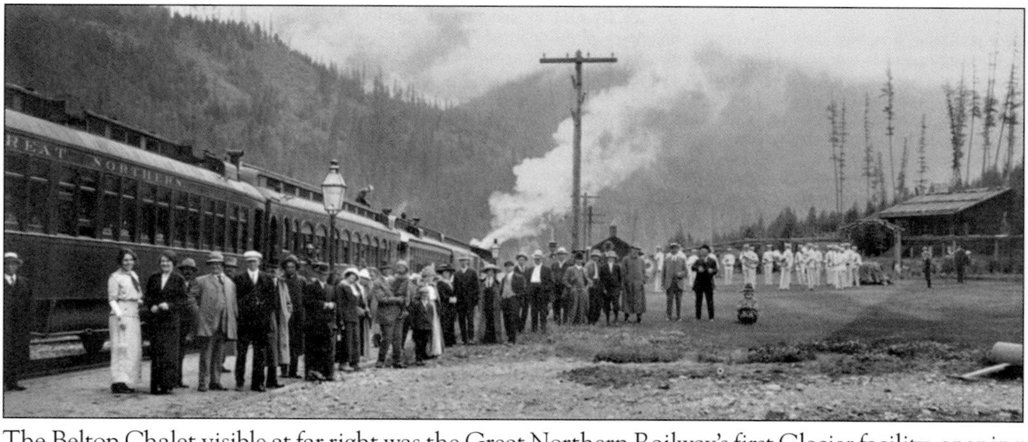

The Belton Chalet visible at far right was the Great Northern Railway's first Glacier facility, opening for business on June 27, 1910. This special seven-car train stopped at Belton in June 1913 to pick up passengers for a visit to the newly opened Glacier Park Hotel at Midvale. (Author's collection.)

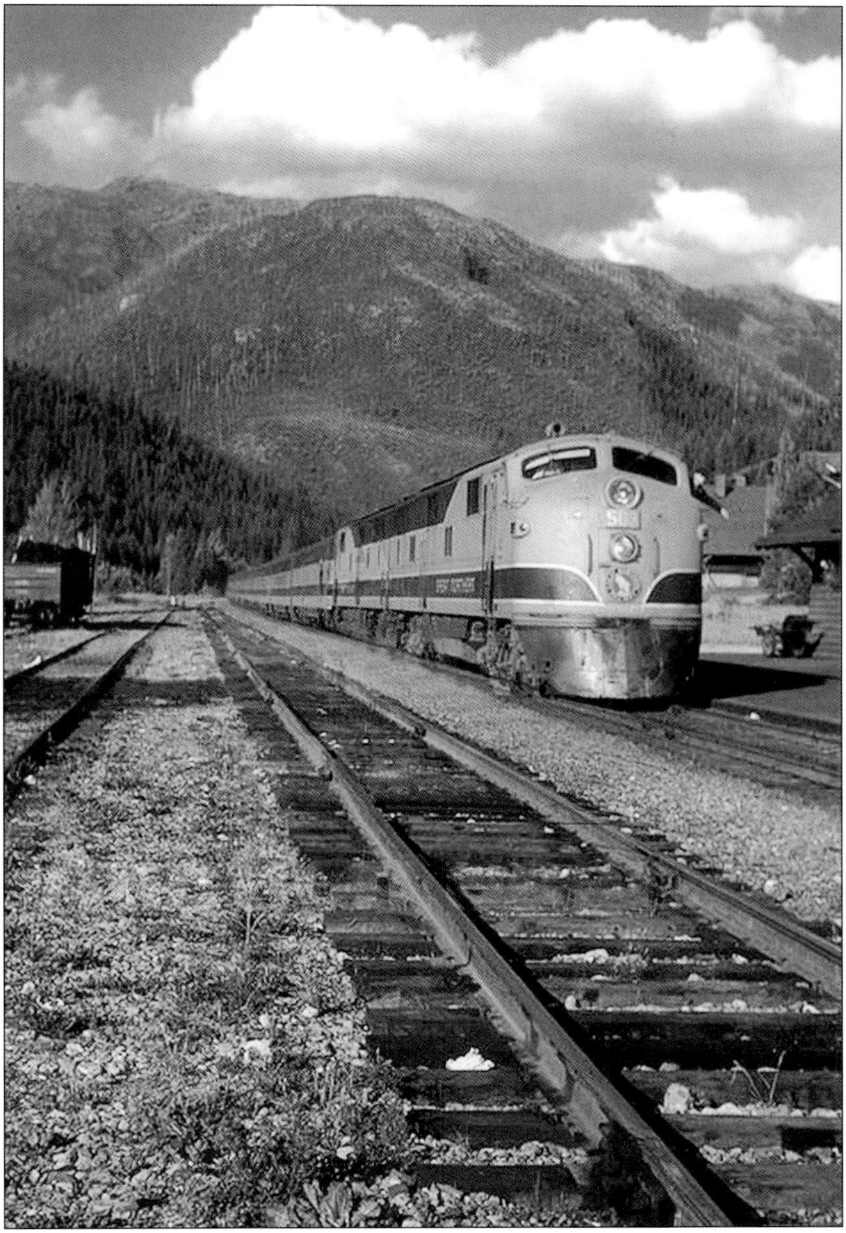

The new, fully streamlined *Empire Builder* was inaugurated in February 1947. The standard configuration included two EMD E7 A units, one railway post office/baggage car, four coaches, one coffee shop/lounge car, one dining car, four sleeper cars, and a sleeper-lounge-observation car. The 503 is one of 13 E7 units the Great Northern purchased for passenger service. A Great Northern travel brochure states: "In order to put in service a second daily streamlined train between Chicago and the Pacific Northwest the Great Northern has obtained 95 new 85-ft cars which make up in six separate new consists. Five of the consists are for the 15-car mid-century *Empire Builder* and the sixth rounds out the Western Star fleet of six 14-car consists so it too can operate over the 2,211-mile route in both directions with daily arrival and departure at all terminals." On a bright summer afternoon, the westbound *Empire Builder* makes the scheduled stop at Belton, the western entrance to Glacier National Park. (Author's collection.)

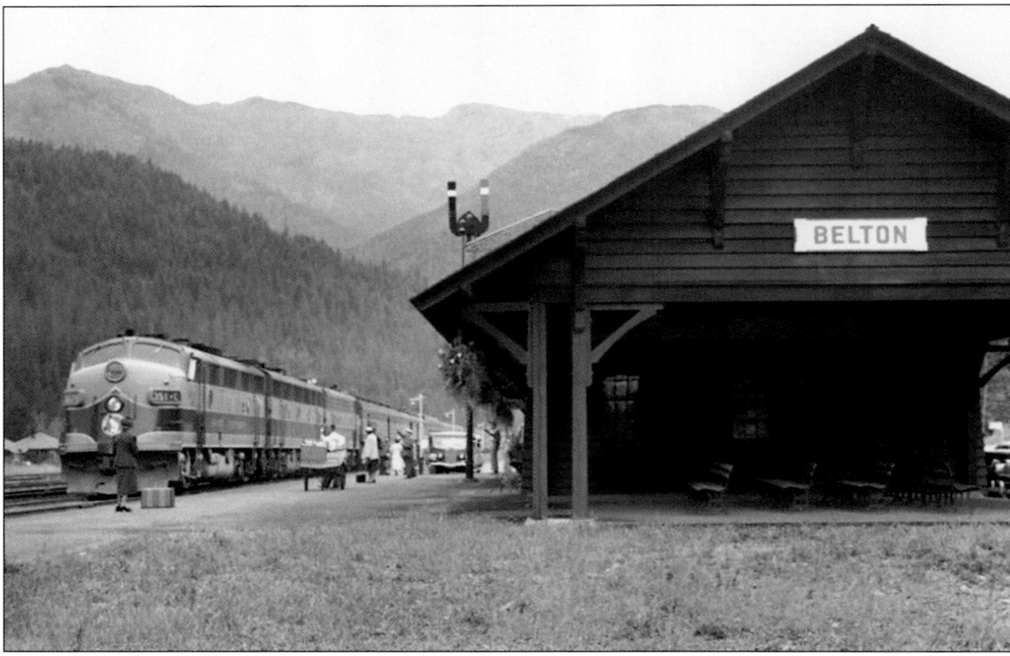

Are Belton and West Glacier the same place? Yes, they are the same location, but West Glacier and East Glacier were not designated railroad station names, as a misunderstanding of west or east in reading train orders could spell catastrophe. To avoid confusion, the correct railroad identifier for West Glacier is Belton and for East Glacier is Glacier Park. (Author's collection.)

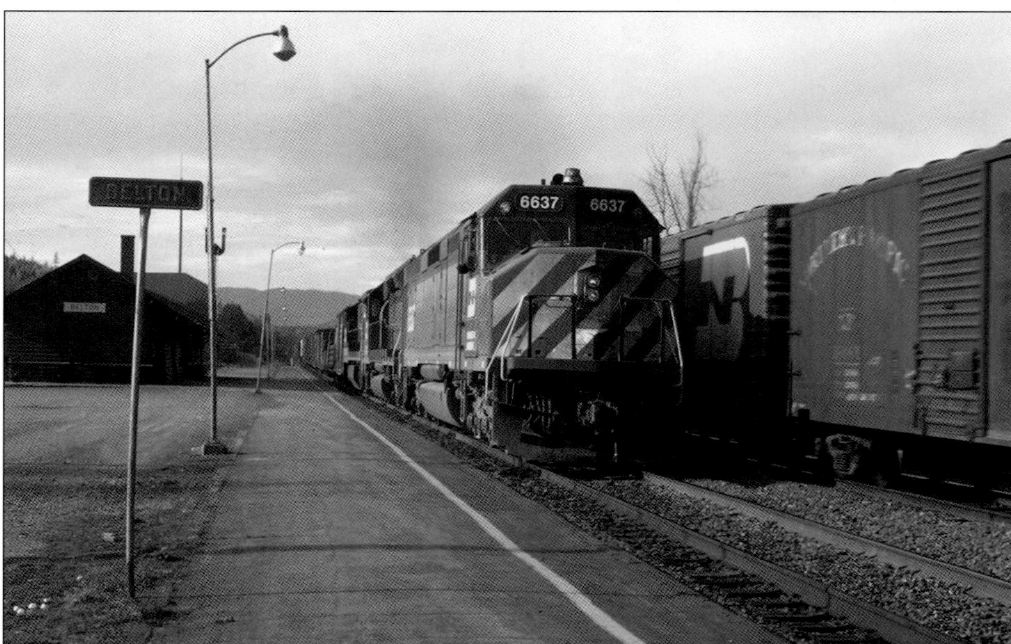

Belton, at an elevation of 3,215 feet above sea level, is considered the western approach to Marias Pass. Eastbound Burlington Northern EMD F45 6637 will gain 2,000 feet in altitude over the next 50 miles, paralleling the Middle Fork of the Flathead River and cresting the Continental Divide at Summit. (Courtesy Jerry Quinn collection.)

The nation's reliance on automobiles and increasing popularity of airplane travel during the late 1960s made the future of America's passenger trains appear doubtful. The National Railroad Passenger Corporation, now known as Amtrak, took control of nationwide passenger rail service on May 1, 1971. Nearly half of all passenger routes were abandoned, but the northern transcontinental route of the *Empire Builder* was one of 182 that survived. In 1975, Amtrak EMD SDP40F 579 and Train No. 7, the westbound *Empire Builder*, exchange passengers at Belton with a 15-passenger car similar to the original 1947 Great Northern streamliner. (Right, courtesy Chuck Hatler; below, courtesy Jerry Quinn collection.)

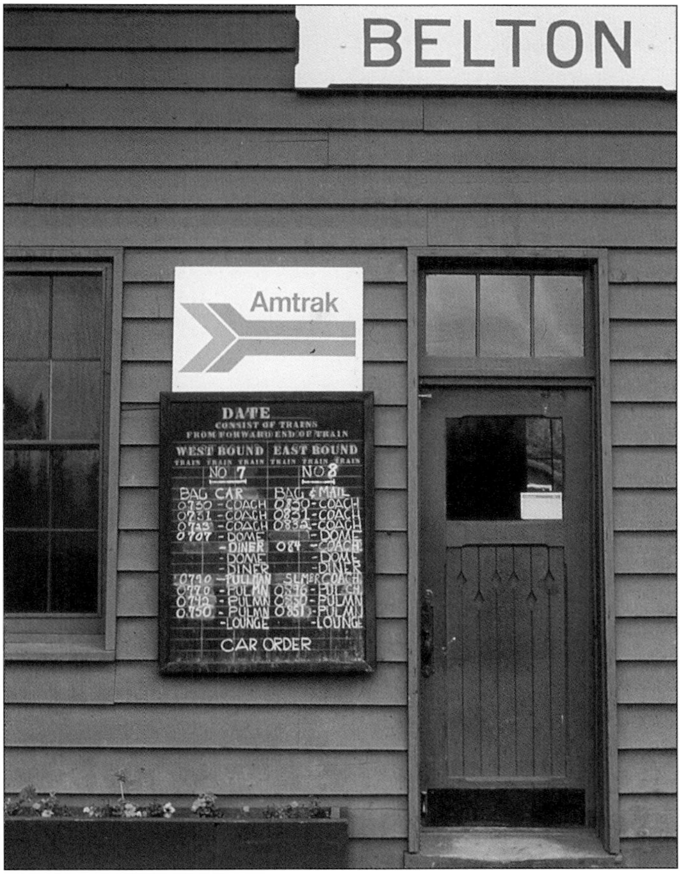

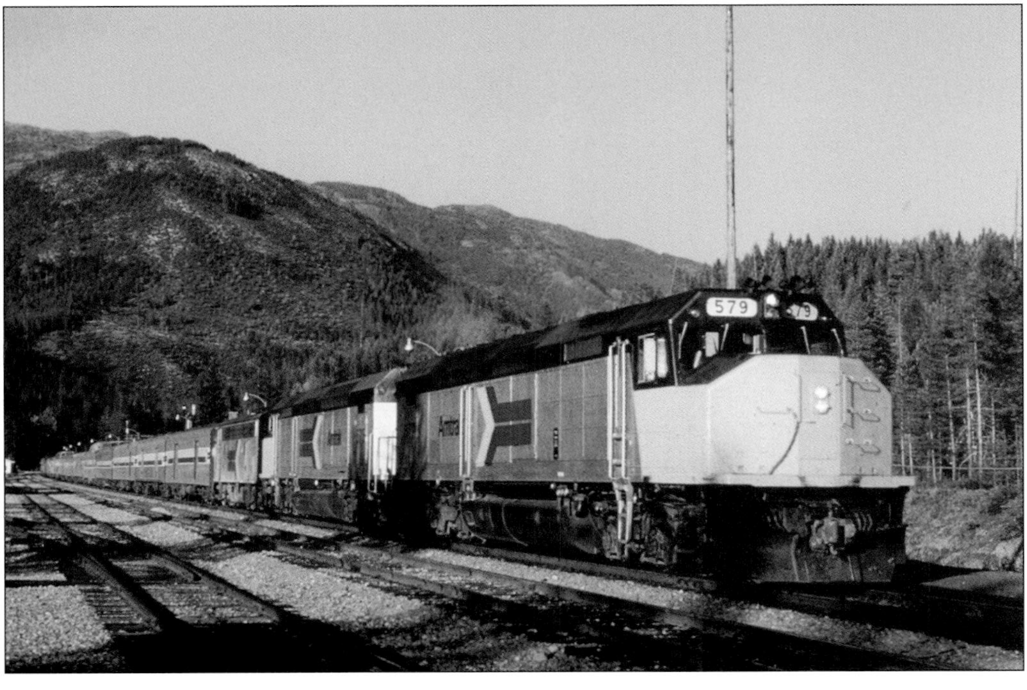

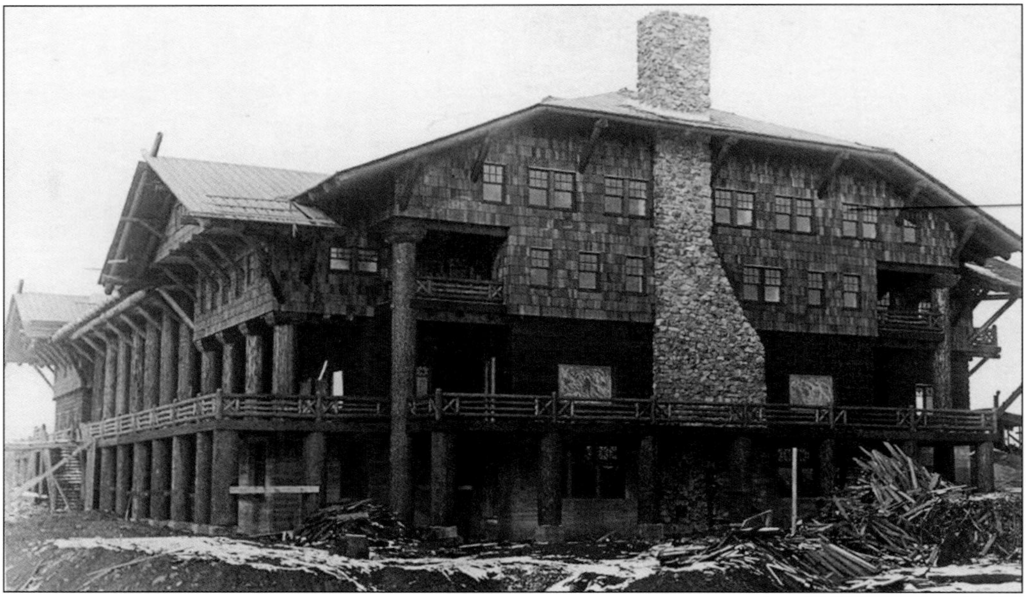

The massive Glacier Park Hotel at Glacier Park Station was Louis Hill's showpiece property. All construction projects required an Authorization for Expenditure (AFE) to maintain accurate financial records. The Glacier Park Hotel was modestly described in AFE No. 20365 as "A Frame Hotel 206 X 110 Feet to Provide Facilities for Taking Care of Tourists in Route to The Glacier National Park," with a total authorized cost of $72,108; a substantial outlay in the early 20th century. A small chalet called Camp No. 1 was used by guests until the hotel was finished in late spring 1913. (Both, author's collection.)

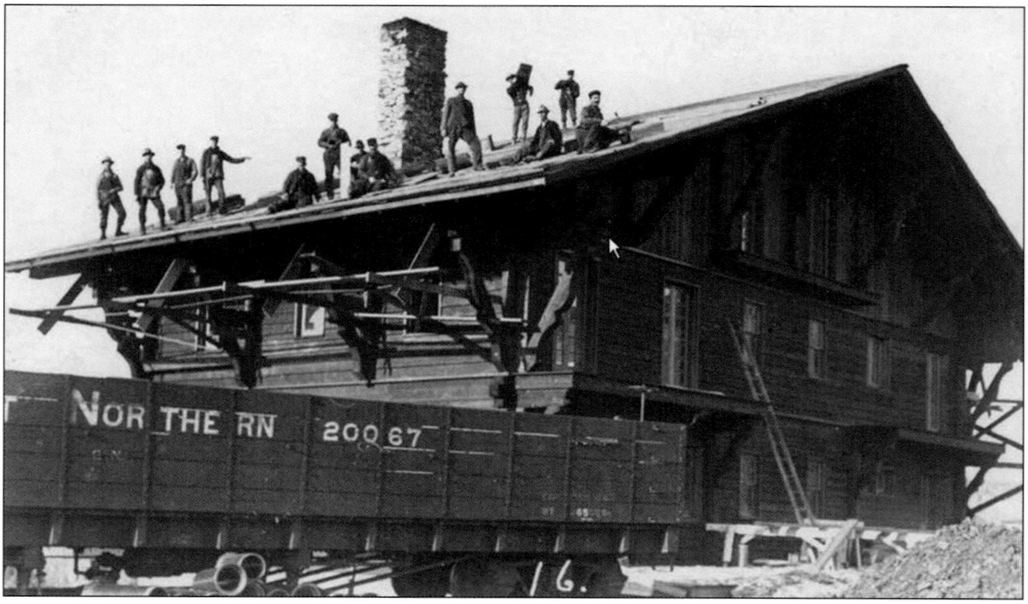

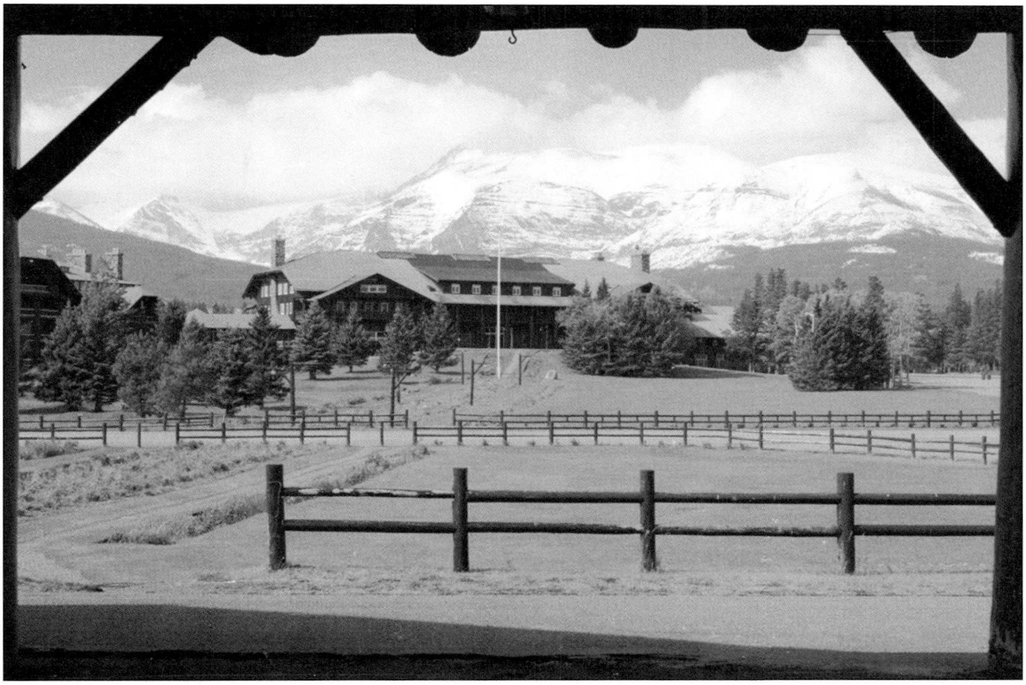

This picture-perfect view of Glacier Park Lodge and Glacier National Park greets passengers as they depart the train at East Glacier Park station. Built in 1912, Glacier Park Lodge is nestled in East Glacier at the foot of Dancing Lady Mountain. (Author's collection.)

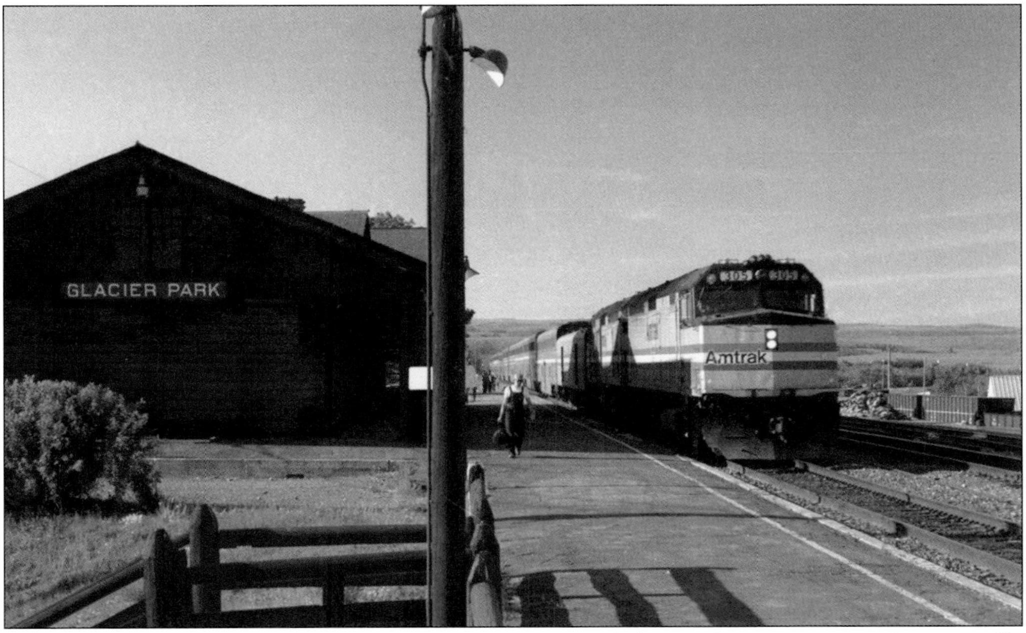

Amtrak makes regular scheduled stops at East Glacier Park during the summer months, normally from mid-April to early October. In June and July, there is enough daylight to enjoy the scenery taking the trip either direction through Marias Pass; this westbound *Empire Builder* leaves East Glacier about 6:30 in the evening with the eastbound train arriving at 9:30 in the morning. (Author's collection.)

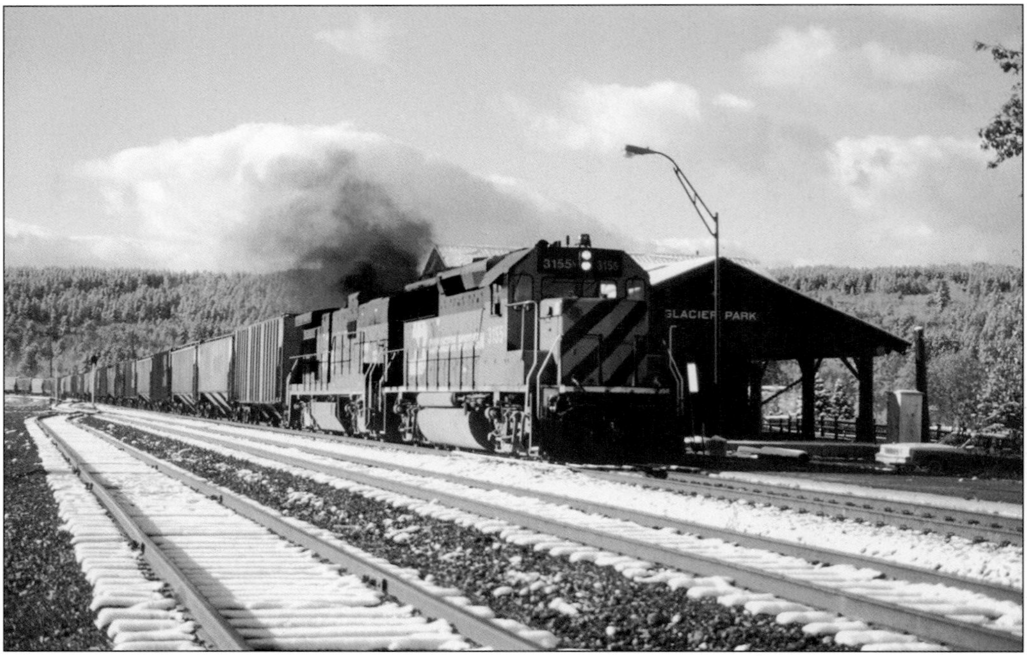

A dusting of snow quickly melts away in the October sun as EMD GP50 3155, in tandem with a General Electric B30-7A, prepares to assault the .08-degree grade to Spotted Robe. The B30-7A, sometimes referred to as "slugs" or "toasters," were cabless units controlled by the lead locomotive. (Courtesy Jerry Quinn collection.)

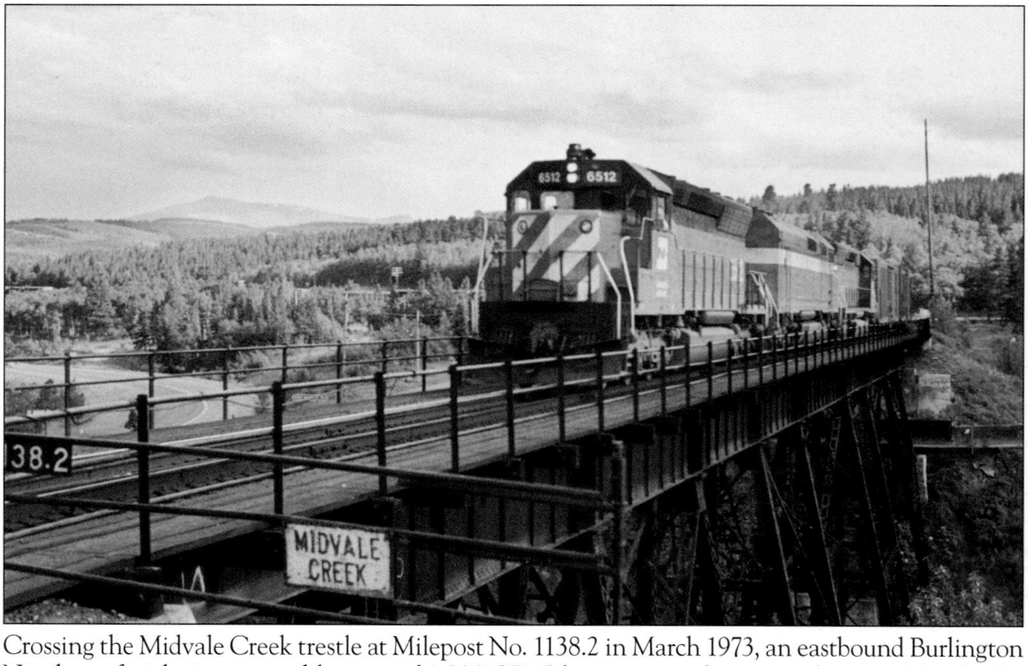

Crossing the Midvale Creek trestle at Milepost No. 1138.2 in March 1973, an eastbound Burlington Northern freight is powered by one of 1,200 SD45 locomotives featuring the new 20-cylinder model 645E3 prime mover producing 3,600 horsepower. The SD45 was one of the most successful EMD locomotives manufactured, and its dependability was a significant reason so many railroads purchased the model. (Courtesy Jerry Quinn collection.)

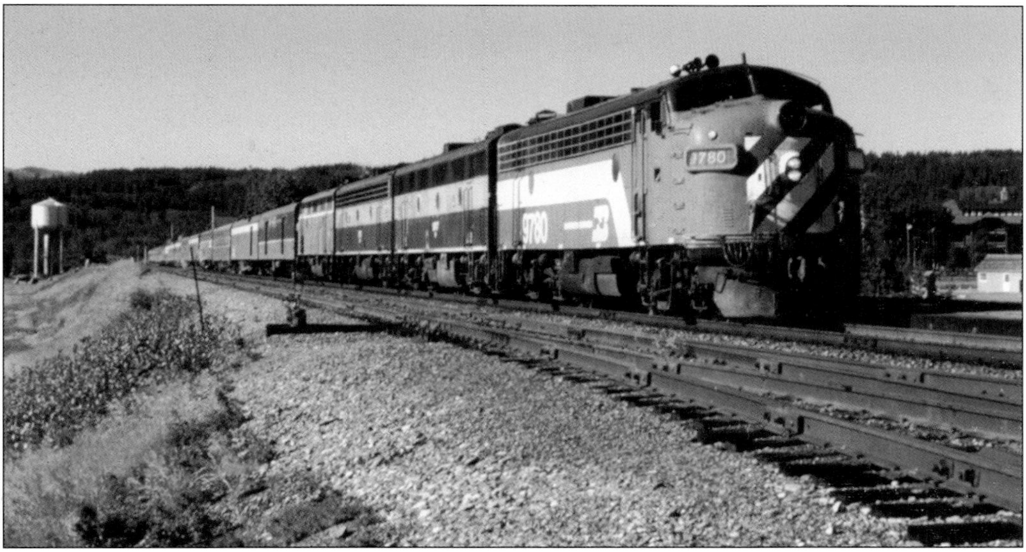

When Amtrak began operation of the nation's passenger rail services in May 1971, it purchased or leased equipment from predecessor railroads. This led to a colorful array of varying paint schemes known as the "Rainbow Era." In August 1972 at Glacier Park, 9780 displays the short-lived Burlington Northern "Hockey Stick" motif. It would take a few years for Amtrak to repaint all the cars with its standard red-white-and-blue scheme. (Author's collection.)

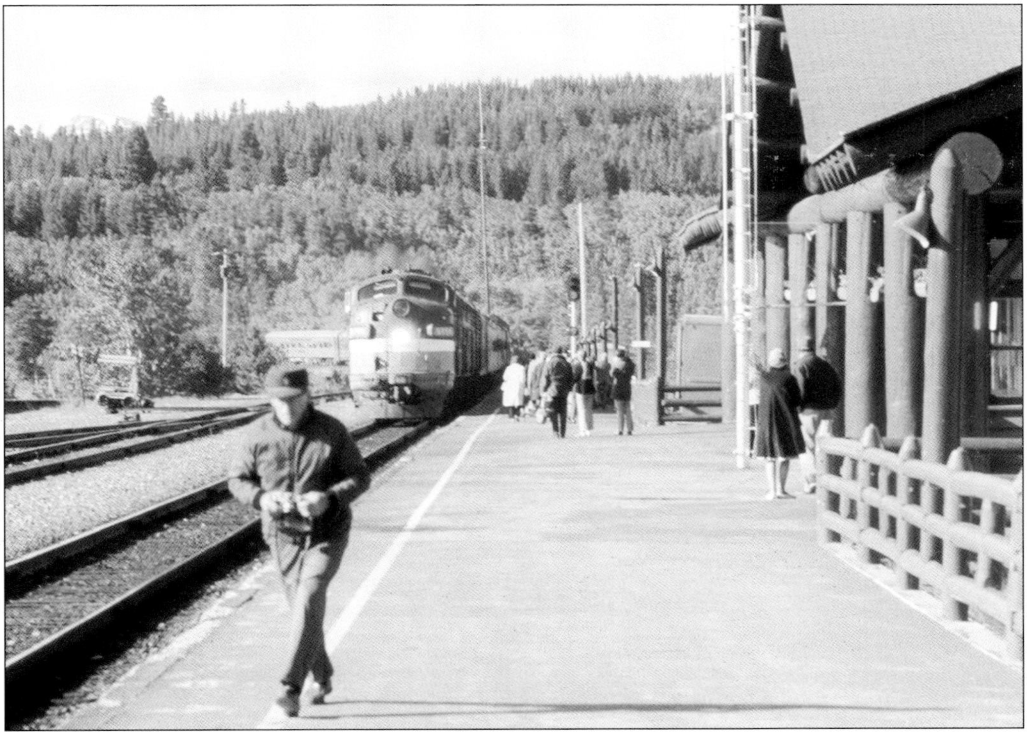

The original 1891 Midvale station was replaced by this 24-by-136-foot two-story depot during the construction of the chalet from 1910 to 1913. A 1972-era eastbound Amtrak *Empire Builder* slowly eases into East Glacier Park Station as a railfan scurries along the platform eager for another photograph. (Courtesy Chuck Hatler.)

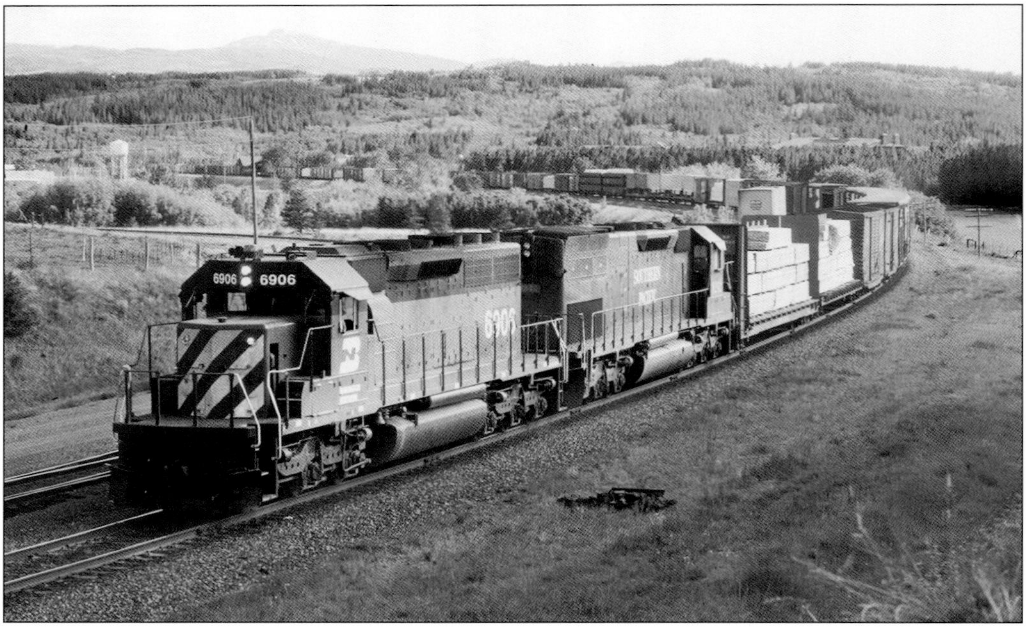

Without the railroad and Glacier National Park, East Glacier would have no raison d'être. On a warm July 1977 afternoon, Burlington Northern Extra 6906 East departs the town; *New York Times* travel writer Stephen Nash wrote: "East Glacier Park . . . is a charming, tumbleweedy throwback with a string of weathered eateries and motor-court lodgings that are only slightly post–World War II." (Courtesy Jerry Quinn collection.)

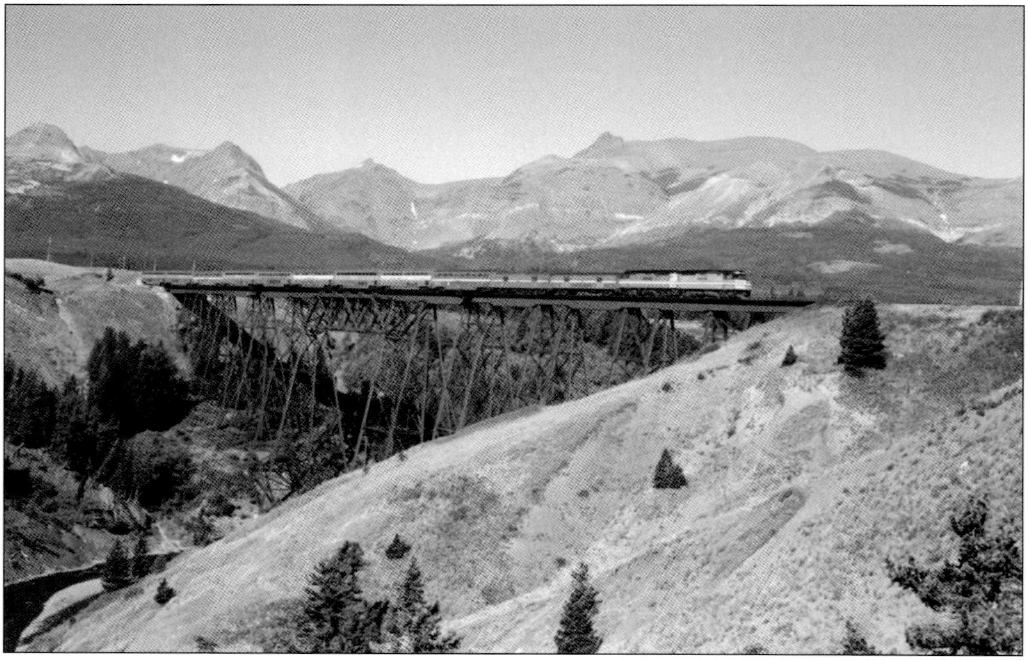

The author's July 15, 1986, photograph of Amtrak *Empire Builder* Train No. 8 stretching out over the 751-foot-long Two Medicine River's trestle attempts to replicate the famous Great Northern Railway public relations images showcasing the Two Medicine River and Rocky Mountain Front used in numerous advertisements. (Author's collection.)

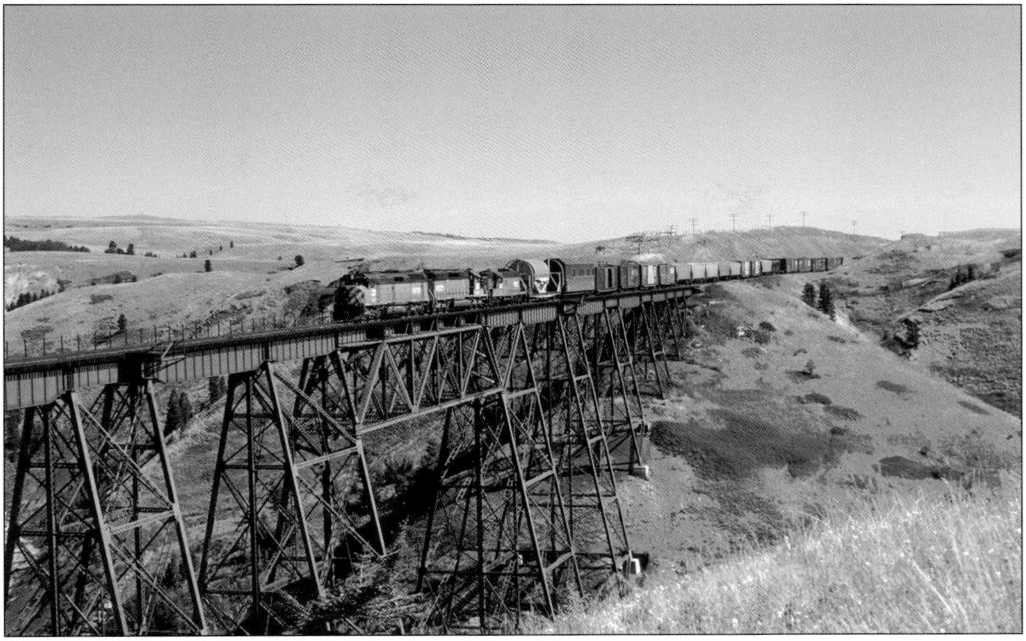
The wheat fields and grasslands of the Montana Hi-Line fade away behind this westbound Burlington Northern freight train approaching East Glacier Park. At nearly 200 feet above the Two Medicine River, Bridge No. 95 ranks as one of the tallest railroad trestles in the world. (Photograph by Kenneth "Ken" Ardinger, author's collection.)

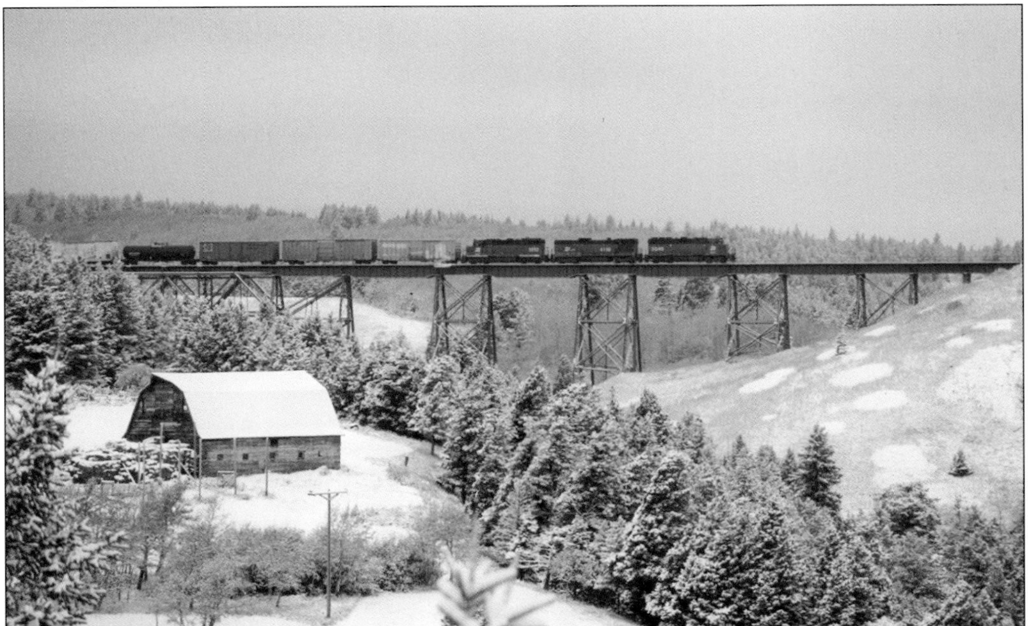
Looking like a scene from a Christmas card, Burlington Northern General Electric B30-7A 4116, sandwiched between EMD GP40-2 3045 and EMD GP40M 3552, slips quietly across the Two Medicine River Trestle in an early-winter Montana snowstorm. For years, the barn in the foreground has been a landmark in nearly all photographs taken at the bridge. (Courtesy Jerry Quinn collection.)

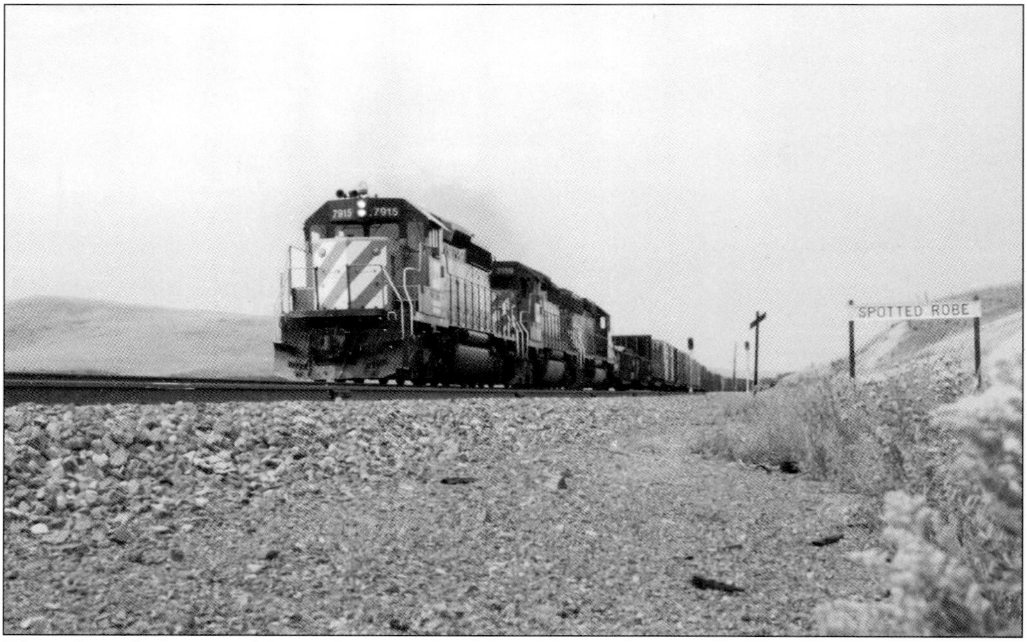

There have been 10 rail line relocations in the 13-mile section of railroad between East Glacier Park and Browning due to "gumbo." The term gumbo applies to much of the soil in the Montana prairie; as one soil scientist remarked, "When the soil is wet, you don't want to be on it. And when it's dry, it's like working concrete." After a heavy rain, the saturated earth triggers hillsides to slip away, causing an unstable roadbed. Here are two views of Spotted Robe. Above, three westbound Burlington Northern SD40-2s pass Milepost No. 1133.22 at the Spotted Robe sign; the picture below shows a 1947 Great Northern public relations photograph of the *Empire Builder* eastbound at Spotted Robe a few miles east of Glacier Park. (Above, author's collection; below, Great Northern Railway.)

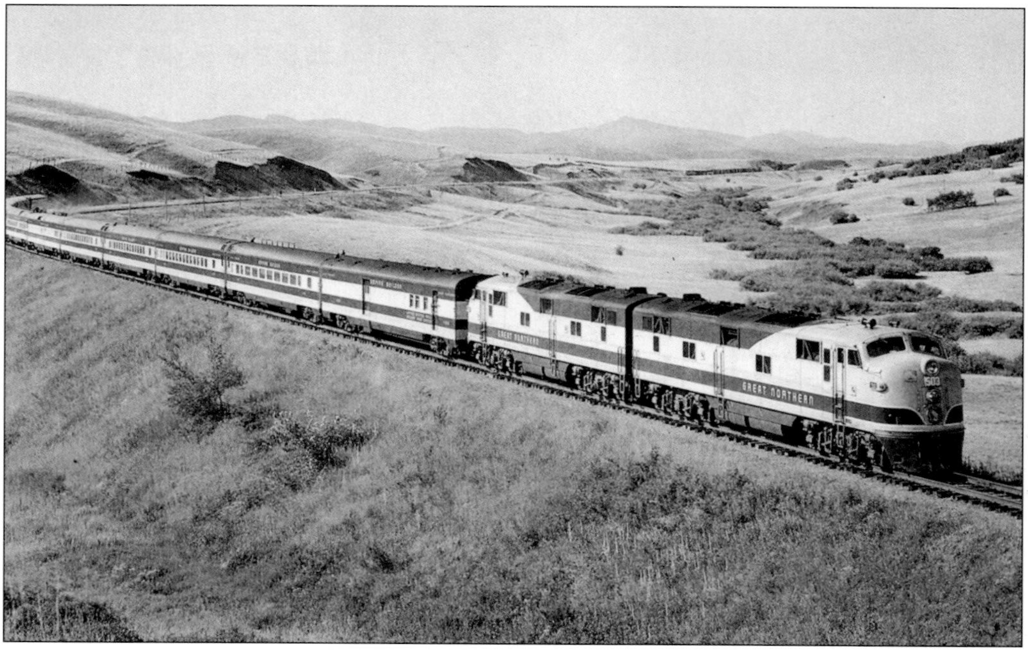

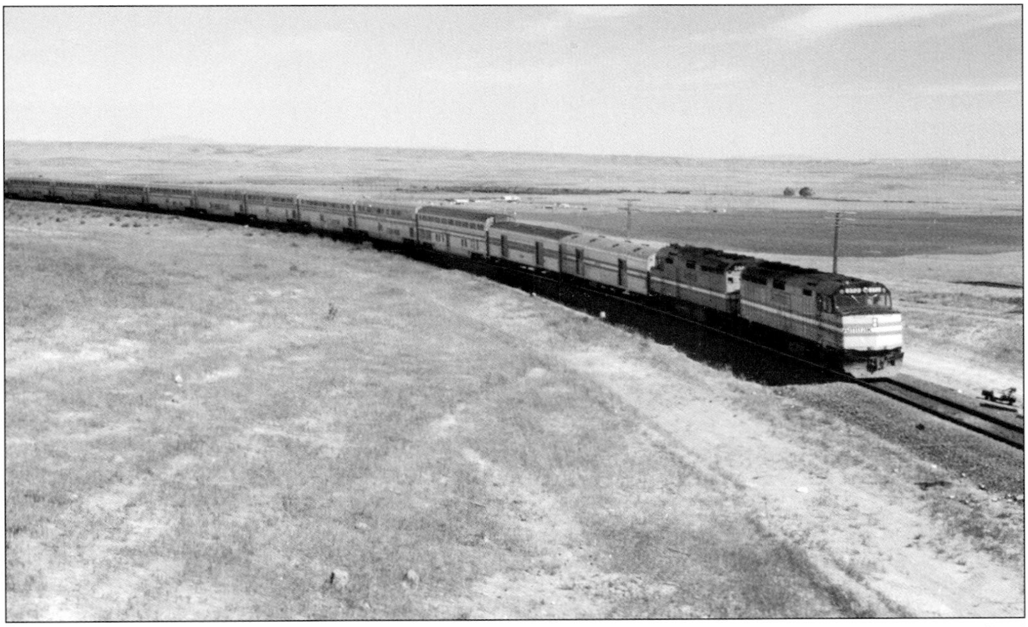

The eastbound *Empire Builder* led by two Amtrak F40PHRs passes the site of former Snowshed No. 1, approximately one mile west of Browning. This 1,118-foot-long shed was built to protect the tracks from drifting snow. There were originally five snowsheds in the 20 miles from Browning to Rising Wolf; since wooden snowsheds are costly to maintain, by the 1960s, the prairie sheds had lost their usefulness. Snowshed No. 1 was the last one removed, in 1967. (Author's collection.)

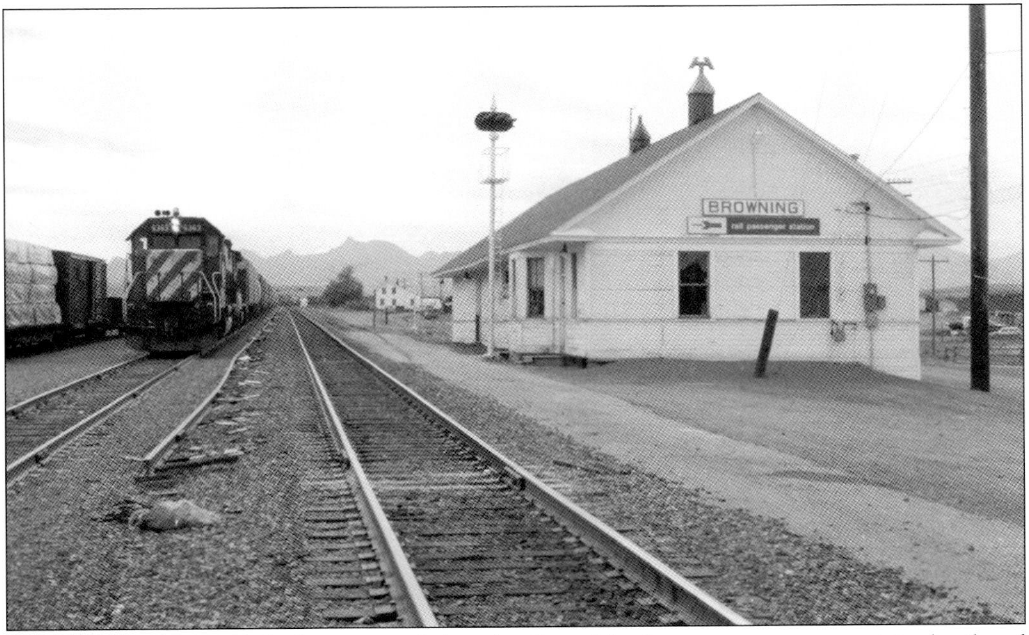

In 1926, James Willard Shultz suggested that the Great Northern rename many original railroad locations with colorful Indian names; Browning was changed to Fort Browning, Essex to Walton, Kilroy to Spotted Robe, and Lubec to Rising Wolf. Many, but not all, locations were returned to their original name by the 1940s. Burlington Northern Extra 6363 East sits on the siding south of the 30-by-112-foot Browning depot. (Author's collection.)

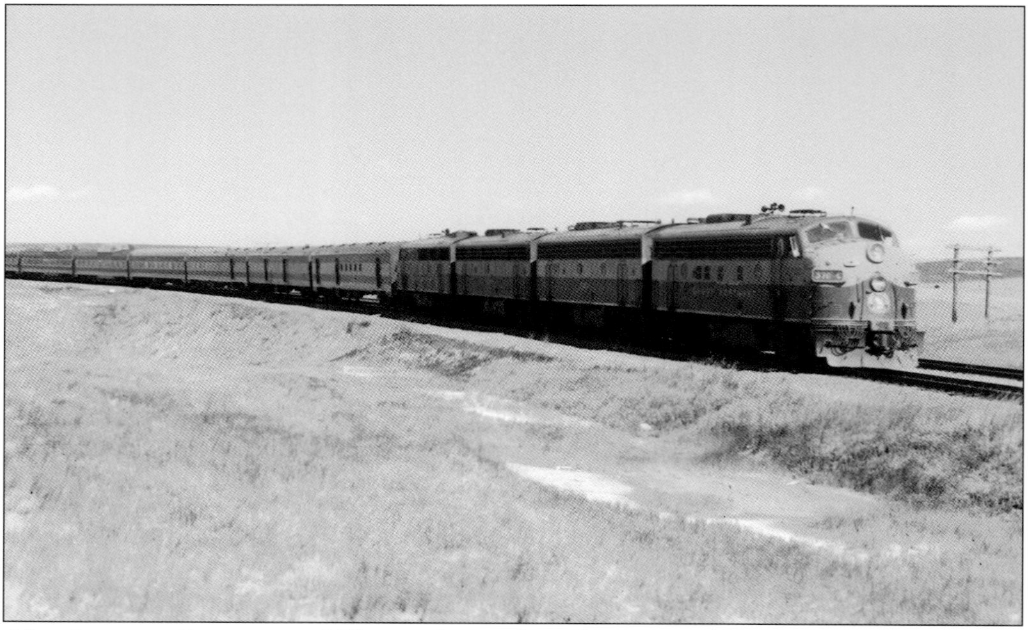

After departing Browning at 3:53 p.m., this eastbound *Empire Builder* will soon be traveling 79 miles per hour on its way to St. Paul, Minnesota. Track speeds for railroads were regulated by the Interstate Commerce Commission, with nine classes of track based on cab and signal controls; the Great Northern had a Class Four designation with a maximum allowable speed of 60 miles per hour for freight trains and 79 miles per hour for passenger trains. (Courtesy Jerry Quinn collection.)

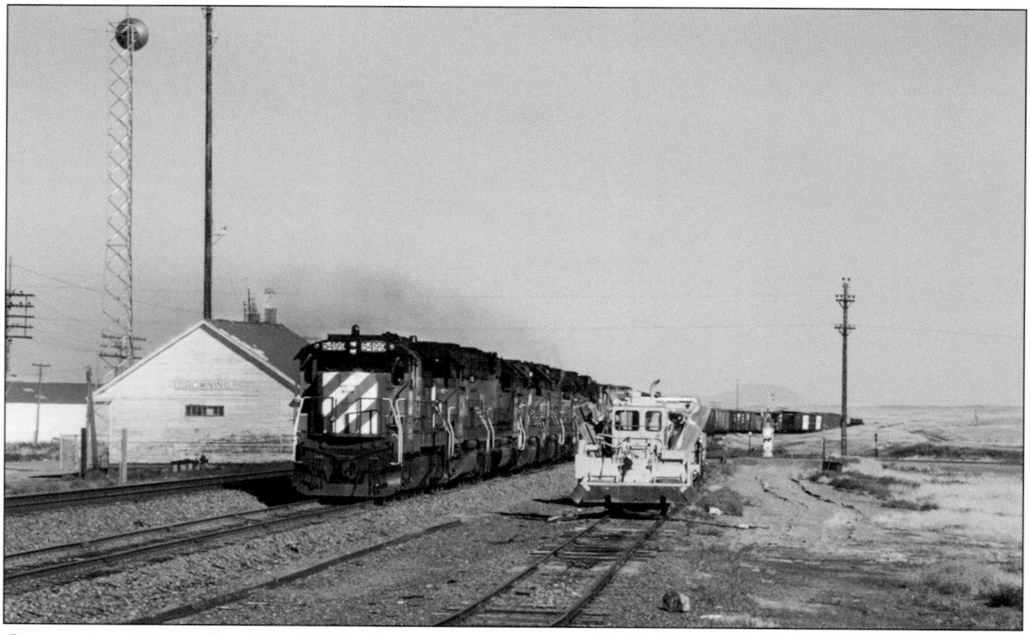

On a crisp November 11, 1987, afternoon, a rarity rolled westward through Browning. The head locomotive 5499 was one of three General Electric B32-8 demonstrator units built for the Burlington Northern in 1984; they were all painted and lettered in Burlington Northern Cascade Green colors. It appears that these locomotives did not meet expectations, as all had been retired by 1991. (Courtesy Jerry Quinn collection.)

Four

The Middle Fork

Views up the Middle Fork of the Flathead River

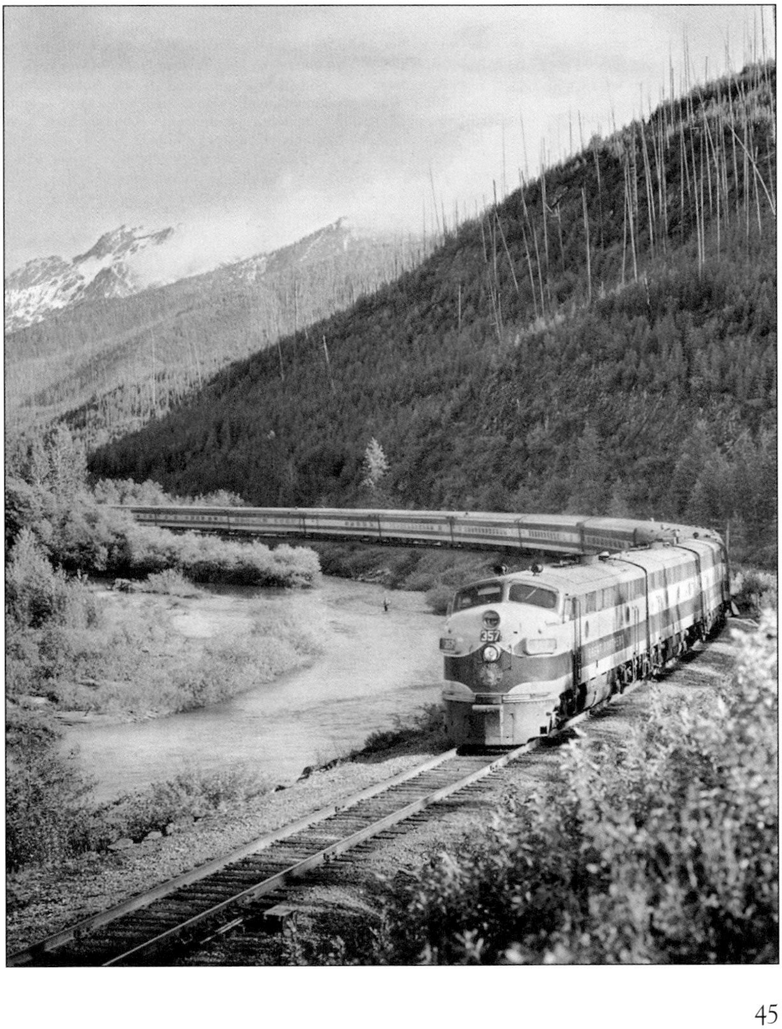

The Middle Fork of the Flathead River originates in the heart of the Bob Marshall Wilderness and flows northwest to form the southern border of Glacier National Park in northwest Montana. This vintage Great Northern Railway public relations photograph taken near Nyack along Deerlick Creek before a 1960s line relocation provides a glimpse of the stunning scenery in the Middle Fork valley. (Great Northern Railway.)

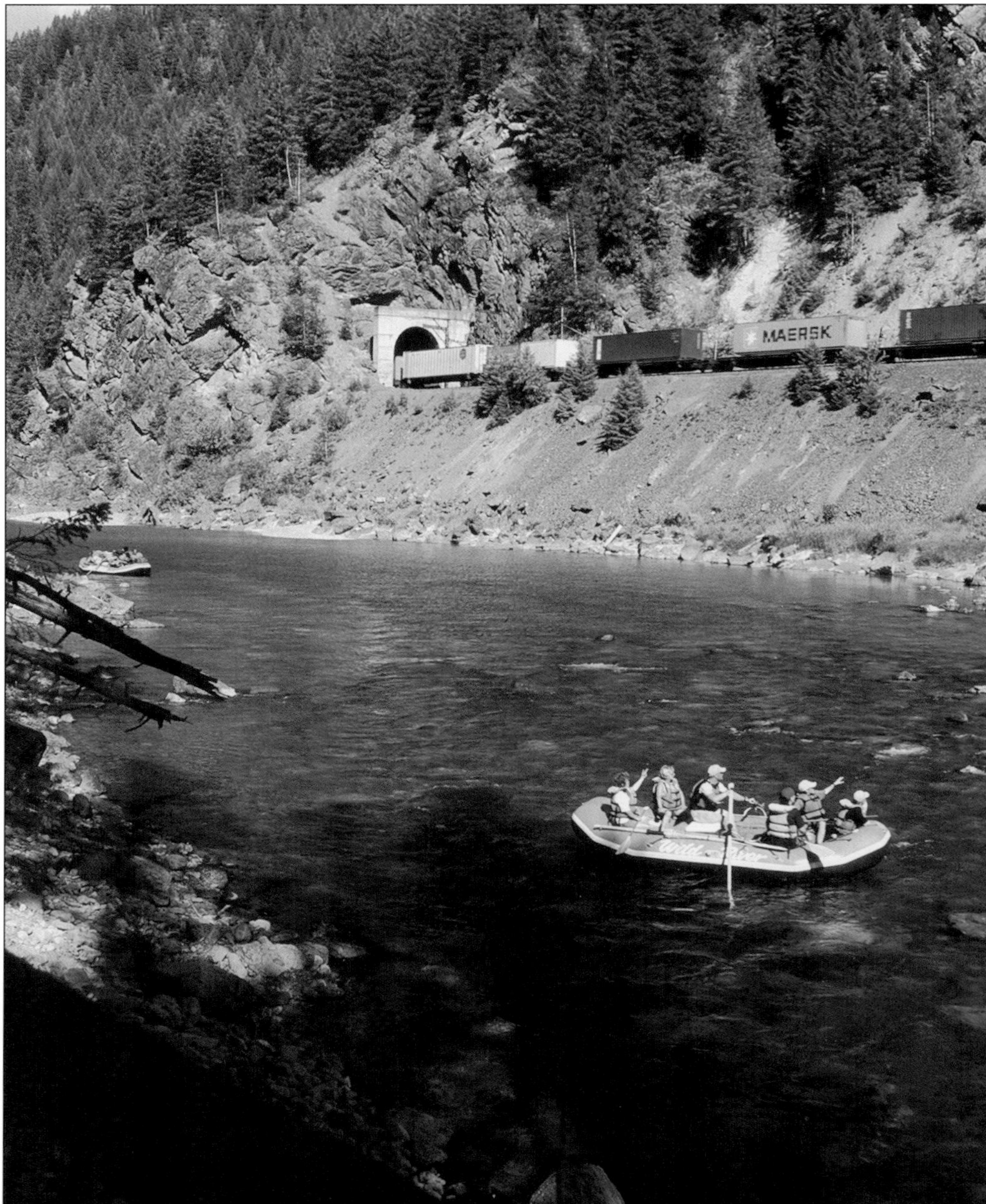

Recognized as a premier whitewater rafting destination, the Middle Fork of the Flathead River hugs the Marias Pass main line from Belton to Nyack. According to one whitewater rafter, "The scenery down the Flathead River, which runs through Glacier National Park, is breathtaking and awesome. There are huge ancient pine tree forests and majestic snow peaked mountain tops. If you are lucky you might see a bald eagle, deer, or even a bear. The water in the Flathead River is crystal clear and ice cold. Even though the water is 20 or 30 feet deep at some points, you can see right to the bottom and it does not appear that deep. Some of the views are so incredible it looks like a postcard or a computer desktop wallpaper." There are six tunnels in Marias Pass located within the 20-mile section of track eastbound from Belton toward Paola. This unique view of trains exiting Tunnel No. 4 is available only to adventurers in whitewater rafts. (Author's collection.)

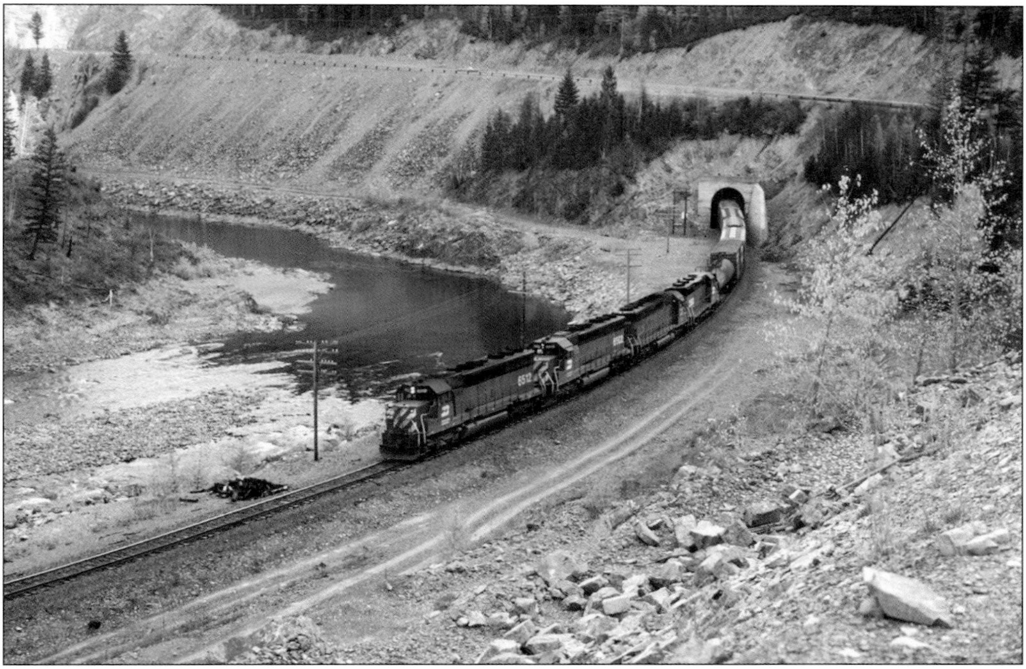

Great Northern milepost and tunnel numbers originated from St. Paul, Minnesota, and increased westward to identify track maintenance locations. At first, the tunnels through Marias Pass were assigned whole numbers—Tunnels Nos. 1 through 5—but as improvements were completed, the railroad needed to specify the position with decimal increments. During the 1940s, there were three tunnel realignments moving the roadbed away from the river, creating Tunnels Nos. 3.7, 3.8, and 3.9. Above, Burlington Northern SD45 6512 exits Tunnel No. 3.8; below, a westbound train drifts downgrade out of Tunnel No. 3.9 in October 1989. (Both, courtesy Jerry Quinn collection.)

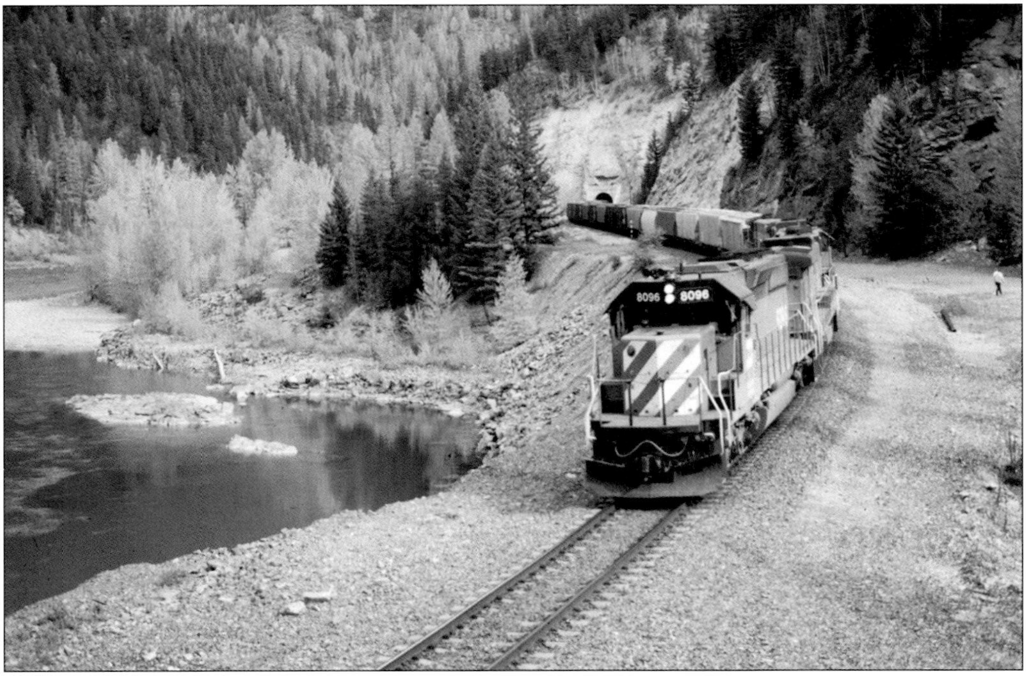

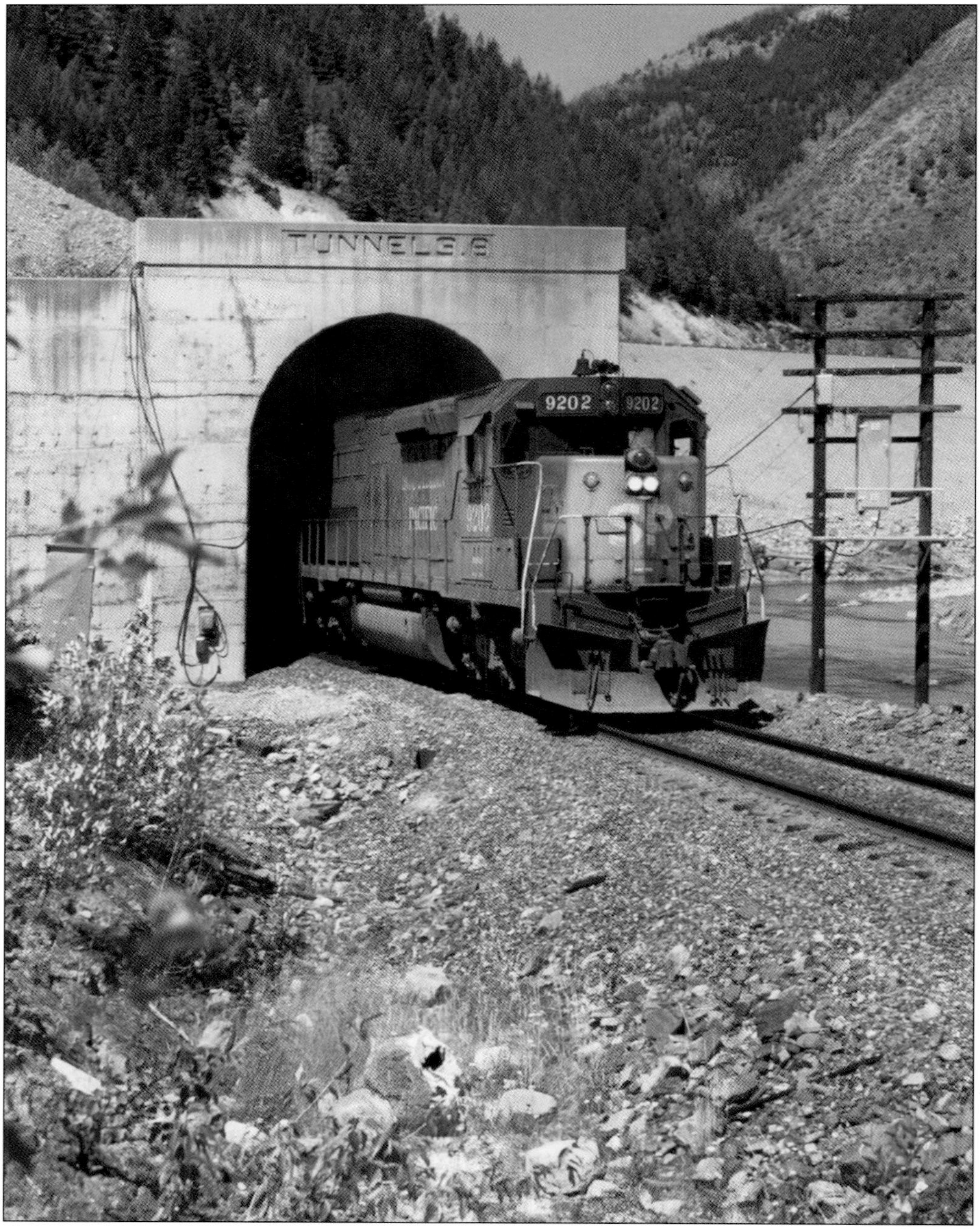

Why is a California-based Southern Pacific locomotive in Marias Pass? Until the 1990s, most locomotives chiefly operated on their "home" rail lines, so in 1986, it was relatively rare to see Southern Pacific SD45T-2 (Special Delivery-Class 45-Tunnel Unit-Second Upgrade) 9202 poke its nose out of Tunnel No. 3.8 into the Middle Fork of the Flathead River sunshine. This unit is operating on the Burlington Northern Railroad in a pool-power arrangement. Railroads exchange, or pool, locomotives for a variety of reasons; for example, a railroad may experience a need for supplementary motive power due to maintenance delays or accidents and request a short-term loan from another company, compensating the other railroad later by loaning a similar locomotive for the same amount of time. (Author's collection.)

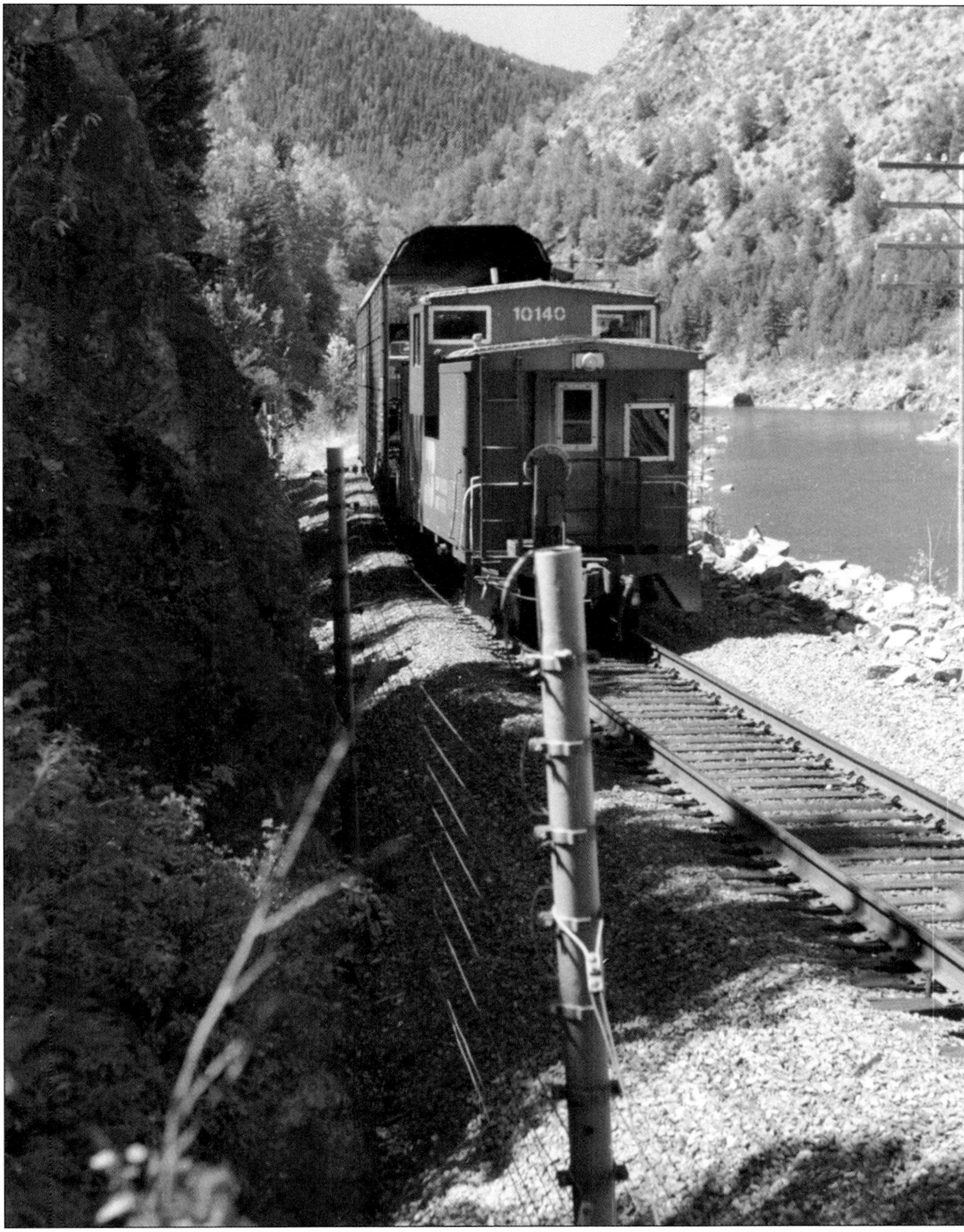

Burlington Northern Caboose No. 10140 on a westbound freight train hugs the hillside in the narrow Middle Fork Canyon, where falling rock is always a potential danger. Note the slide fence in the foreground; energized cables are stretched out on poles that trigger a red warning signal if a rockslide breaks the wire. Where are the cabooses today? By the mid-1980s, new labor agreements reduced the hours of service for train crews, including provisions for the removal of cabooses from the rear of freight trains. The labor agreements also cut crew size from five to four, and finally to two, an engineer and conductor, both of whom could ride comfortably in the locomotive cab. Today, an electronic device called a flashing rear-end device (FRED) is mounted on the end of freight trains in lieu of a caboose. (Author's collection.)

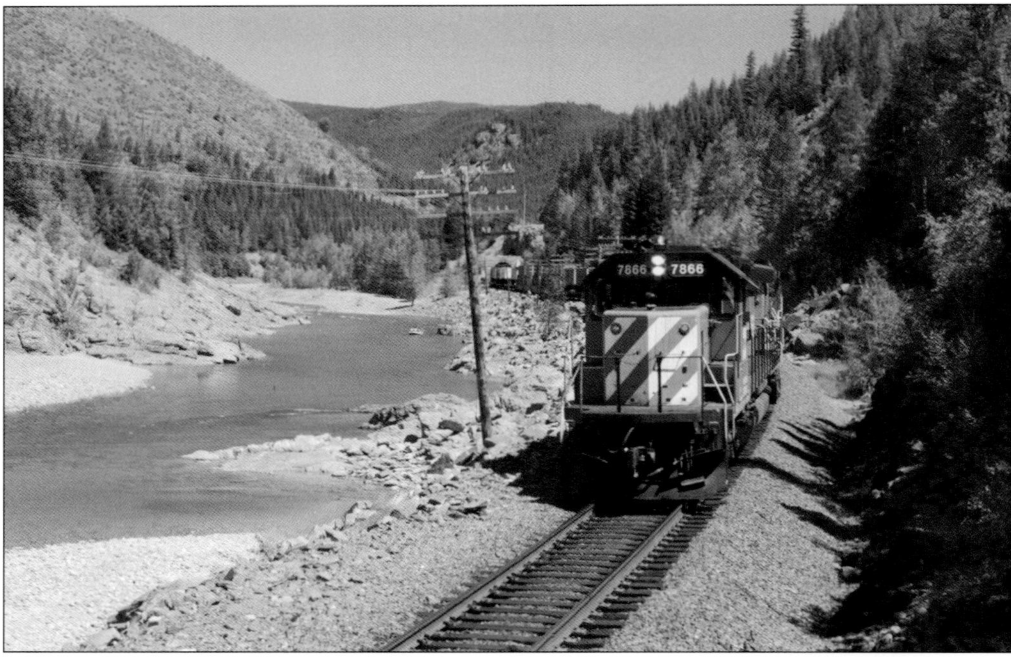

In the author's opinion, this image best captures the essence of railroading along the Middle Fork of the Flathead River. The photograph features a clear mid-July Rocky Mountain afternoon, the glacier blue-tinged water in the Middle Fork, Tunnel No. 3.7 in the background, and a westbound Burlington Northern SD40-2 in the classic Cascade Green paint scheme. (Author's collection.)

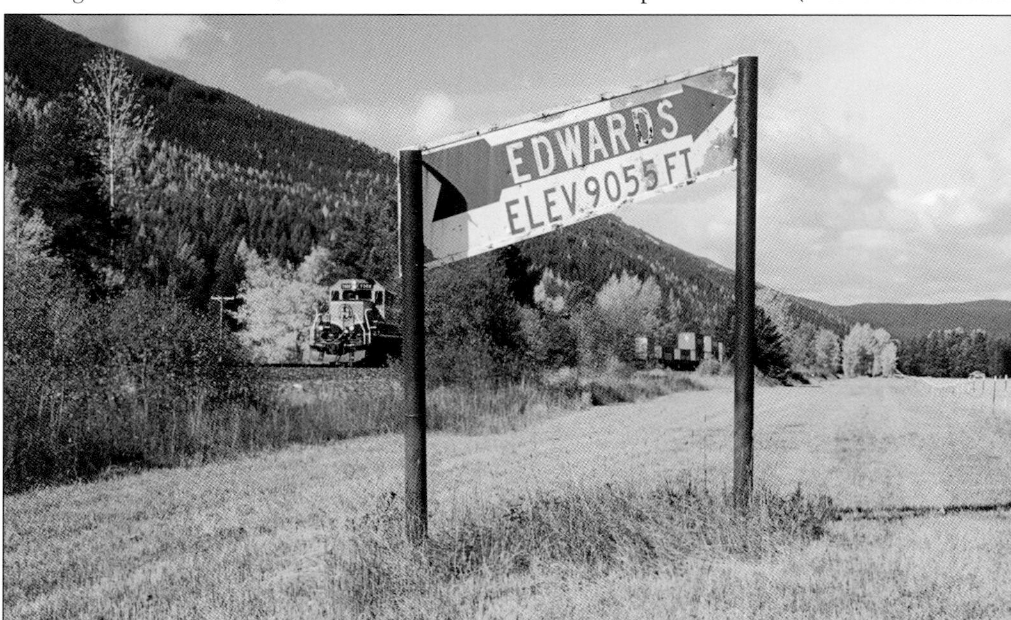

During the 1920s, the Great Northern Railway enthusiastically promoted visiting Glacier National Park. The railroad sought to increase public interest in the park and improve passenger revenue, and so, 19 signs pointing out mountain peaks in the park were erected along the right-of-way from Belton to Paola in 1925. Most of the signs are now overgrown by trees or removed, but the Mount Edwards sign in the Nyack Flats may still be visible today. (Author's collection.)

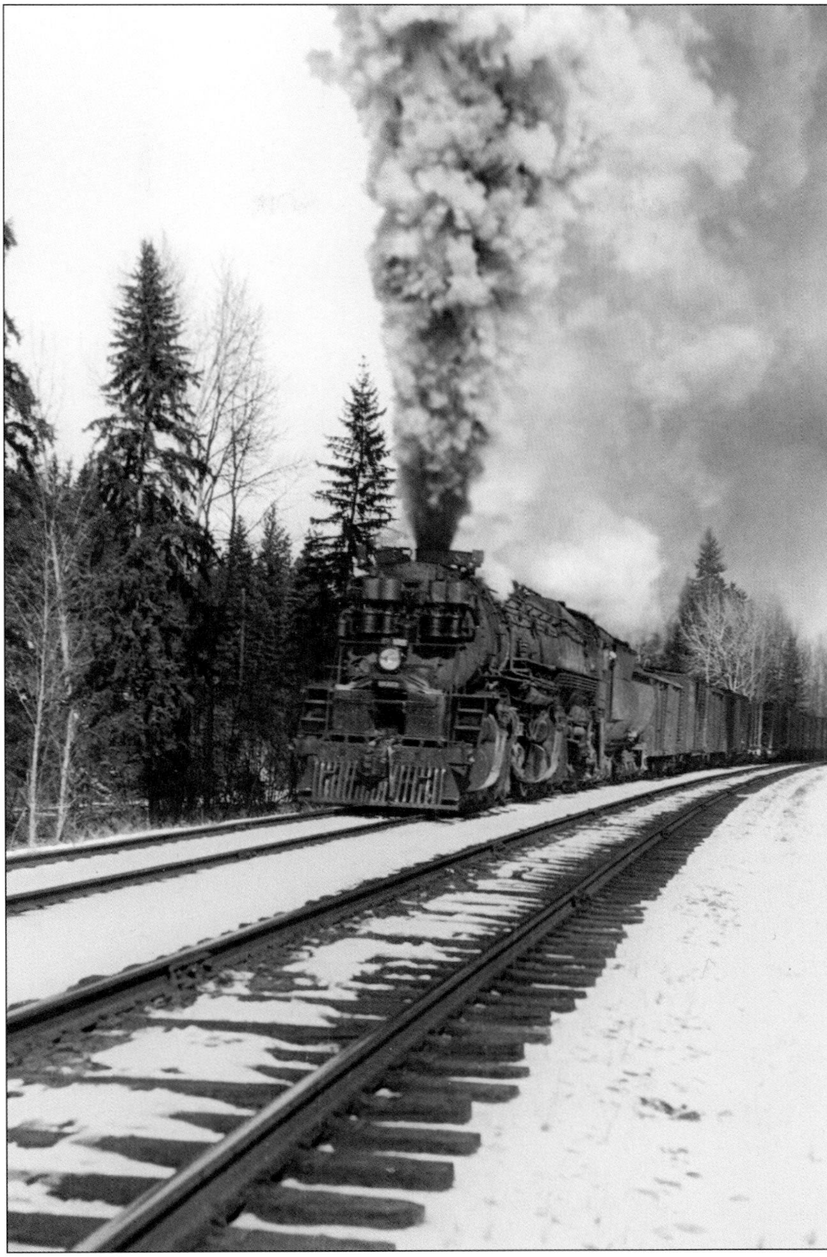

Great Northern Railway's 2-8-8-2 Class R-2 locomotives produced 153,000 pounds of tractive force and were reputed to be the most powerful steam engines in North America. Beginning in March 1929 through November 1930, the 16 R-2 units were erected at the company's Hillyard, Washington, shops. The Great Northern needed considerable horsepower to move heavy freight trains through Marias Pass, and all 16 of these massive oil-burning locomotives were assigned to the Kalispell Division from Whitefish to Blackfoot. To prevent the spread of forest fires from burning coal embers, most Great Northern steam engines on Lines West were converted to oil burners during the 1920s. On this early winter day at Red Eagle in Nyack Flats, the dense steam engine exhaust will not pose any wildfire danger as Class R-2 2048 slowly drags an eastbound train up the nearly one-percent grade to Essex. (Courtesy Ed Krona collection.)

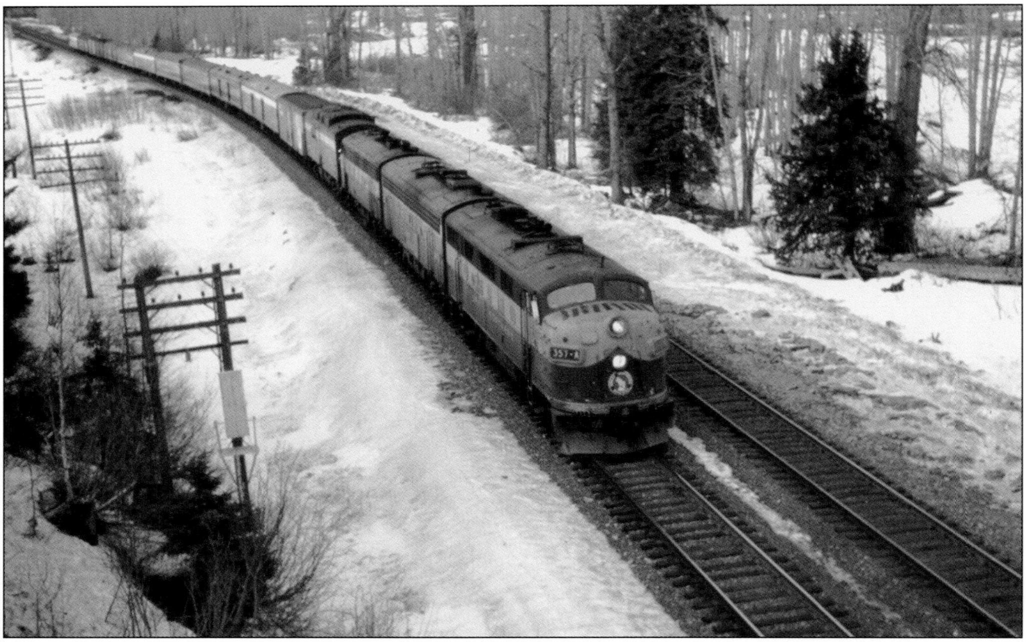

Looking north from the US Highway 2 overpass at Red Eagle, P7 367-A leads a consist of mainly mail and express cars on an eastbound *Western Star*. In 1950, the Great Northern held a "name-the-train" contest to identify its new secondary streamliner; one entry was *The Evergreen*. Railroad officials chose *Western Star* after the Stephen Vincent Benét poem about the westward migration of the pioneers and their journey through America toward the West. (Courtesy Cordell Newby collection, Great Northern Railway Historical Society.)

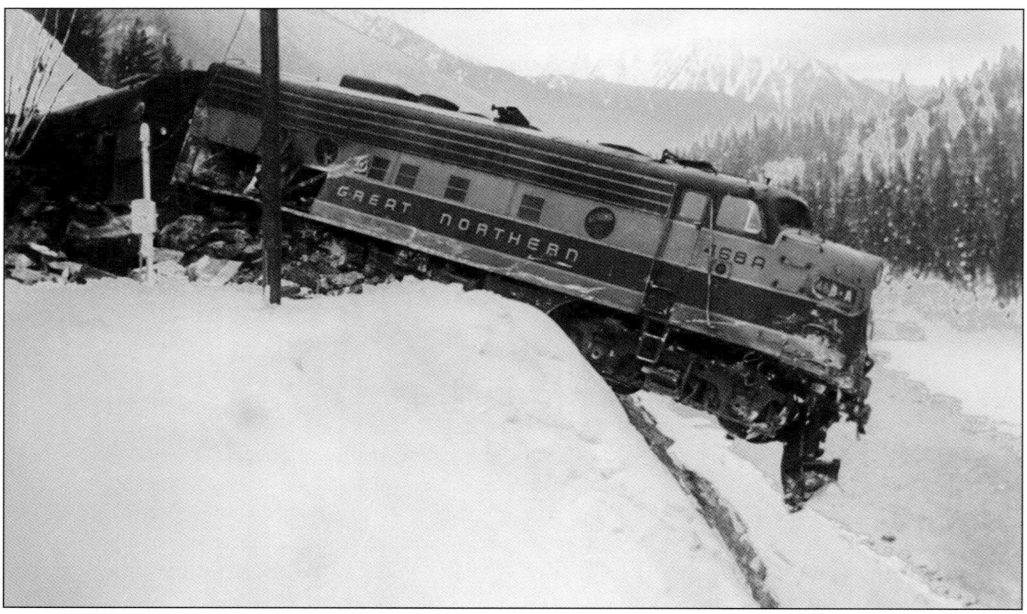

After encountering a rockslide, this accident at Twin Bridges just west of Hidden Lake could have been catastrophic for the crew in F7 468-A had it bounced a few more feet toward the canyon. It appears this eastbound train struck the pile of rocks in the foreground, but the slow uphill ascent prevented a disaster. (Courtesy Ed Krona collection.)

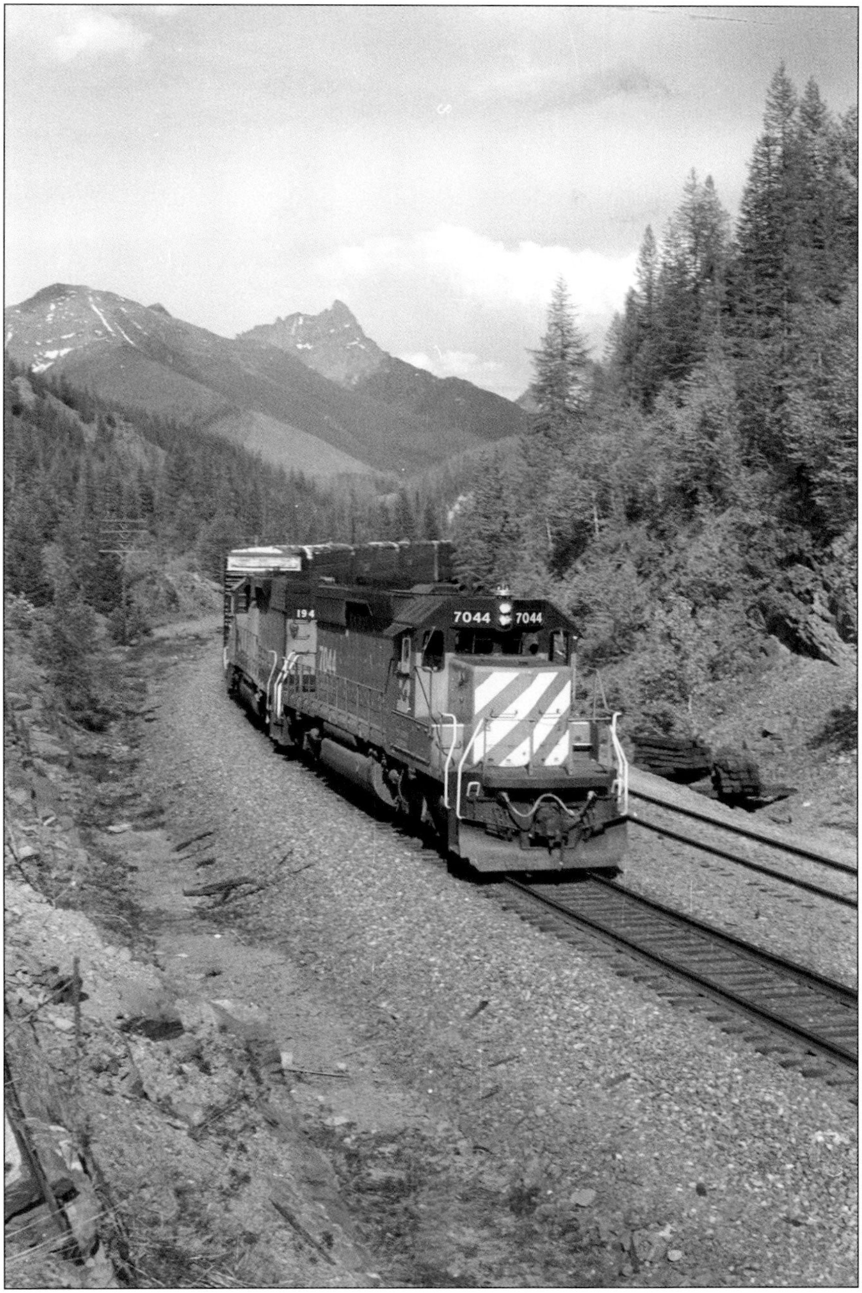

This view of southwest Glacier National Park at Milepost No. 1181 looking east from the US Highway 2 overpass is magnificent. In the past, the Great Northern public relations department used the landscape behind Burlington Northern SD40-2 7044 in a variety of publications. Looking up the Coal Creek drainage to 8,830-foot Battlement Mountain on the left and Mount St. Nicholas on the right provides a glimpse into one of the most inaccessible areas in Glacier National Park. In 2016, the National Park Service issued an official warning concerning backcountry access in the Nyack–Coal Creek zone due to fallen trees and snags left from the 2015 fires: "Currently, we do not recommend backcountry travel in the Nyack unless you are very fit and are willing to climb over and around hundreds, possibly even thousands of blackened trees." (Author's collection.)

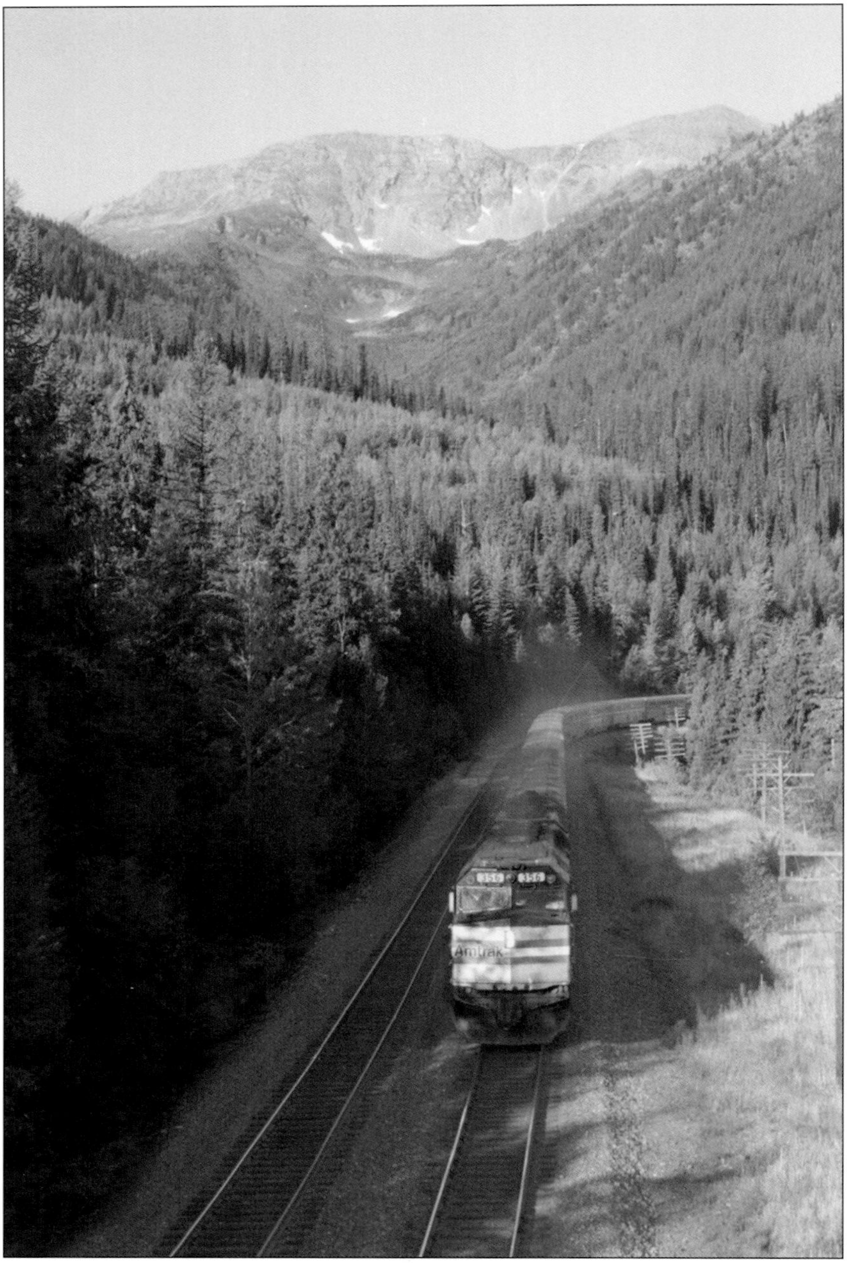

Little did Boies Penrose, a senator and avid sportsman from Pennsylvania, know that when he climbed the mountain in the background, his name would later be associated with the peak. The locale has become a popular spot for railfans to snap photographs of eastbound trains in Marias Pass, like this 1986 Amtrak *Empire Builder*. According to Jack Holterman in his book *Place Names of Glacier/Waterton Parks*, the three Penrose brothers were hiking at about the 7,000-foot level in the mountains near Nyack on September 1, 1907, when Dr. Charles Penrose and A.A. Stiles went deer hunting and killed a young grizzly bear. Almost instantly, the mother attacked Dr. Penrose, mauling a large part of his body. Despite the injuries, after an arduous trip bushwhacking down the mountain, they reached the Nyack depot the next day and were rescued by flagging down an eastbound passenger train. (Author's collection.)

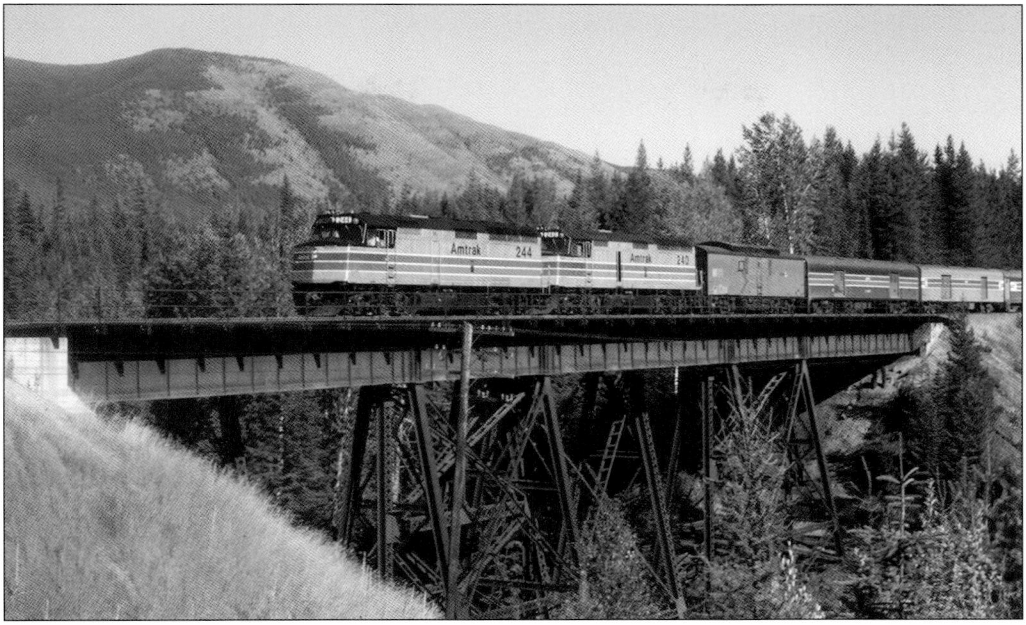

Several locations around Glacier National Park have been identified by multiple names. Amtrak Train No. 7, the westbound *Empire Builder*, crosses Stanton Creek, which is named after H.T. Stanton, a Montana railroad commissioner from the early 1900s. The Great Northern station at this site was originally called Garry, but in 1926, it was renamed Hidden Lake in reference to nearby Stanton Lake; currently, it is nameless. (Courtesy Jerry Quinn collection.)

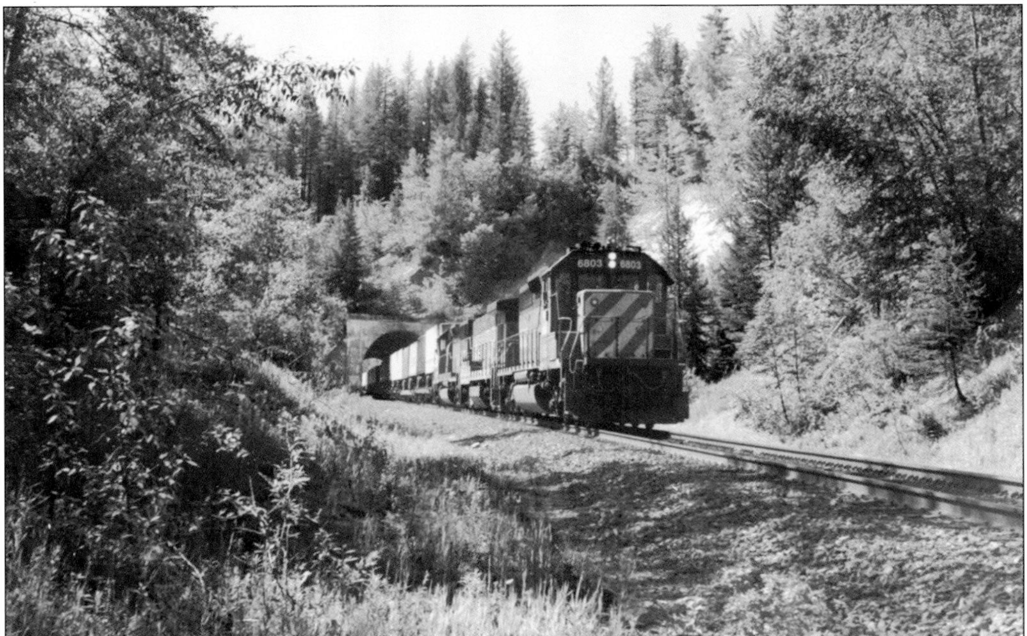

A Burlington Northern westbound freight leaves Tunnel No. 3; at 453 feet, this is the shortest of all six tunnels in Marias Pass. The two tunnels in the Paola area are not lengthy but are required to keep the tracks a safe distance from a steep embankment that has a history of sliding into the Middle Fork. (Author's collection.)

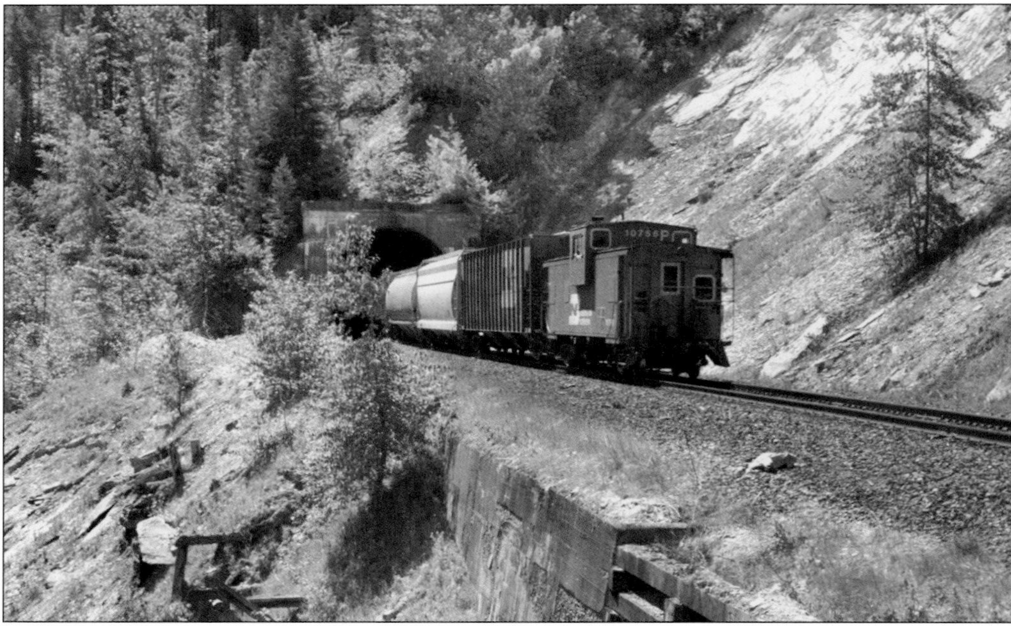

Burlington Northern Railroad Caboose No. 10756 on the rear of an eastbound train enters the darkness of Tunnel No. 3. Improvements to the right-of-way have been ongoing since 1898. Note the approach to the tunnel, with its concrete cribbing and retaining walls. The approach could potentially still be involved in a landslide, but none have been recorded for decades. (Author's collection.)

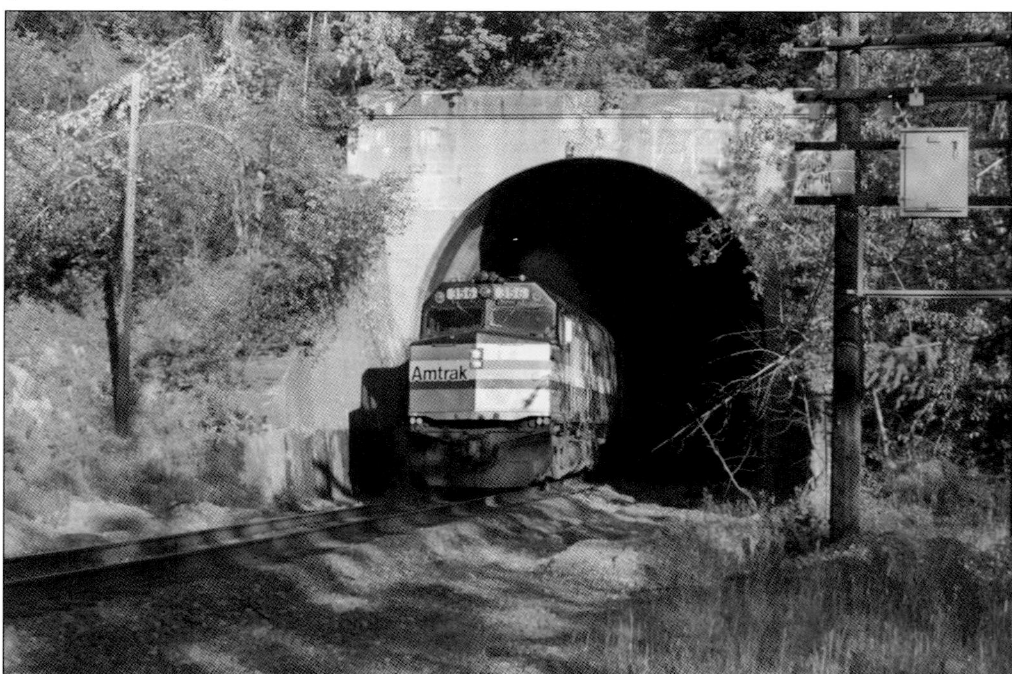

At 8:30 in the morning on a warm summer day, the eastbound Amtrak *Empire Builder* led by F40PH 356 hustles out of Tunnel No. 2 at the 50-miles-per-hour maximum track speed between Paola and Pinnacle, arriving on time at the next scheduled stop of Essex. (Author's collection.)

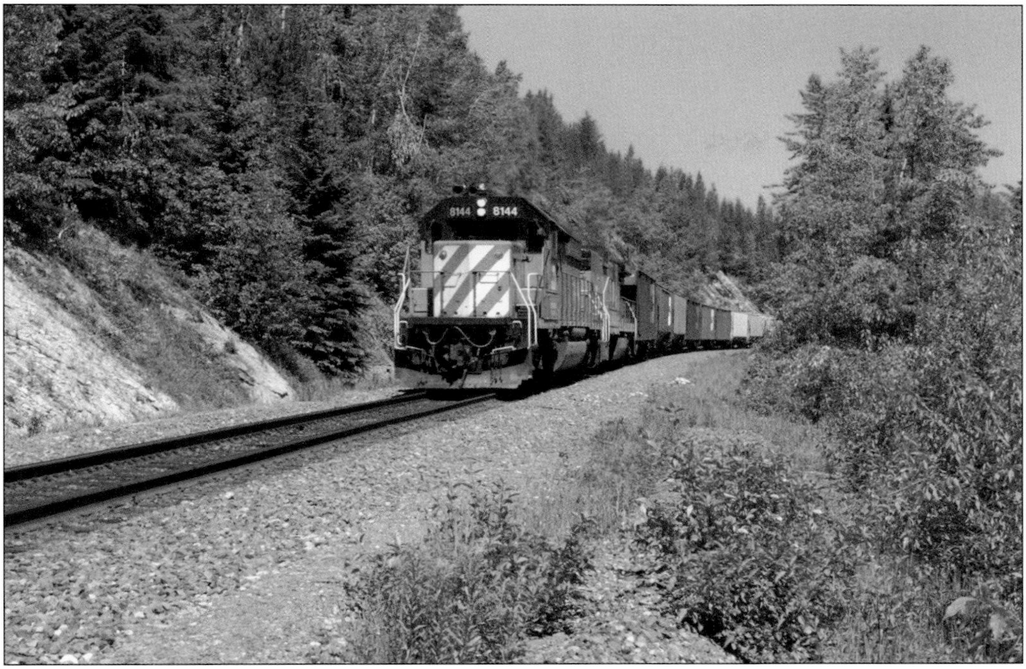

Two photographs of Burlington Northern trains at Tunnel No. 3 reveal the years of undergrowth that have stabilized the hillsides around Paola, but that has not always been the case. The July 9, 1897, *Kalispell Daily Interlake* reported: "Harry Landis and August Urback had a narrow escape last Saturday morning. They were running the engine up the grade from Essex to the summit. They had helped a freight up and were returning . . . near Paola the track gave way beneath the engine and it went off and down the hill 30 feet or more. Landis . . . was pretty badly bruised and shaken up. Urback had his head cut quite badly and one rib was broken." (Both, author's collection.)

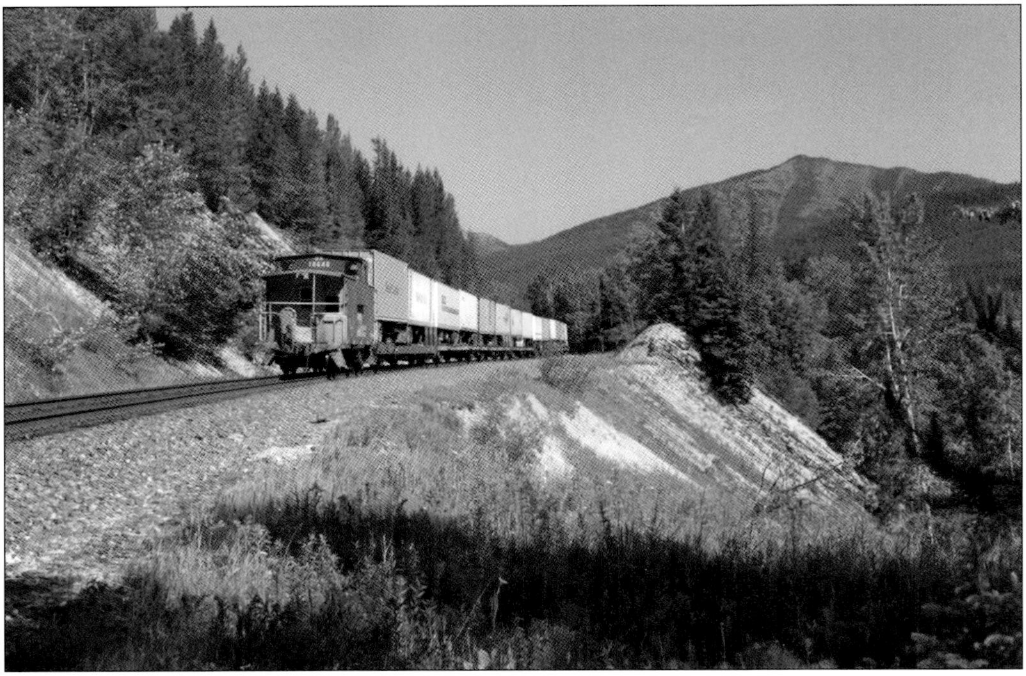

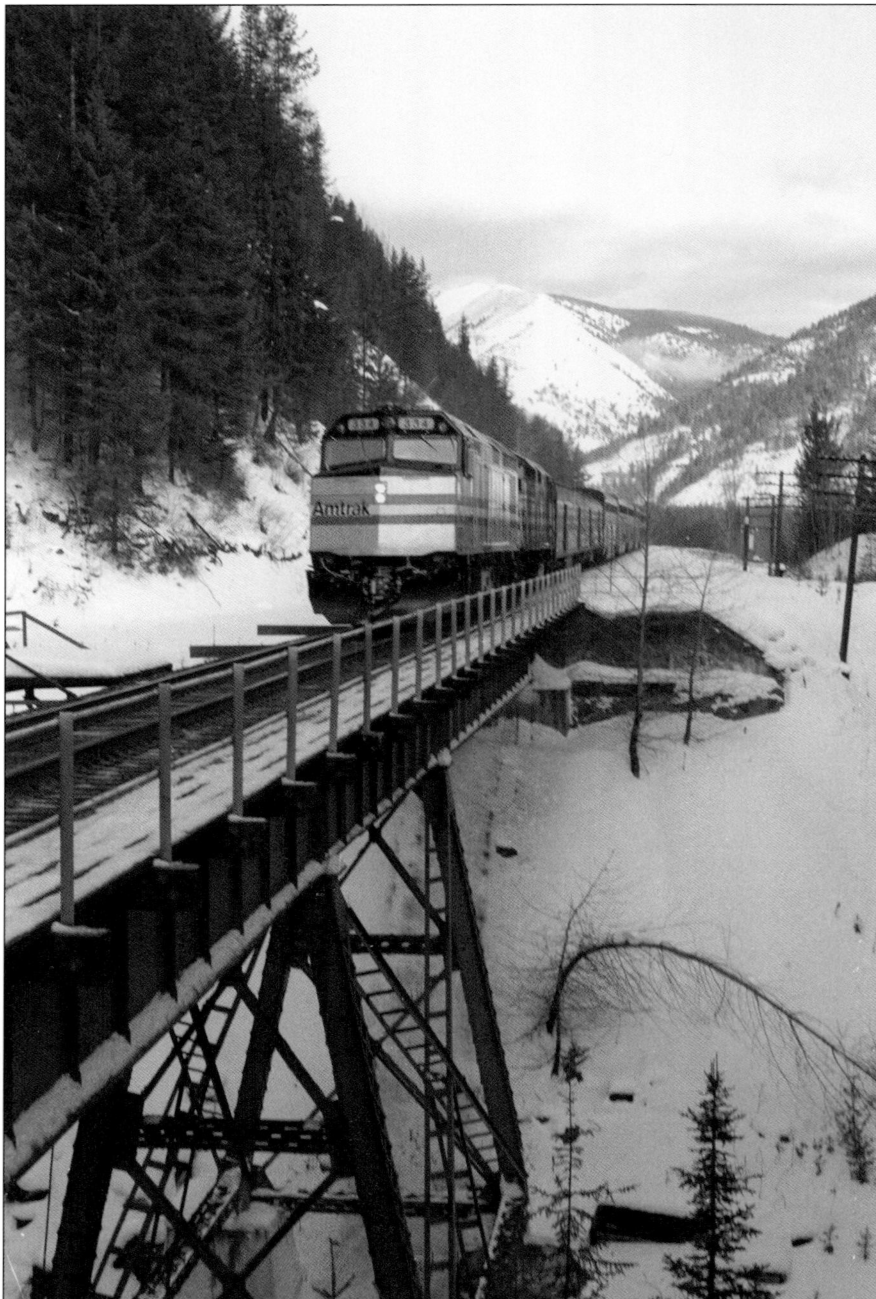

Amtrak *Empire Builder* Train No. 8 approaches Bridge No. 122 spanning Paola Creek at Milepost No. 1173.7 on a cold winter's day. The railroad between Paola and Pinnacle once had a track configuration known as a gauntlet: a parallel set of rails spiked to a single crosstie with a switch that aligns a single track onto either the inside or outside set of rails, allowing the railroad the flexibility of double track running without the need for additional right-of-way. The single-track gauntlet was removed in 1941 and replaced with physical double-tracking. The empty space in the bridge abutment to the right of the train is where the westbound track and second span of the double-track bridge were removed in 1956. (Author's collection.)

Five

Essex

Operations Headquarters for Marias Pass

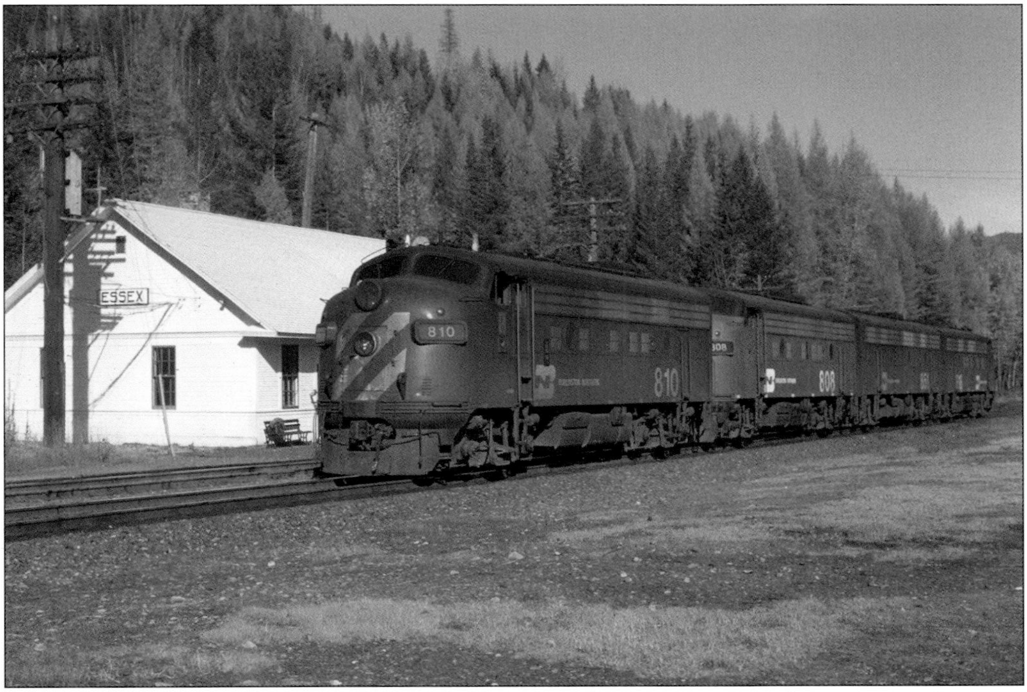

The steep mountainous terrain in Marias Pass required maintenance facilities to provide minor locomotive and railcar repair and to act as home base for freight train helpers. Coincidently, Essex is halfway between Whitefish and Browning, with the only level area large enough to accommodate these services. Burlington Northern F-9 helpers pause in front of the Essex depot waiting to assist the next eastbound train. (Courtesy Jerry Quinn collection.)

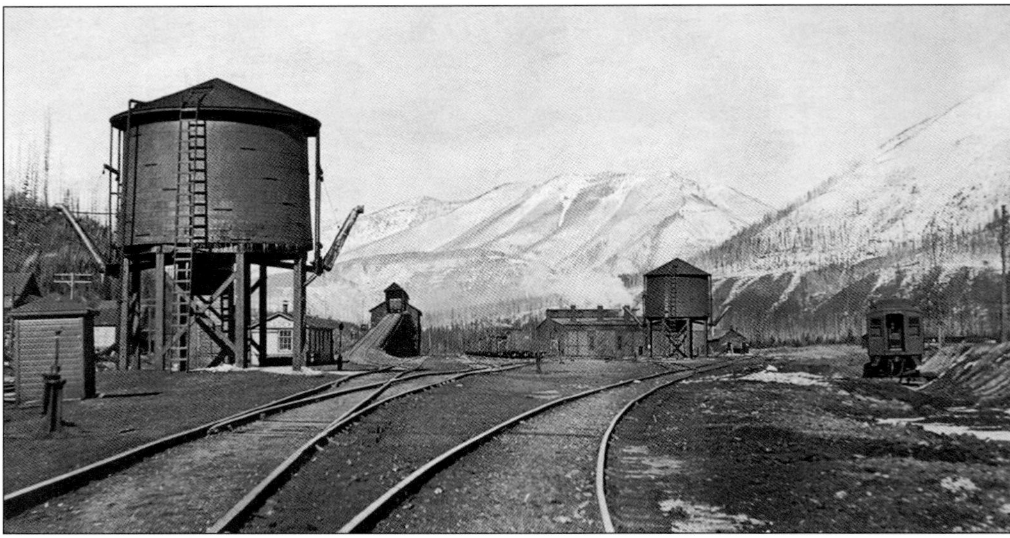

The railroad has witnessed many changes throughout the years, but the mountains always remain the same. Every photograph taken at Essex looking north has the same backdrop—Scalplock Mountain is prominent to the east, continuing down the Middle Fork is Rampage Mountain, and next is Riverview Mountain with Double Mountain in the far distance. In the photograph above, barren hillsides dominate the early-20th-century landscape while providing a glimpse of the maintenance infrastructure essential to mountain railroad operations. Notable are two 50,000-gallon dual spout water tanks, a 10-pocket coal chute, and a four-stall engine house. Below, 70 years later, Scalplock Mountain still dominates the background and locomotives still receive servicing at Essex, but the trees have grown. (Above, courtesy Ed Krona collection; below, author's collection.)

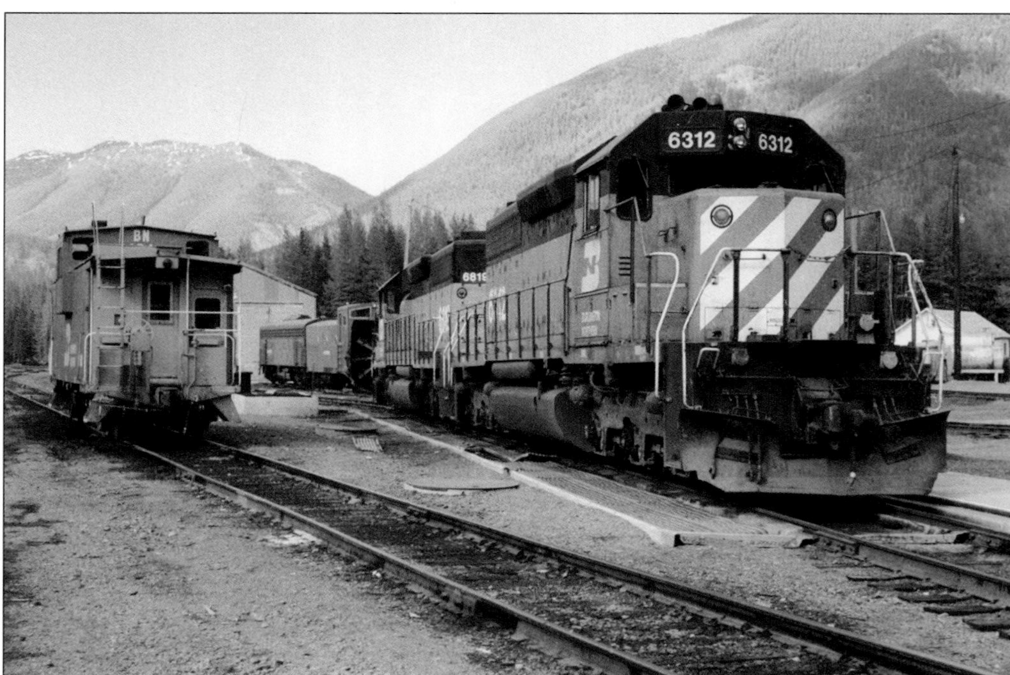

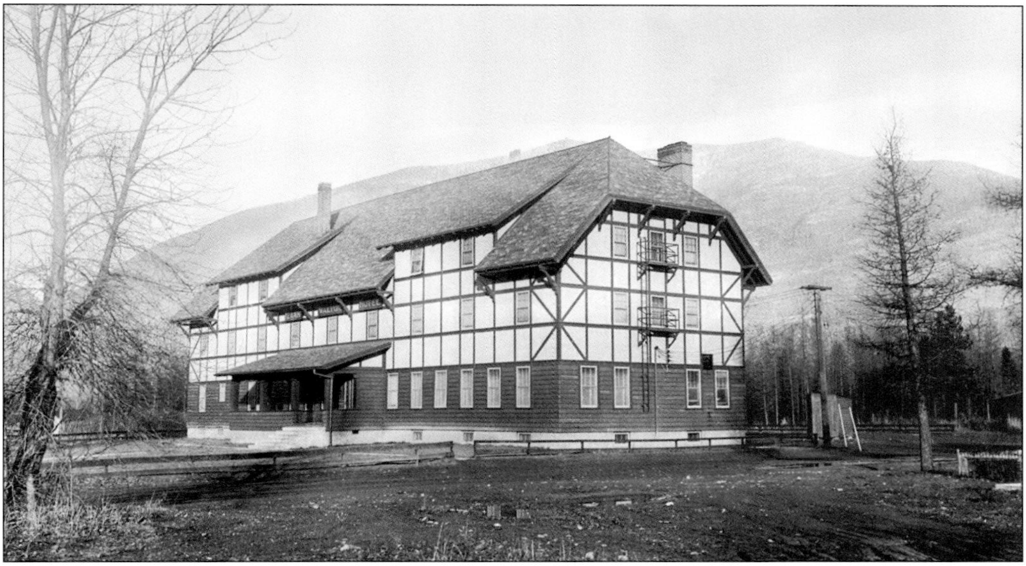

The scores of employees who worked in Marias Pass needed room and board. Accommodations were minimal, as a 1909 AFE16917 instructed: "Furnish and Place 28' Car Body for Car Men," with meals provided at "Beanery's," a colorful nickname for lunchrooms. In 1935, the last beanery burned, leaving Essex without a lunchroom or adequate lodging. The railroad saw a need to improve employee lodging and foresaw the potential for future tourism. A new two-and-a-half-story, 36-by-114-foot structure was built with 29 bedrooms, 10 bathrooms, a lobby, dining room, and kitchen that opened on November 15, 1939. The name Izaak Walton Inn was embraced to attract tourists in addition to serving the needs of railroad employees. As seen in the 1940s photograph above and the 1980s photograph below, there were but slight changes to the Izaak. (Above, courtesy Ed Krona collection; below, author's collection.)

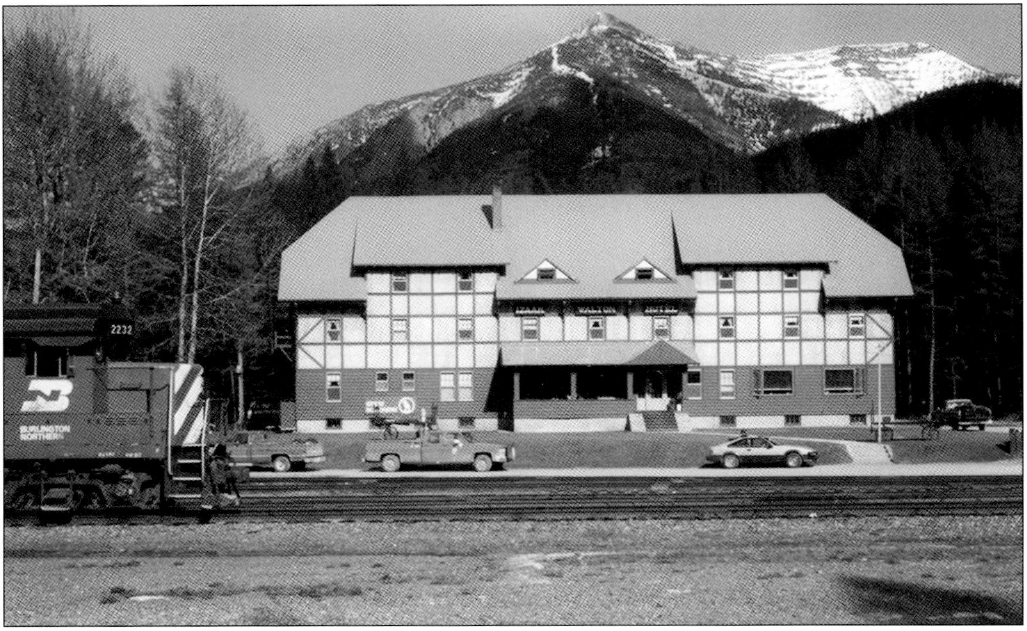

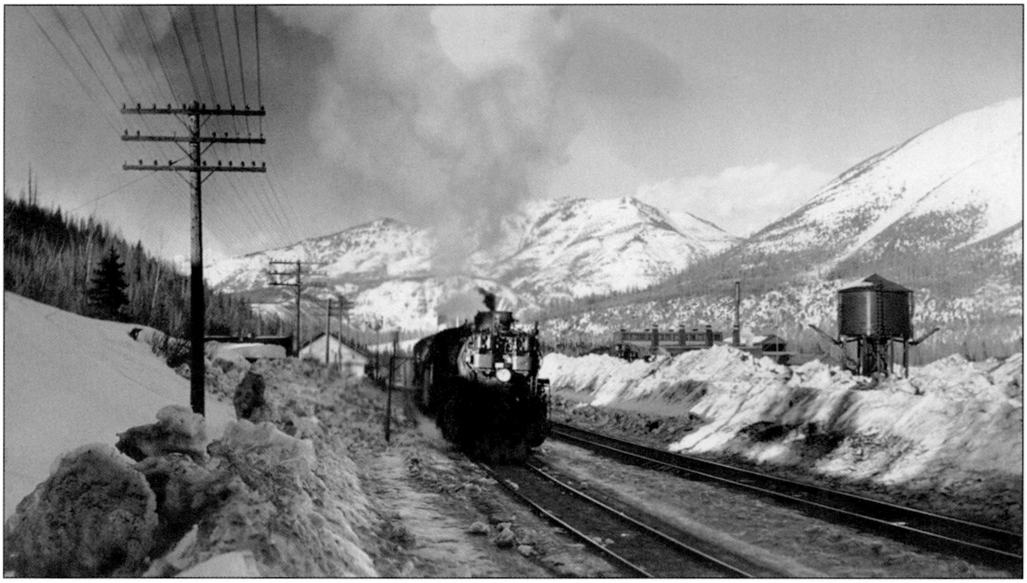

In winter, the mountains surrounding Essex cast a shadow allowing sunlight for only brief periods in the afternoon. The unmistakable Twin Westinghouse Cross Compound air pumps on the smokebox of a 4-8-4 Class S steam engine shine in the low angle of the sun on an eastbound *Empire Builder* during the 1940s. (Courtesy Ed Krona collection.)

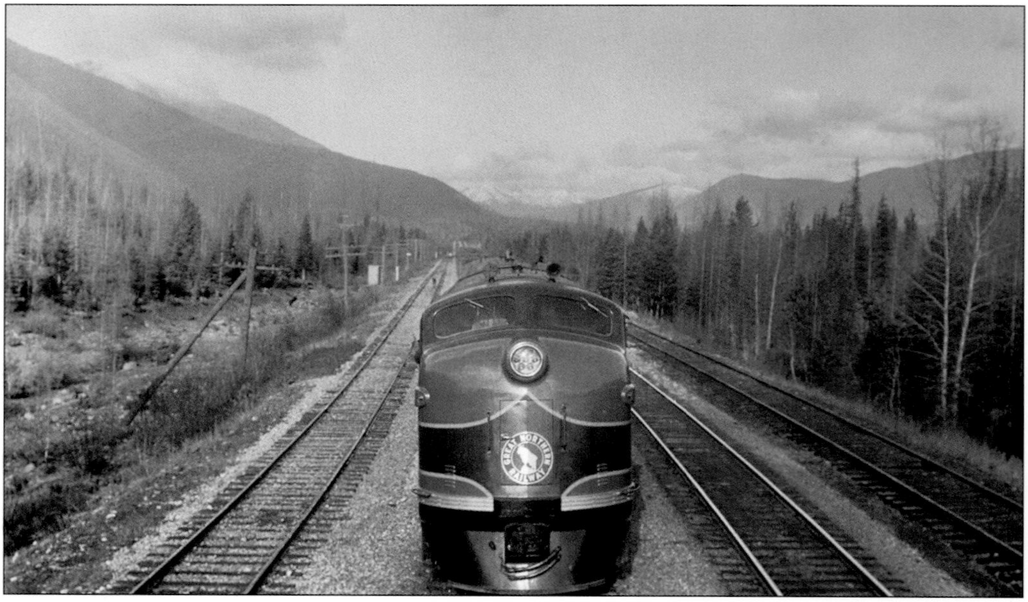

In March 1940, EMD's famous FT demonstrator set toured the Great Northern system, convincing management to incorporate diesel locomotives into their roster. A three-unit A-B-A FT set was built specifically for Marias Pass helper service. In April 1942, the 5900 displays the new colorful paint scheme of Omaha Orange and Pullman Green at the west end of Essex yard. (Courtesy Ed Krona collection.)

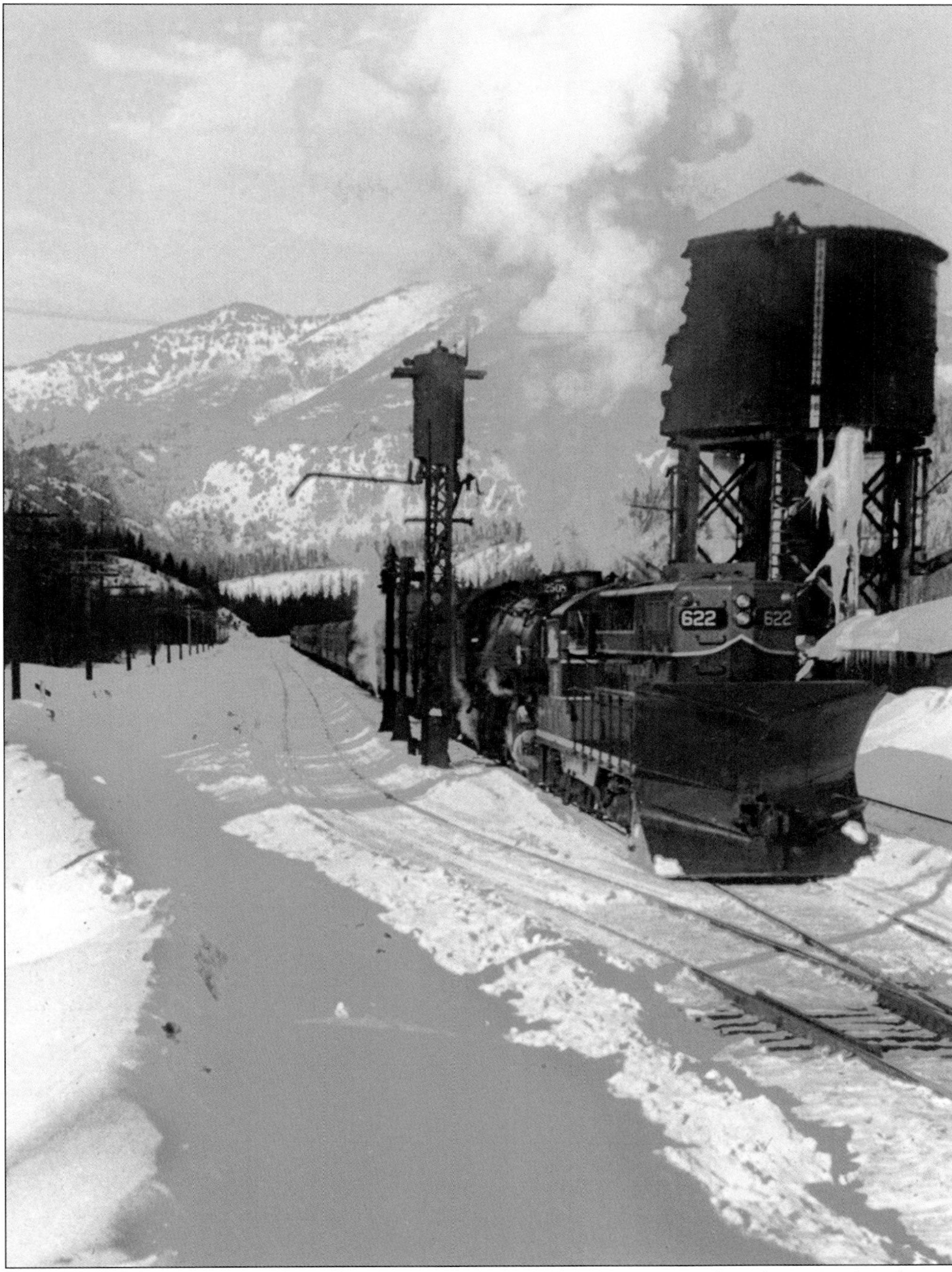

The transition between the steam and diesel eras is quite evident in this photograph. There is only about a five-year timeframe in which all the elements in this image could have coincided. The first hint is EMD GP-7 622, with the huge front-end plow, which was purchased in 1950; next, the steam engine, a 4-8-2 Class P Mountain 2508, was retired in 1955; for the final clue, the train appears to be a nine-car *Western Star* that began operating from Spokane to Havre in the mid-1950s. After all the factors are tallied up, this unique winter scene from 1950 to 1955 documents one of the last steam-engine trips though Marias Pass. (Courtesy Ed Krona collection.)

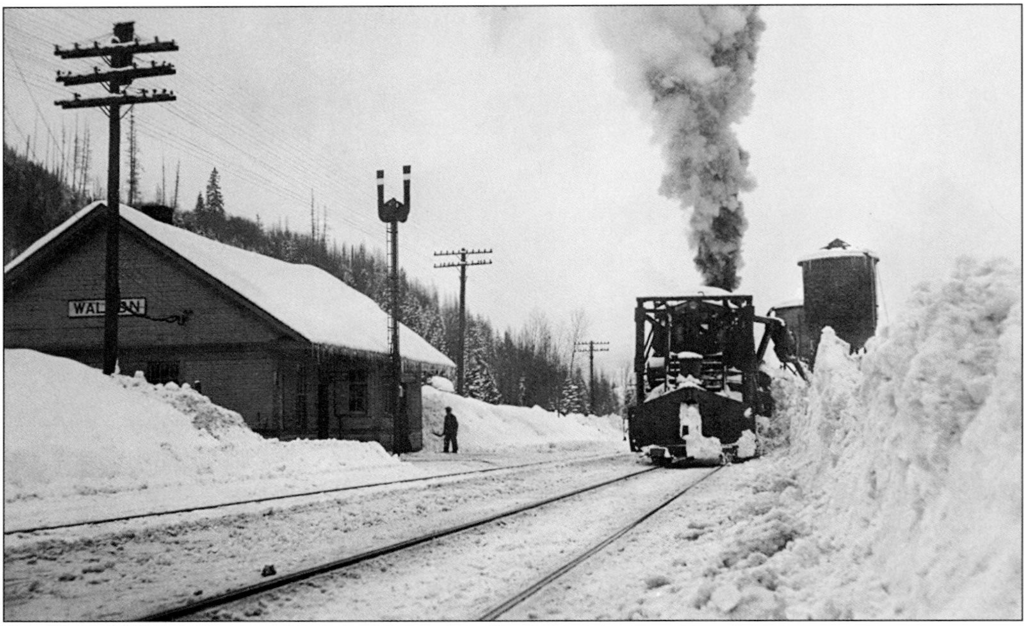

Winter in Essex is normally expected anytime from October to April and is considered a five-month struggle; the average January snow depth is between five and six feet, with some years receiving a 22-foot accumulation during the height of winter. The Great Northern has an arsenal of snow-removal equipment, divided into four categories. The primary point of attack is the wedge plow attached to the front of locomotives, as shown below. The second choice, the snow-dozer, is located behind the steam engine; this heavily-weighted car has rail-level and side-plow surfaces to clear more area. Next is the Jordan Spreader, with adjustable arms capable of spreading snow away from the tracks. Finally, there is the rotary snowplow, which will be examined in a later chapter. (Both, courtesy Ed Krona collection.)

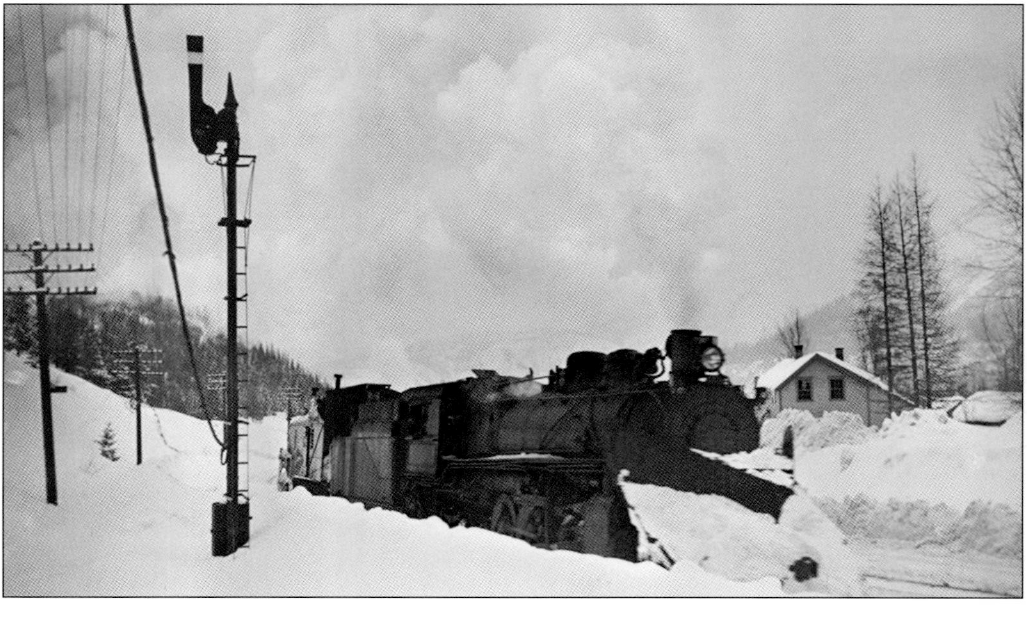

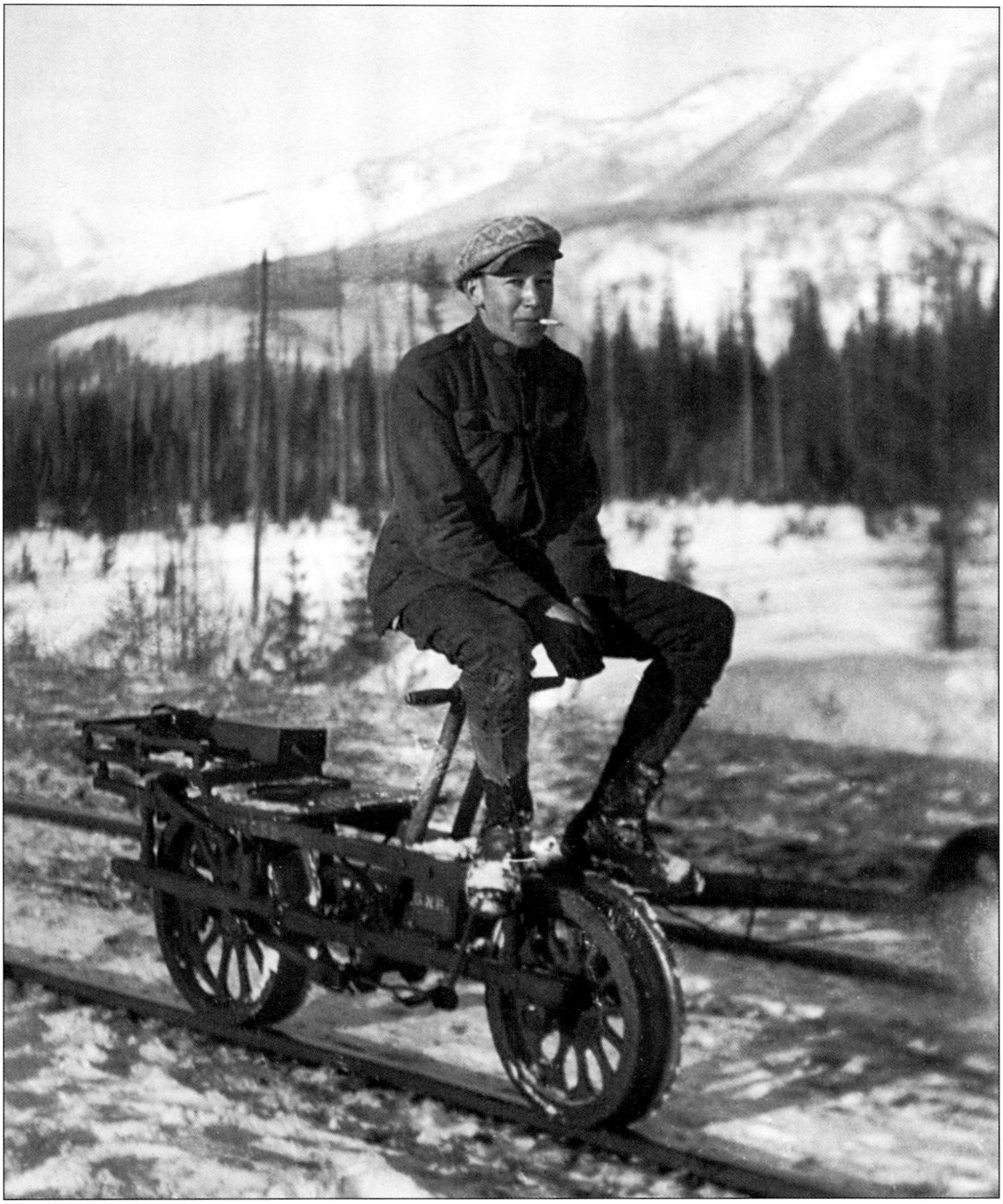

Track walkers or track inspectors have the serious responsibility of ensuring the safety of railroad operation. There must be a daily examination of the roadbed, tunnels, and bridges, checking the rails for fractures and inspecting the condition of joint bolts, fishplates, angle bars, spikes, and other crucial factors. Before gasoline-powered maintenance equipment was available, track inspection was accomplished by hand-powered velocipedes and handcars. At the west end of Essex yard, Bob Roberts proudly shows off a new Sheffield velocipede; this three-wheeled railroad handcar was propelled by a combination of hand and foot power and was designed by Michigan farmer George S. Sheffield. Commenting on the cars' practicality, one railroad superintendent stated, "I have found it exceedingly convenient in inspecting track and bridges, with one or two men. I can make 15 miles per hour over ordinary grades without difficulty." (Courtesy Ed Krona collection.)

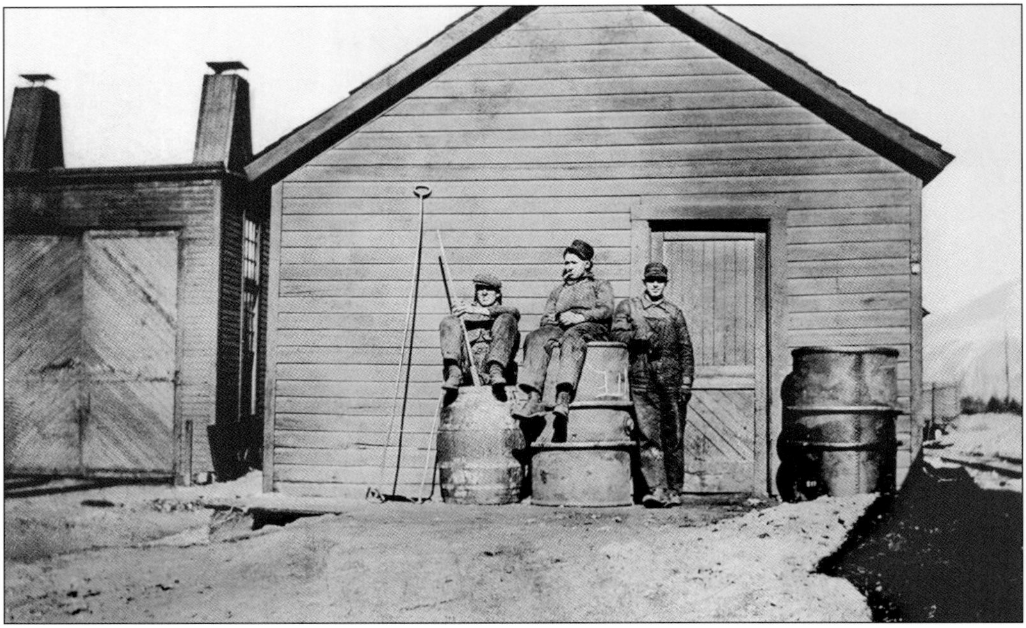

Maintaining steam locomotives under ideal conditions is a labor-intensive and grimy endeavor that becomes even more demanding in winter. One maintenance manual states, "A steam locomotive needed extensive daily maintenance: ashpans needed to be emptied; valves, valve gear, side rods and other reciprocating parts needed regular lubrication and inspection . . . along with boilers and fireboxes." Another observer noted, "For a given size, the steam engines generated a lot less power and were limited in terms of their speed by the mechanics of their pistons and connections to the wheels. A steam engine's tractive force was limited by the pressure in its boiler and cylinder size, and thus at low speeds could only generate low amounts of power." The smoky behemoth pictured below in the Essex yard is one of 35 Class M 2-6-8-0 articulated locomotives purchased in 1910 from the Baldwin Locomotive Works. (Both, courtesy Ed Krona collection.)

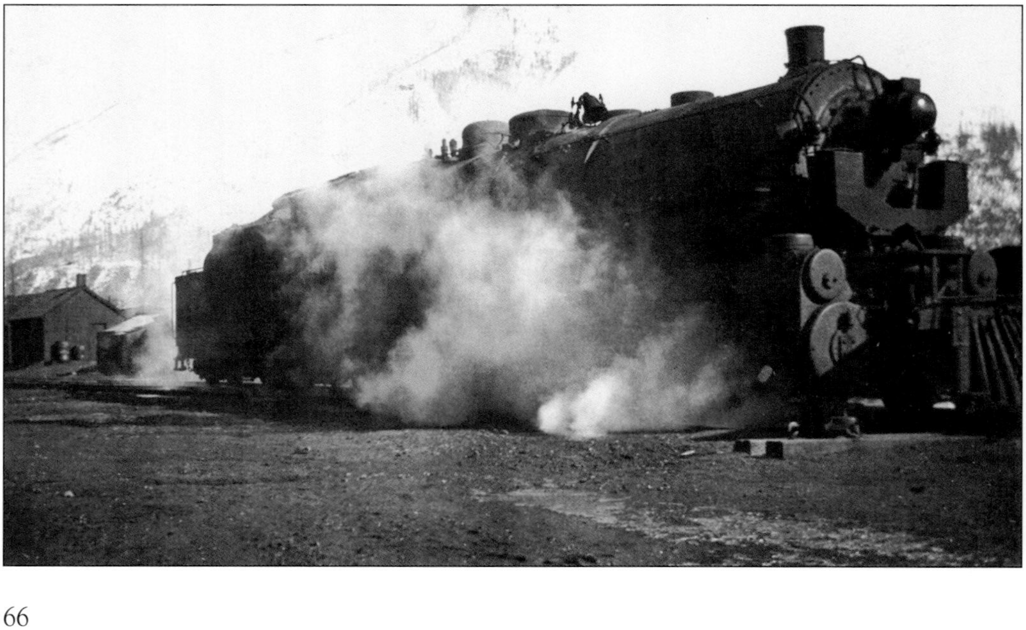

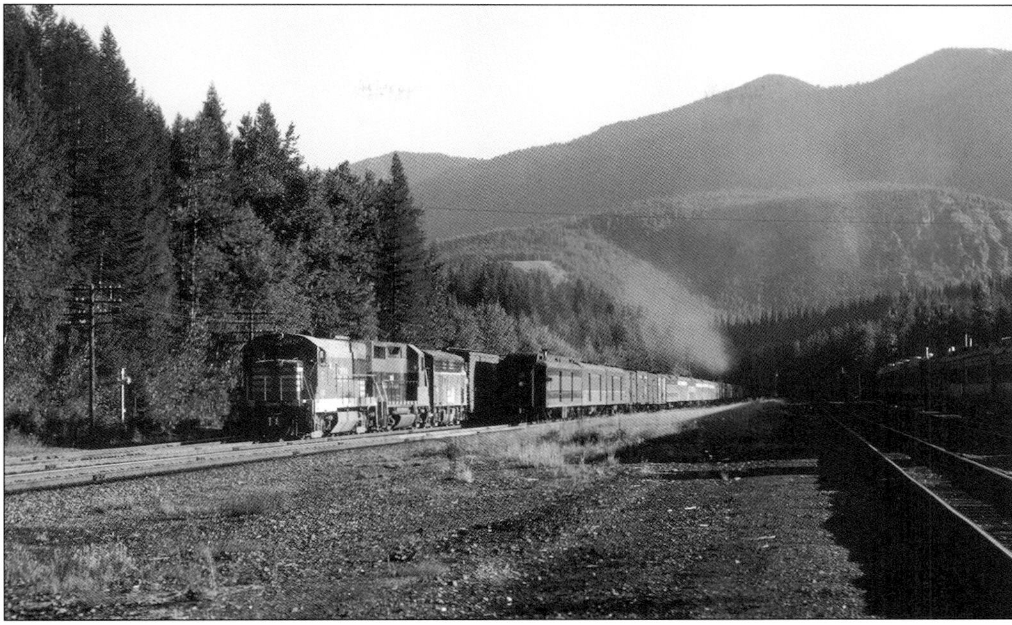

On March 2, 1970, the Great Northern Railway; Northern Pacific Railway; Spokane, Portland & Seattle Railway; and the Chicago, Burlington & Quincy Railroad merged to create the Burlington Northern Railroad. It would take several years to repaint hundreds of locomotives into Burlington Northern colors; in August 1970, a former CB&Q General Electric U28B passes the westbound *Western Star* at Essex. (Photograph by Ronald Hill, author's collection.)

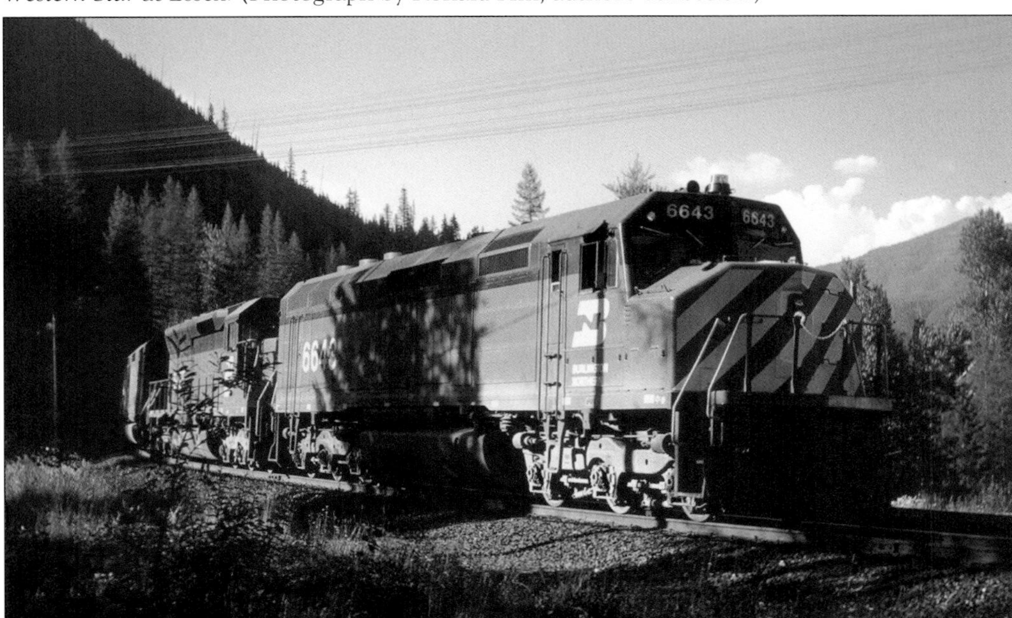

The EMD F45 was designed with internal walkways to minimize the danger of crewmembers slipping on ice or snow-covered walkways. Burlington Northern owned a total of 46 of these locomotives that were assigned as regular power on the trains from Chicago to the West Coast. Burlington Northern No. 6643 East stops at the east end of Essex waiting for a rear-end helper to be connected. (Author's collection.)

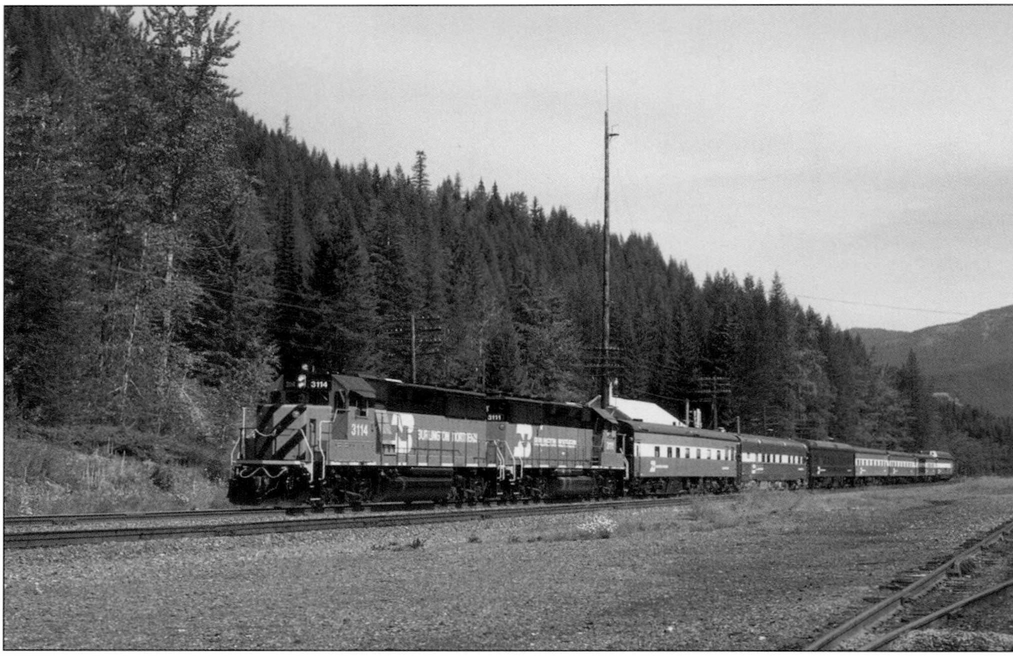

Railroads often own specially designed passenger cars for official company business and public relations functions; in July 1985, this eastbound seven-car Burlington Northern *Officer's Special* with two new tiger-stripe EMD GP50s slows through Essex offering prospective customers or grateful community leaders a glimpse of the Montana Rockies. (Author's collection.)

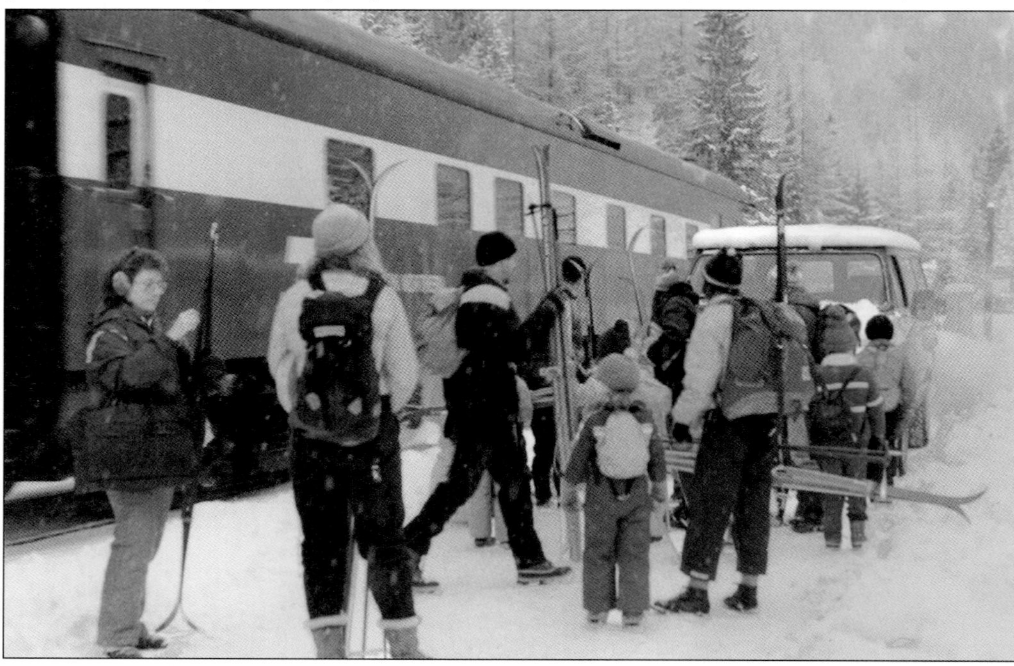

Cross-country skiing was nearly unknown when the hotel at Essex was built in the 1930s; during the 1980s, Izaak Walton Inn owners Larry and Lynda Vielleux were influential in designing the ski trails and campaigning to have Essex listed as a flag stop for Amtrak, one of the few listed in the system. (Author's collection.)

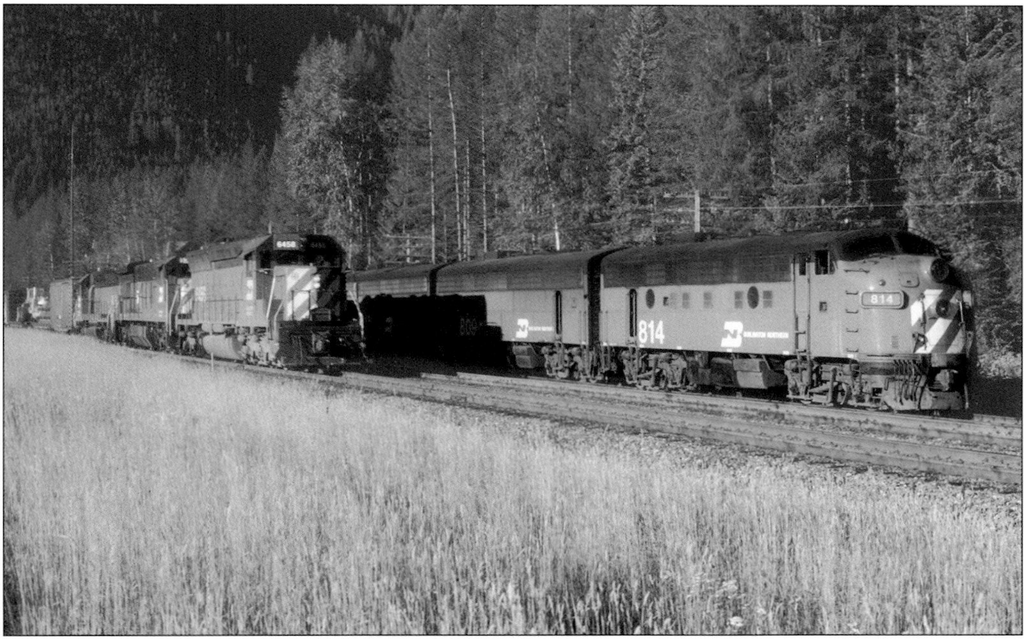

Throughout the history of railroading in Marias Pass, helpers have been considered a necessity on most eastbound trains at Essex. The Burlington Northern F-series locomotives dubbed "covered wagons" were the primary helpers during the 1970s until the early 1980s, when EMD SD40-2s took over the assignment. Most of the Fs were numbered in the 600, 700, and 800 sequences and upgraded to more powerful F9 specifications from existing lower-horsepower units. The photograph above is of a four-unit helper waiting to assist an eastbound train while a westbound freight glides quietly past the Essex depot. Below, the tamaracks glow on the hillside on a warm October 1974 afternoon as Burlington Northern 2204 Extra East pulls by the four-unit helper at the depot. (Both, courtesy Jerry Quinn collection.)

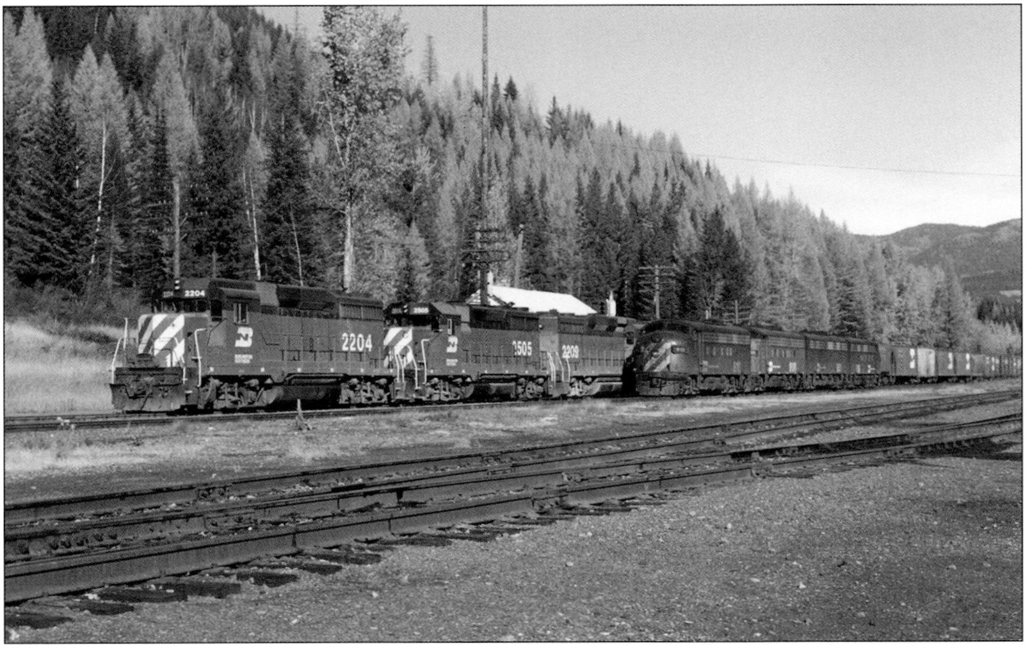

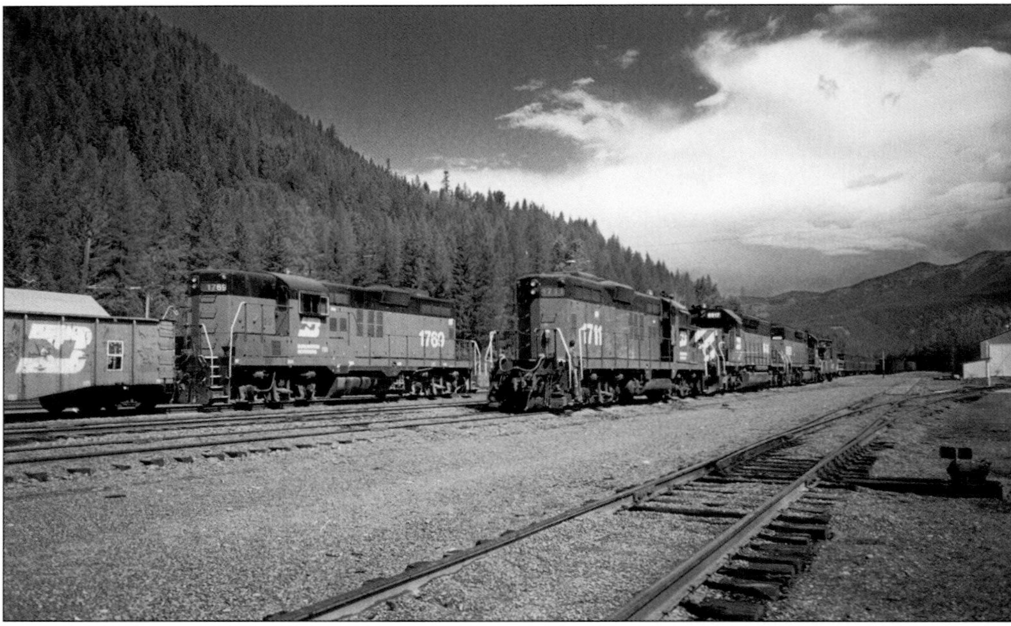

Summertime at Essex is a flurry of track maintenance activity as the winter months of damp, unstable weather take their toll on the roadbed, culverts, bridges, tunnels, snowsheds, railroad ties, ballast, fishplates, angle bars, spikes, track gauging and alignment, rail integrity, and all other aspects of keeping a mountain railway operating smoothly and safely. In the summer of 1985, two EMP GP9s shuttle various work cars in the Essex yard. (Author's collection.)

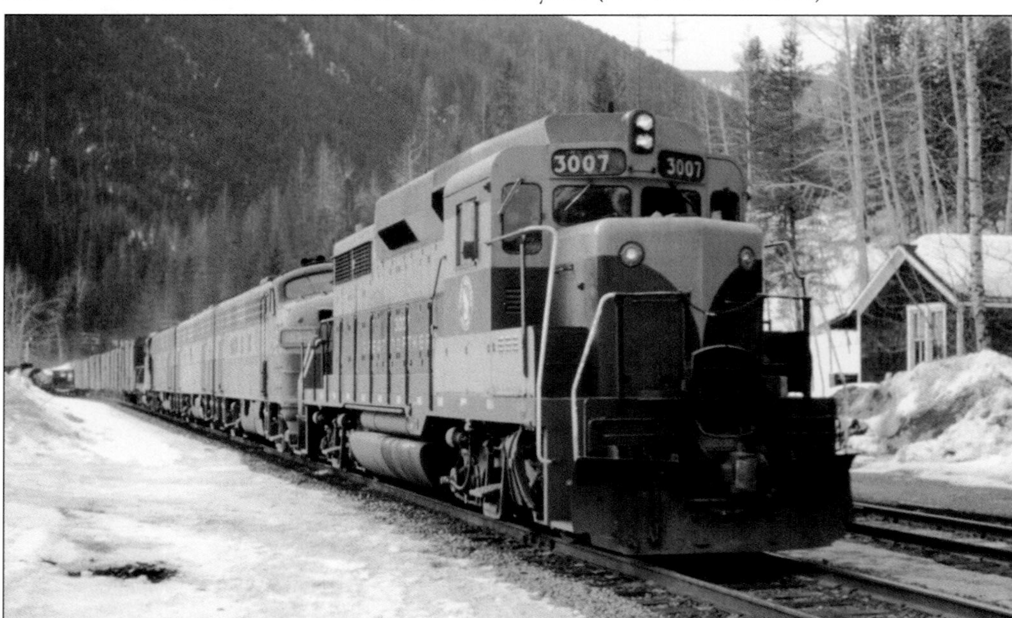

In the author's estimation, EMD's second-generation GP30 was the most handsome of all the locomotives built by the General Motors Electro-Motive Division. Great Northern GP30 3007 on the point of a westbound freight with three F7s and one GP9 is stopped at the Essex depot on a gray spring afternoon. (Courtesy Cordell Newby collection, Great Northern Railway Historical Society.)

Six

Snowsheds

Protecting the Railroad in Winter

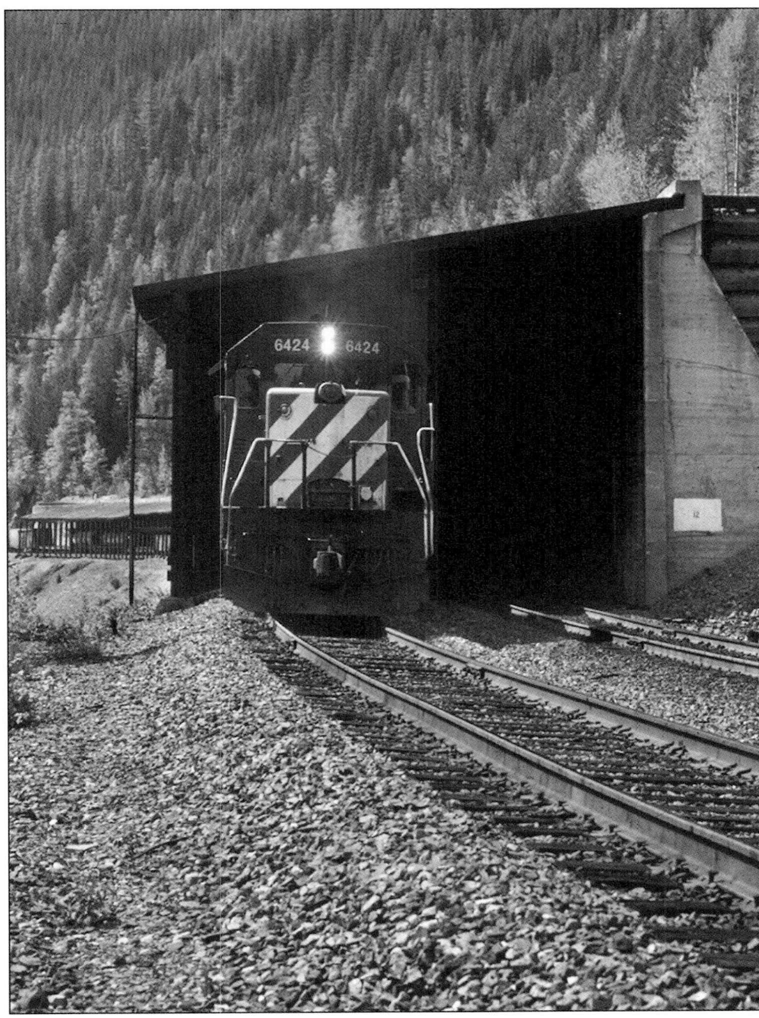

The terrain along the route through Marias Pass is steep, making the tracks vulnerable to dangerous winter avalanches. Mountain snowsheds are constructed across avalanche chutes, sheltering trains from destructive snowslides; the many snowsheds in Marias Pass comprise the largest collection of existing wooden railroad snowsheds in the world. Burlington Northern SD45 6424, built in 1968 as Northern Pacific 3624, exits Snowshed No. 12 in June 1975 near Essex. (Courtesy Gerald "Jerry" Quinn collection.)

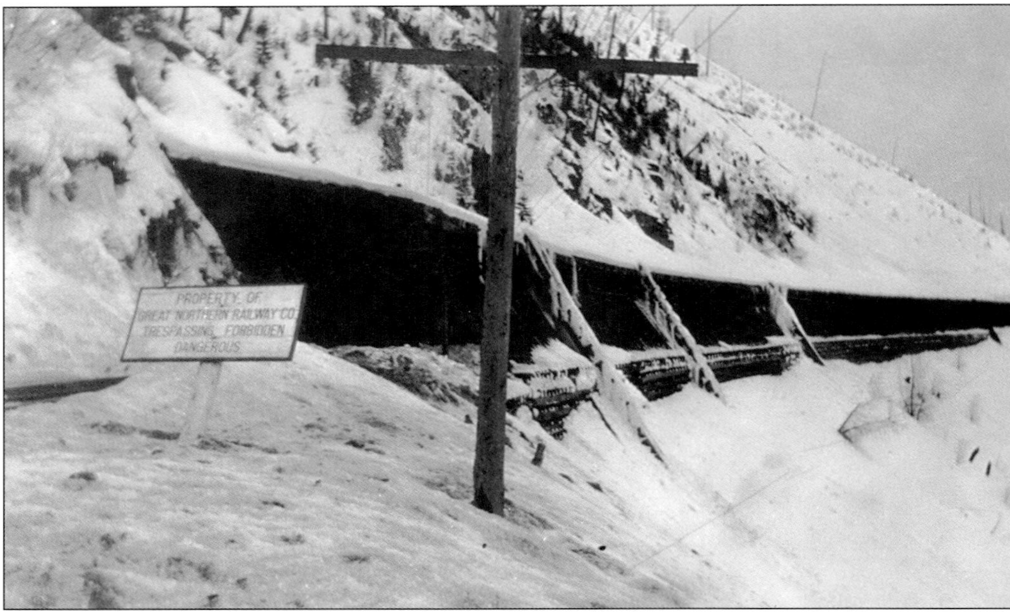

Snowshed No. 12 was the last mountain snowshed built from Browning to Essex in Marias Pass; about a mile east of Essex, it is the longest remaining snowshed in Marias Pass protecting the railroad from snowslides on the barren hillside of appropriately named Snowshed Mountain. (Courtesy Ed Krona collection.)

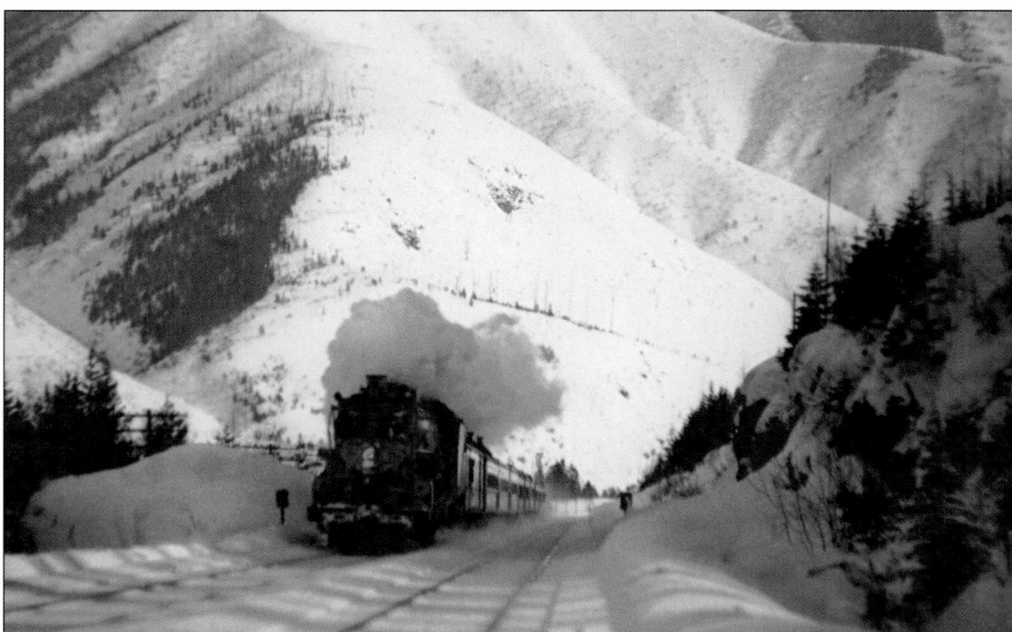

There are not many trackside photographs of Great Northern steam-powered trains operating in the three-mile stretch between Essex and Nimrod-Java. Massive Running Rabbit Mountain in Glacier National Park casts a perennial shadow in the canyon, so this winter image of a westbound 1930s *Empire Builder* running late into Essex is unusual. (Courtesy Ed Krona collection.)

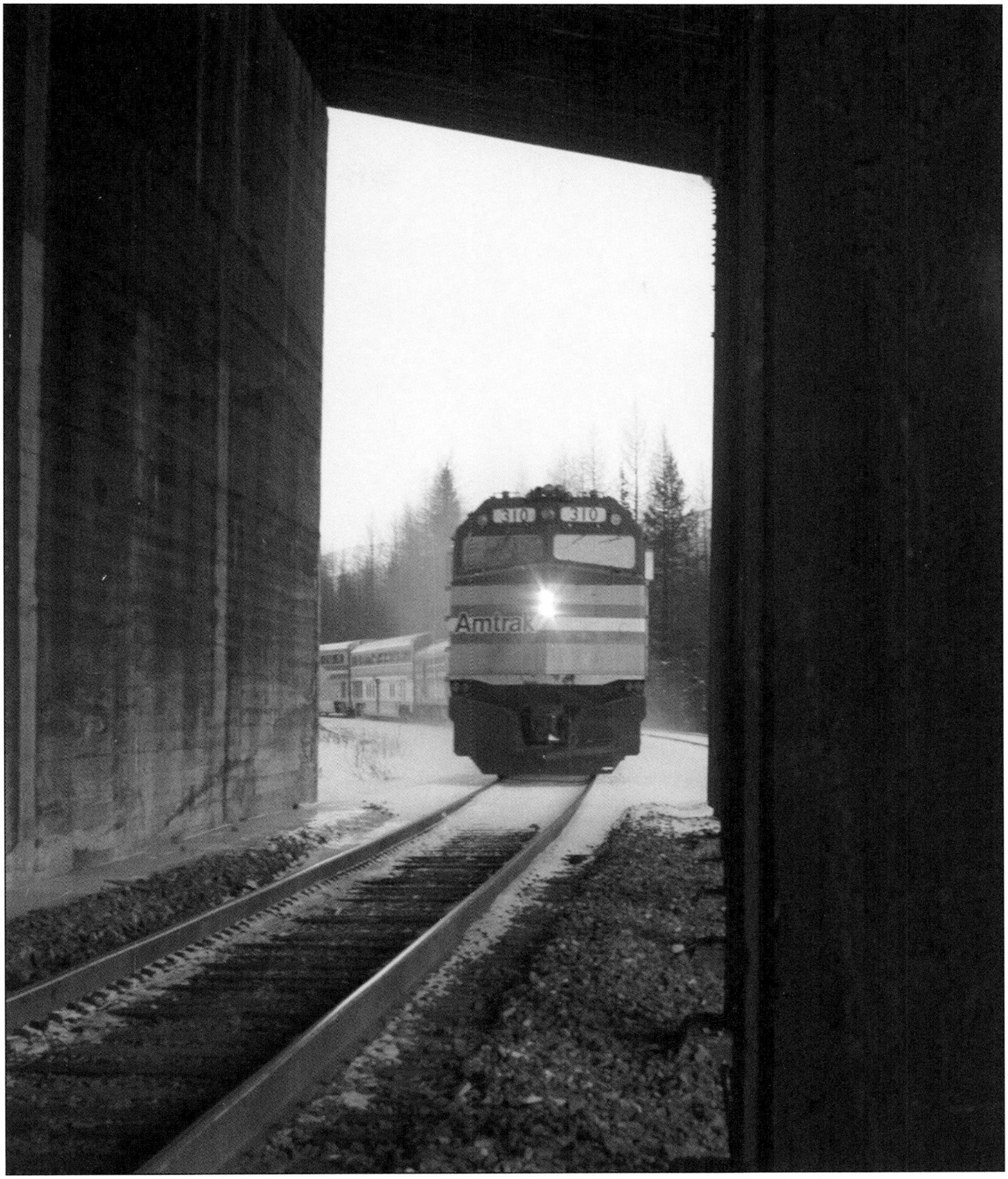

Amtrak *Empire Builder* Train No. 8 with EMD F40PHR 310 enters Snowshed No. 12 one mile east of Essex on a cold February 1986 morning. Snowshed No. 12 was originally built in 1913 as a 202-foot single-track shed with a gauntlet-interlocking track until 1919, when the shed was replaced and extended to 1,420 feet in the 1920s with a double-track combination shed. In 2004, a study was commissioned to examine the viability and status of Marias Pass snowsheds; in part, it was determined that, "Maintenance of these sheds costs around $40,000 per year according to BNSF personnel . . . From the standpoint of protection against avalanche hazards, snowsheds provide almost complete protection when they are long enough to prevent breach on the ends. They cost approximately $7,000 per foot to build according to recent BNSF estimates. Track structure inside snowsheds is somewhat more difficult to maintain than track outside the sheds, so there is either a resulting higher cost to maintenance of track or lowered maintenance standards" (Author's collection.)

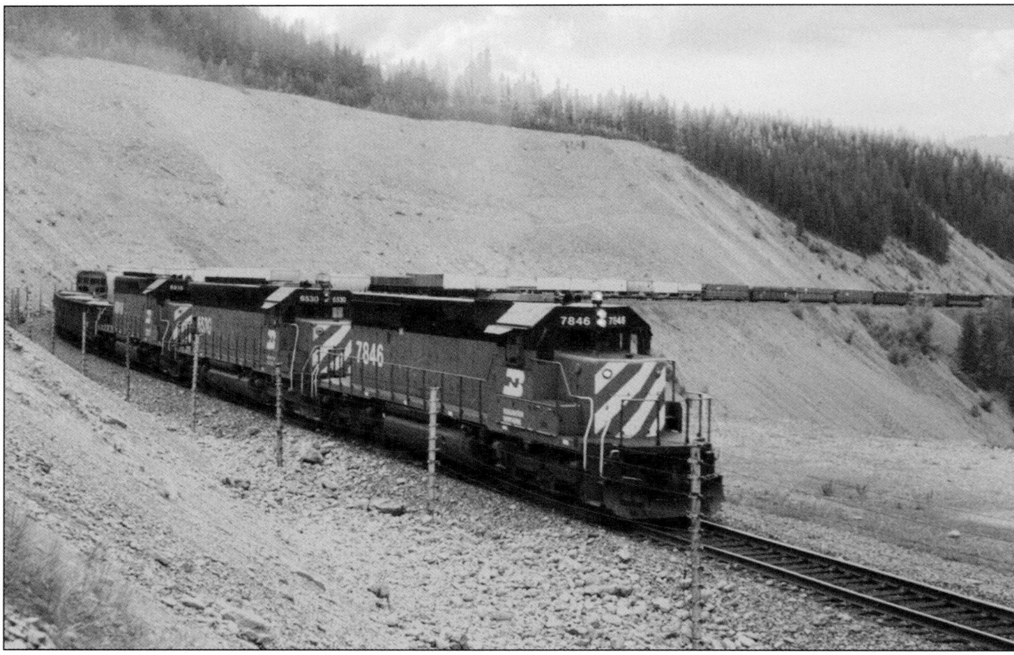

Burlington Northern SD40-2 7846 leads an eastbound freight across the gauntlet. As precarious as the barren rock slope appears, damaging washouts are not as common here as at other locations along the Middle Fork. From 1925 to 1955, this half mile of gauntlet track from Java West to Java East was the longest in Marias Pass. (Author's collection.)

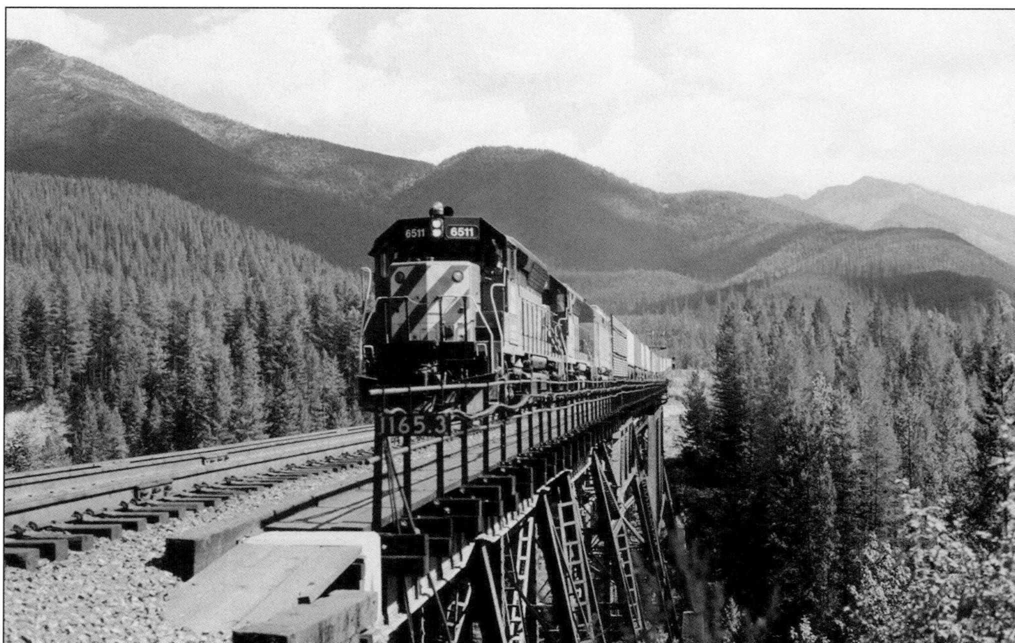

Spanning Java Creek and the Middle Fork of the Flathead River at Milepost No. 1165.3 east of the gauntlet is Bridge No. 116, a 778-foot-long Pratt deck truss trestle. Looking south behind Burlington Northern SD45 6511 on a warm 1978 summer afternoon, the Great Bear and Bob Marshall Wilderness Complex looms in the distance. (Courtesy Jerry Quinn collection.)

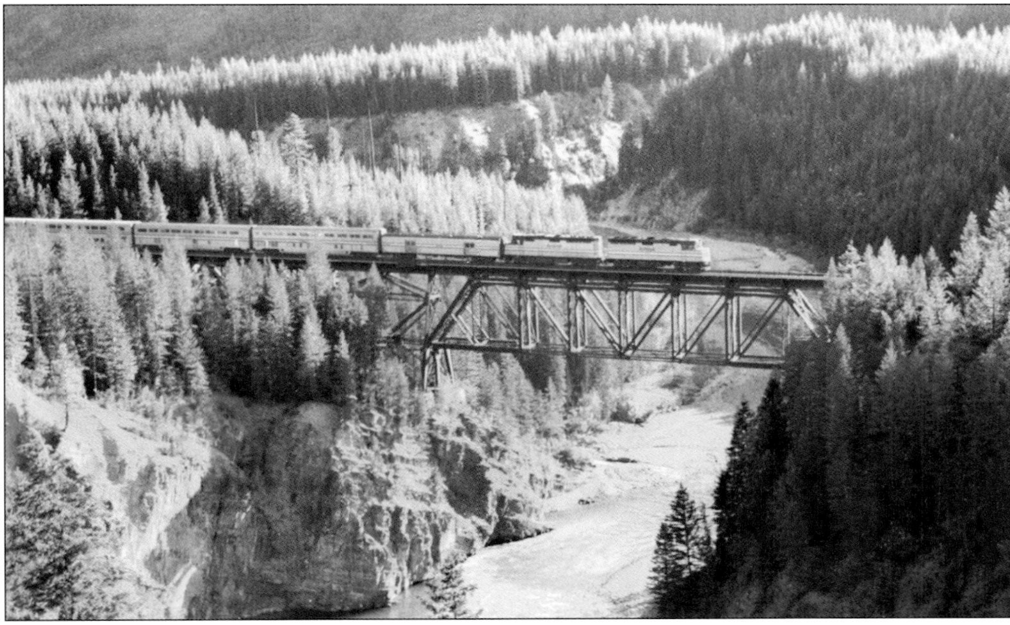

The scenery surrounding Bridge No. 116 is spectacular from all vantage points. This photograph of eastbound Amtrak Train No. 8 was taken from the Great Bear Wilderness looking across the Middle Fork into Glacier National Park; capturing this image involved crossing the Middle Fork trestle, fording cold Java Creek, and climbing a steep trail to this location—though this trek is not recommended. (Author's collection.)

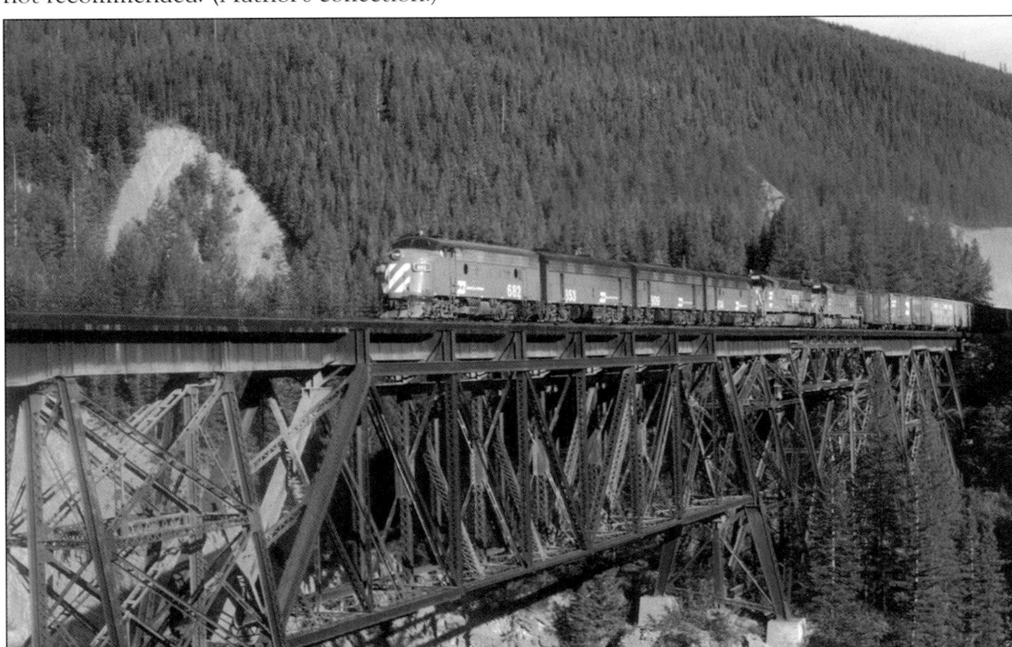

The early morning light in August 1978 offers a dramatic view of this F9 682 four-unit helper set assisting an eastbound freight at the beginning of the steep 1.8-percent grade at Java. Helpers were placed in the train depending on how the tonnage was distributed; here, they are attached to the front. (Courtesy Jerry Quinn collection.)

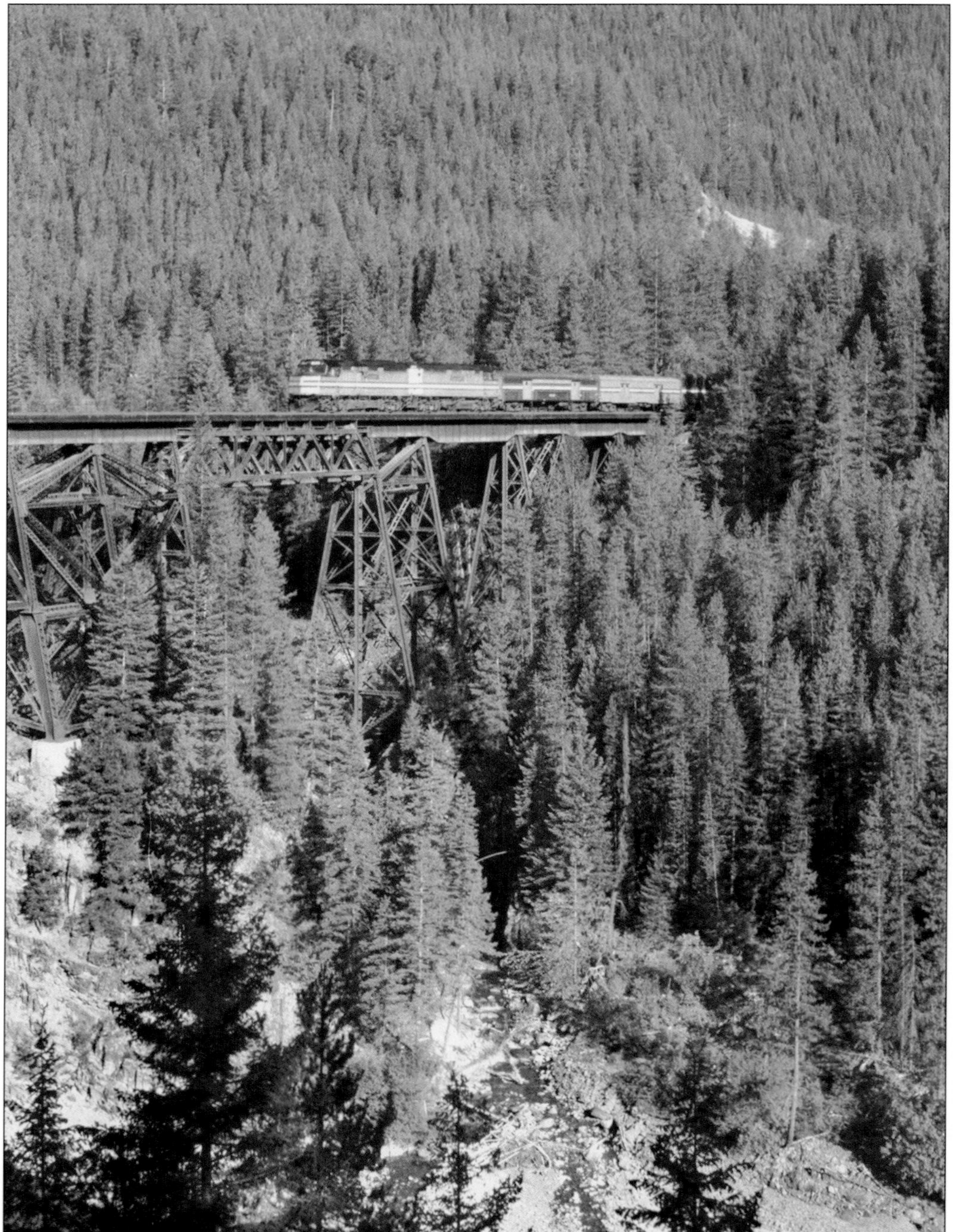

Amtrak *Empire Builder* Train No. 8, appearing quite small, glides past a long-forgotten spot called Briggs onto the spindly looking Bridge No. 116 high above the Middle Fork Canyon along the border of the Great Bear Wilderness. In the 1920s, many locations in Marias Pass were renamed by the railroad to reflect its advertising campaign promoting Glacier National Park. Java was renamed Nimrod in 1926 and remained known as such until 1973–1974, when the Burlington Northern Railroad restored the name Java; today, the Burlington Northern Santa Fe has defined the location even further as Java West and Java East. (Author's collection.)

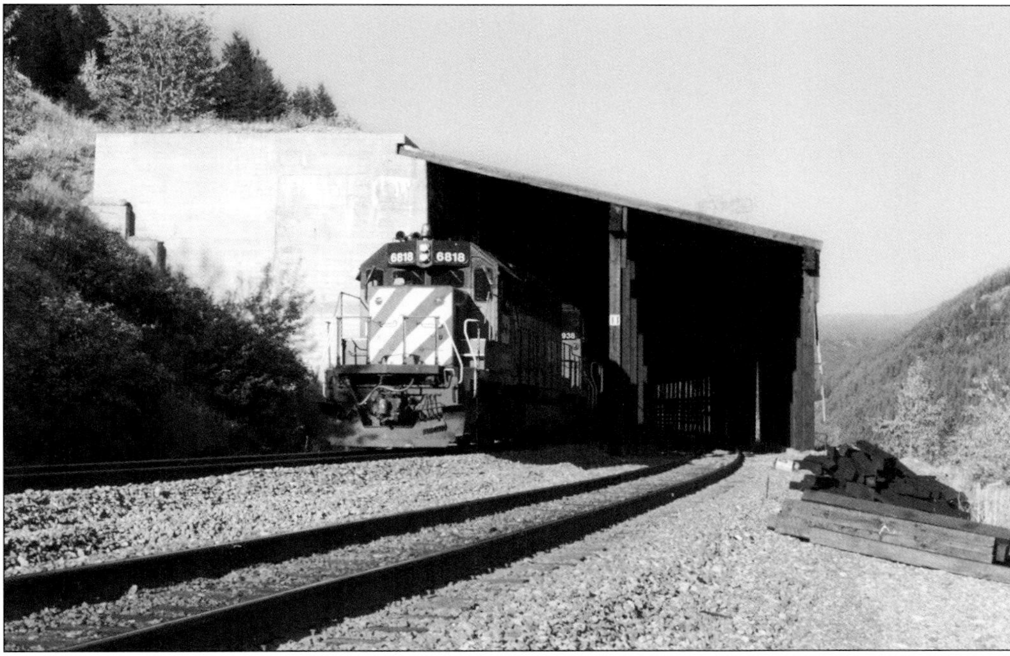

Exiting Shed No. 11, Burlington Northern SD40-2 6818 returns westbound to Essex after assisting an eastbound freight to Summit. There are nine active snowsheds in Marias Pass from Java to Summit; the number assignment from Java East begins with Sheds Nos. 11, 10.5, 10, 9, 8, 7, 6,5, 4-D, and former 4-C, which burned in the late 1970s. (Author's collection.)

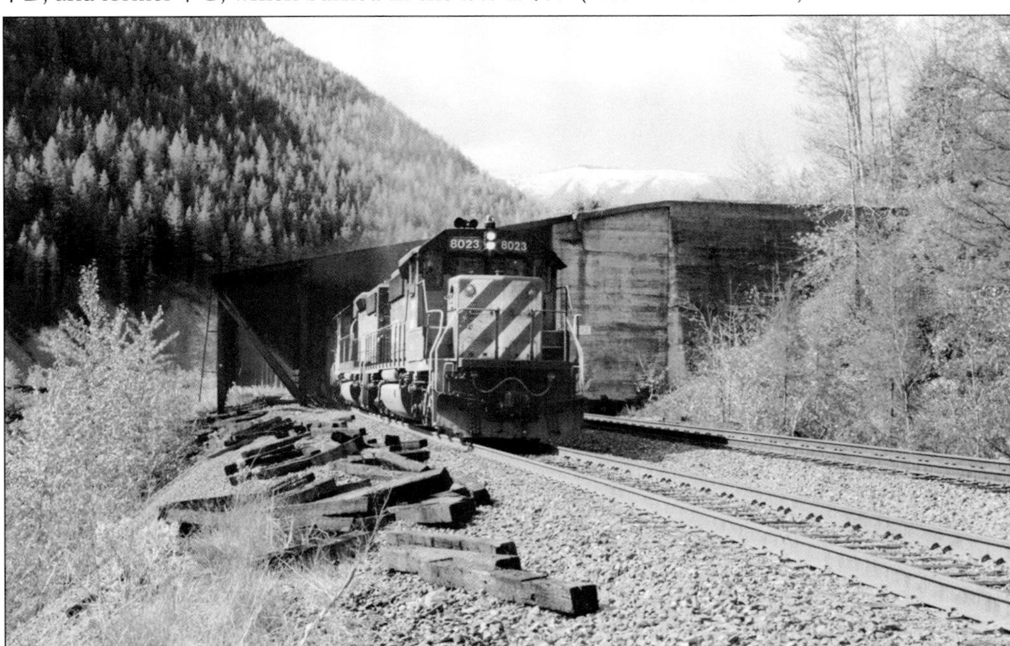

All the Marias Pass snowsheds accommodate double-track operation, but only Shed No. 10 has an extension beyond the tracks for added protection from snowslides originating on Running Rabbit Mountain in Glacier National Park. In 1986, Burlington Northern SD40-2 8023 slowly drags an eastbound freight toward Summit. (Author's collection.)

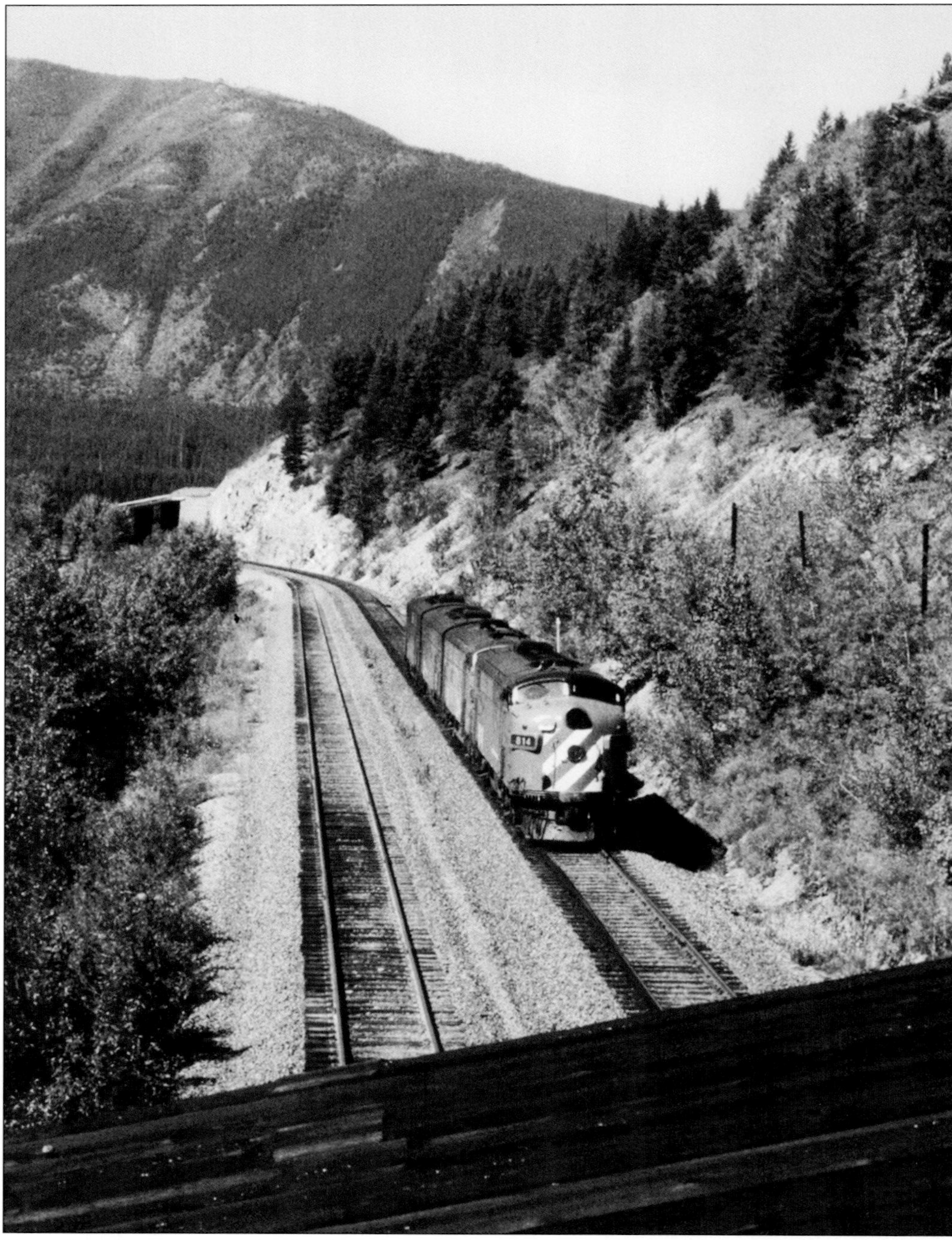

Several of the images in this book were taken during simpler times. From the 1960s to 1990s, the author and his associates often freely strolled along railroad right-of-ways, climbed signal towers, and scaled snowsheds and other trackside structures to document many of the scenes captured here. Today, due to heightened security and common sense, railroads have instituted a zero-tolerance policy toward trespassers on their property. This situation presents photographers with a chance to view railroads in a new light. Here on this warm, bright July 1971 day, the avalanche danger and snowslides of winter are but a distant memory as a four-unit Burlington Northern F9 helper runs "lite" downgrade to Essex between Sheds 10.7 and 11. (Author's collection.)

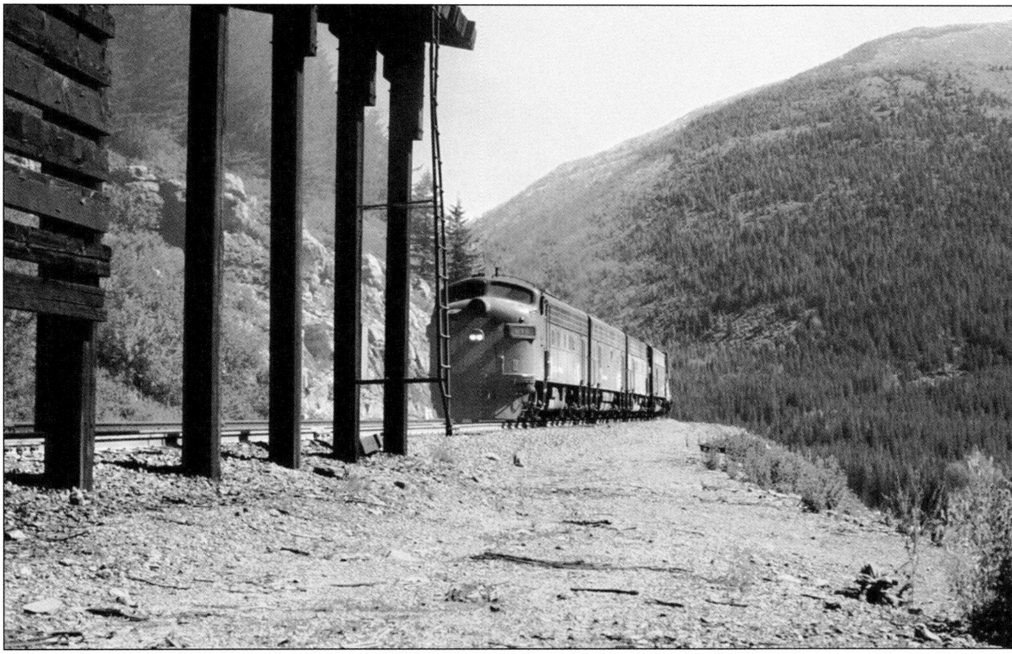

The 567C internal combustion diesel engines in these Burlington Northern F9s produced a blue haze of exhaust when the engineer revved up the locomotive into a higher notch of power pushing on the rear of eastbound freights through the snowsheds. These helpers are exiting Shed No. 7 on the way to Summit. (Author's collection.)

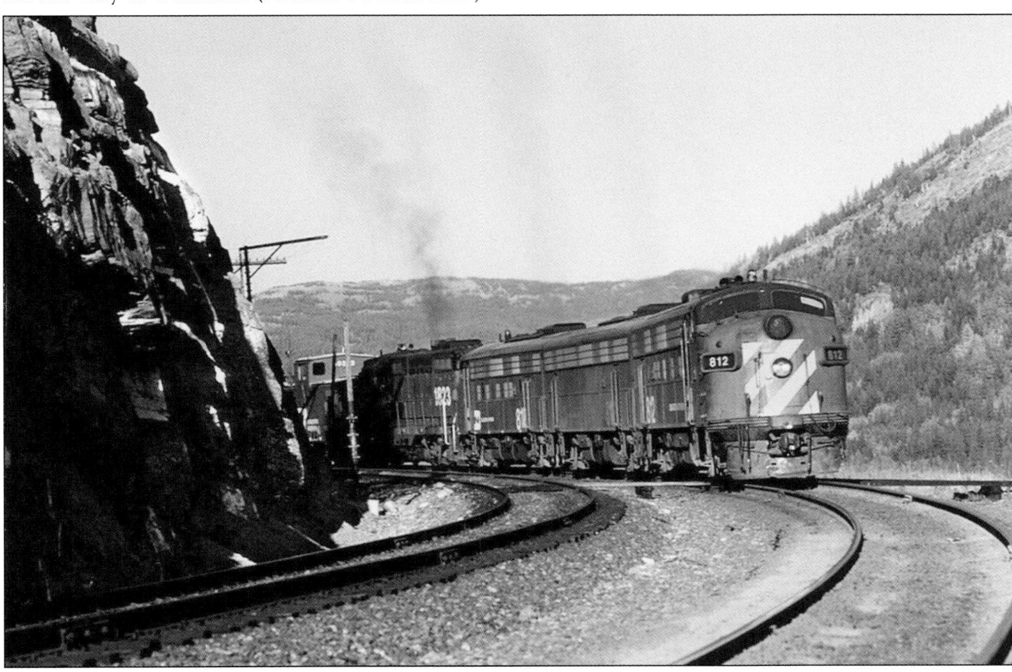

Three Burlington Northern EMD F9s led by 812 and a GP9 are straining the drawbars on Caboose No. 10223 of an eastbound extra freight at Windy Point. Windy Point was the location of 321-foot-long Tunnel No. 1.5, which was demolished in 1969 to allow larger freight loads to be moved without special handling. (Author's collection.)

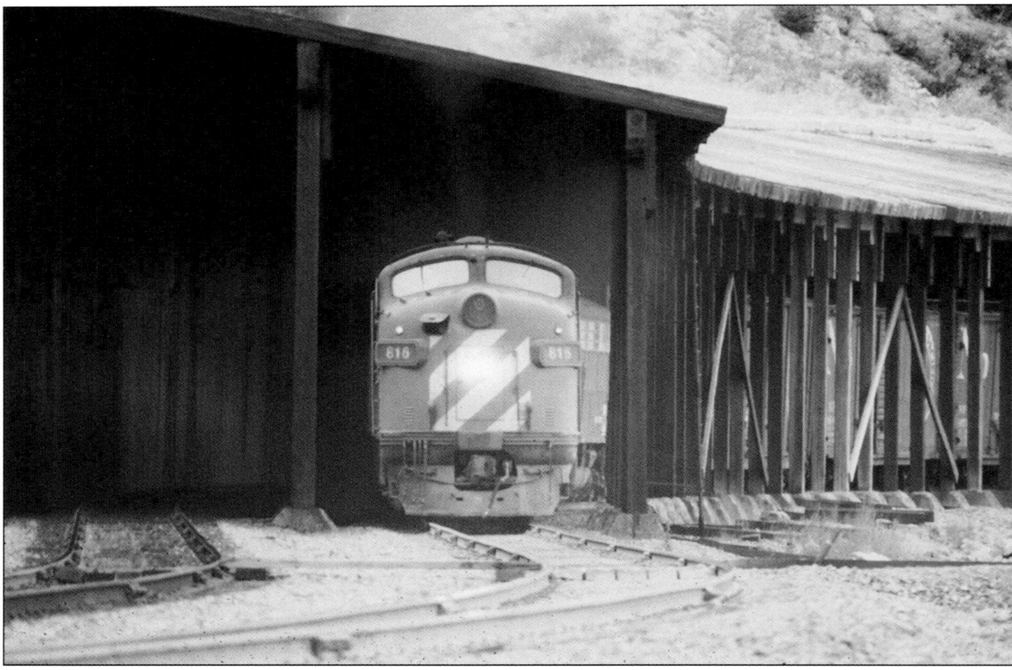

A telephoto lens foreshortens this image of a rear-end helper with F-9 816 pushing an eastbound train entering Sheds 5 and 6; the railroad between Java and Summit in Marias Pass is double track to allow trains to ascend and descend without waiting at passing sidings. (Author's collection.)

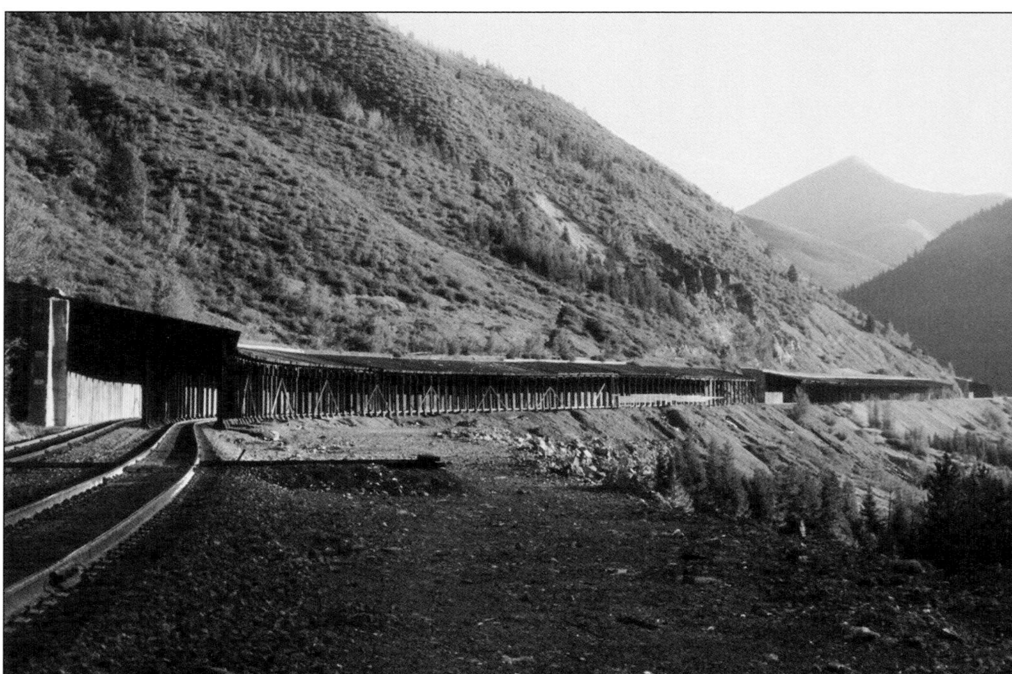

The Great Northern skirts the Glacier National Park boundary for about 25 miles from Java East to Bison; looking north from Windy Point, Sheds 5, 6, 4-D, and 4-C provide shelter from snowslide-prone 35-degree hillsides for over 1.5 miles of track. (Author's collection.)

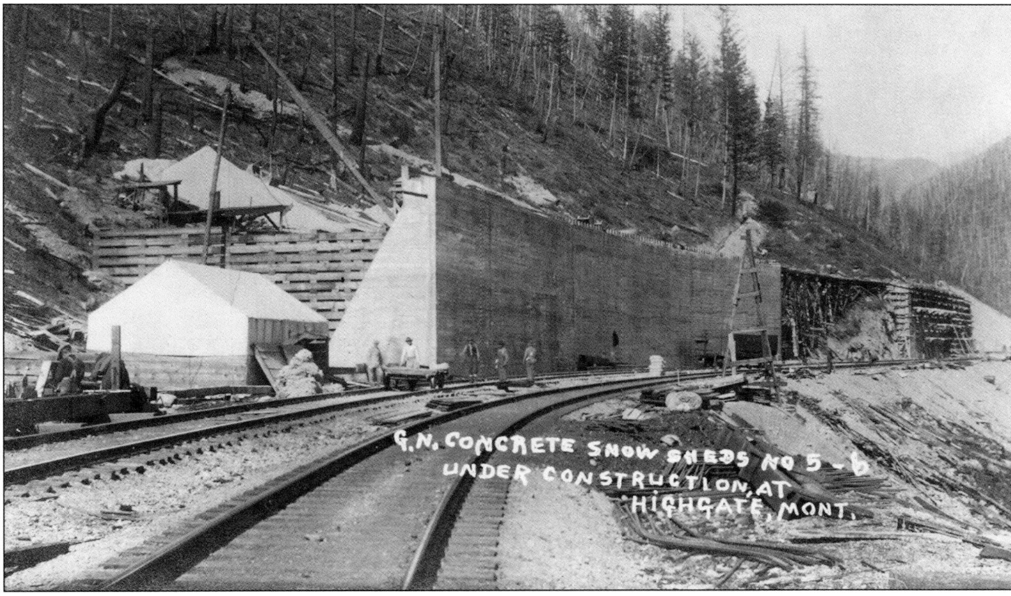

Photographic documentation of snowshed construction in Marias Pass is relatively rare, as access to the building sites was limited. In 1912, a photographer captured the primitive beginnings of Sheds 5 and 6 near Highgate in the avalanche-prone area near Tunnel No. 1.5 at Singleshot. (Author's collection.)

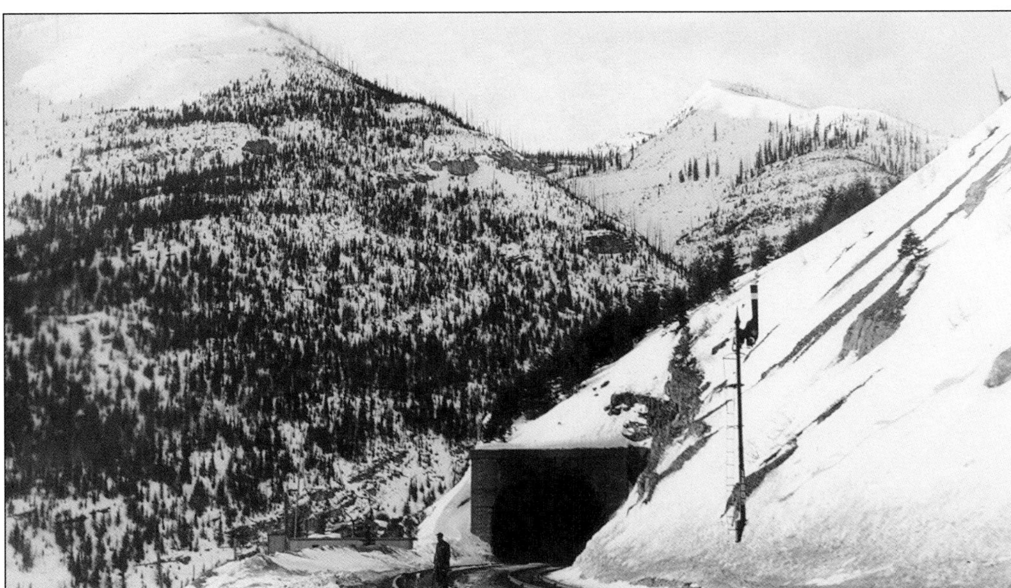
For nearly 20 years, the railroad hugged the steep embankment at the confluence of Devil and Bear Creeks. In 1910, the 321-foot concrete-lined Windy Point tunnel was built; it shifted the tracks away from landslide danger and shielded them from snowslides. Regardless of the protection, sentries were employed to monitor current conditions. (Courtesy Ed Krona collection.)

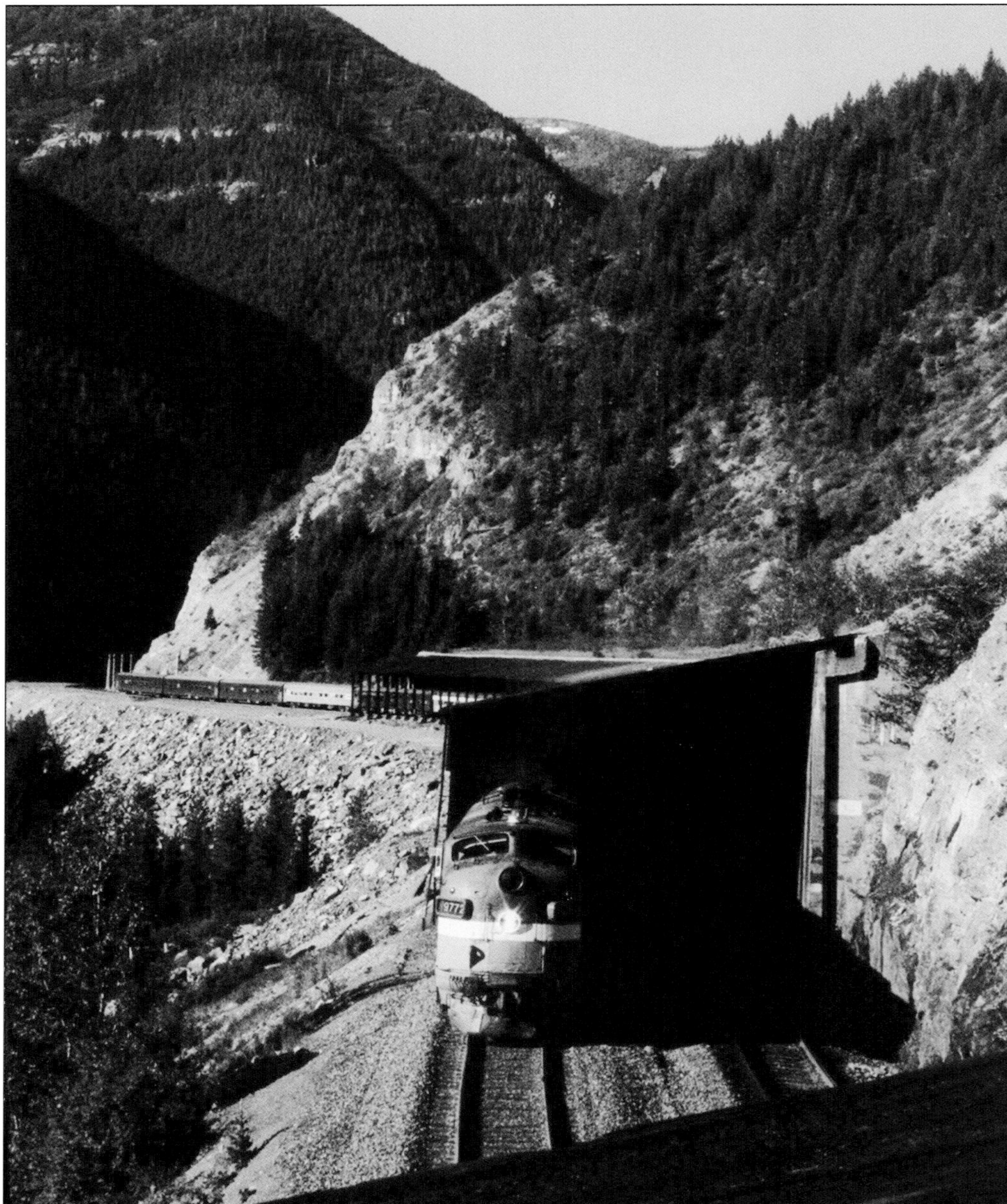

This dramatic image of the eastbound Amtrak *Empire Builder* in July 1971 showcases an array of passenger car equipment, trackside structures, and stunning scenery. Looking south from atop Shed No. 6, Amtrak F7-A 9772 (former Northern Pacific 6507C) heads upgrade through Shed No. 5 with the recently demolished Windy Point Tunnel No. 1.5 and Devil's Hump in the Great Bear Wilderness as a backdrop. The 2004 National Park Service avalanche survey states, "The Shed 6 avalanche path has a steep, rocky starting zone with dispersed timber in bands. The timber is not dense enough to provide good anchors for snow stability, although analysis of old photographs show that it is thickening over time. The slope angles remain steep all the way to the shed, which is well placed. Shed 6 path has a history of producing large events in the past. Looking at photographs from the 1960s, it has since re-vegetated and large events do not seem likely with the present timber growth." (Author's collection.)

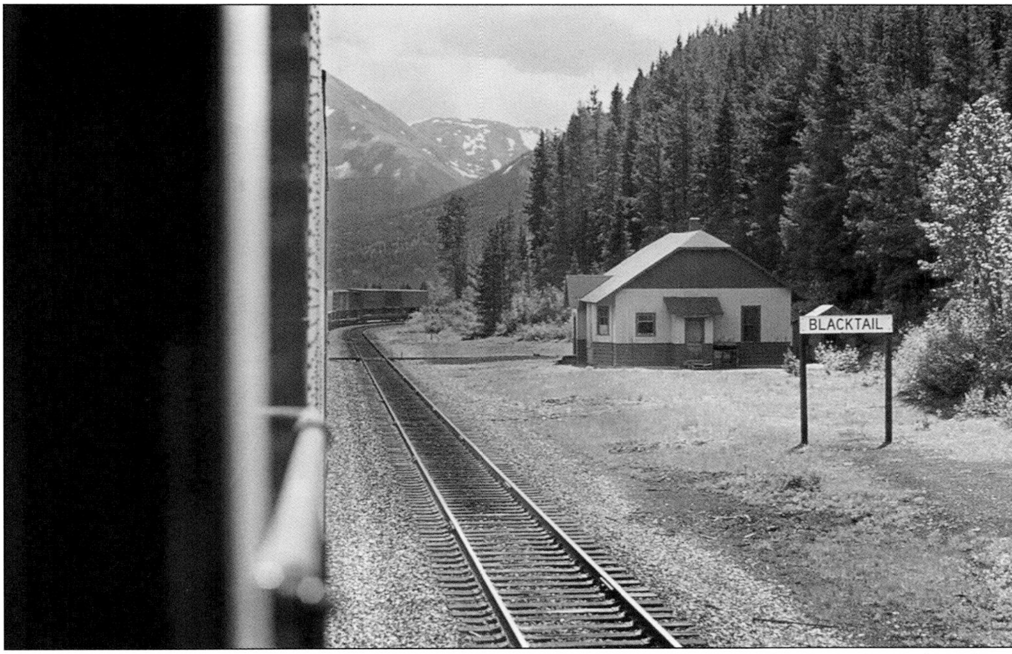

The only horseshoe curve in Marias Pass was originally called Bear Creek when the railroad was built in 1891. The name was changed to Fielding in 1907, and since 1926, the station has been known as Blacktail. The original 1910 depot was a 30-by-48-foot structure; it was split in 1944 to create this new section house that has since been destroyed. (Courtesy Chuck Hatler.)

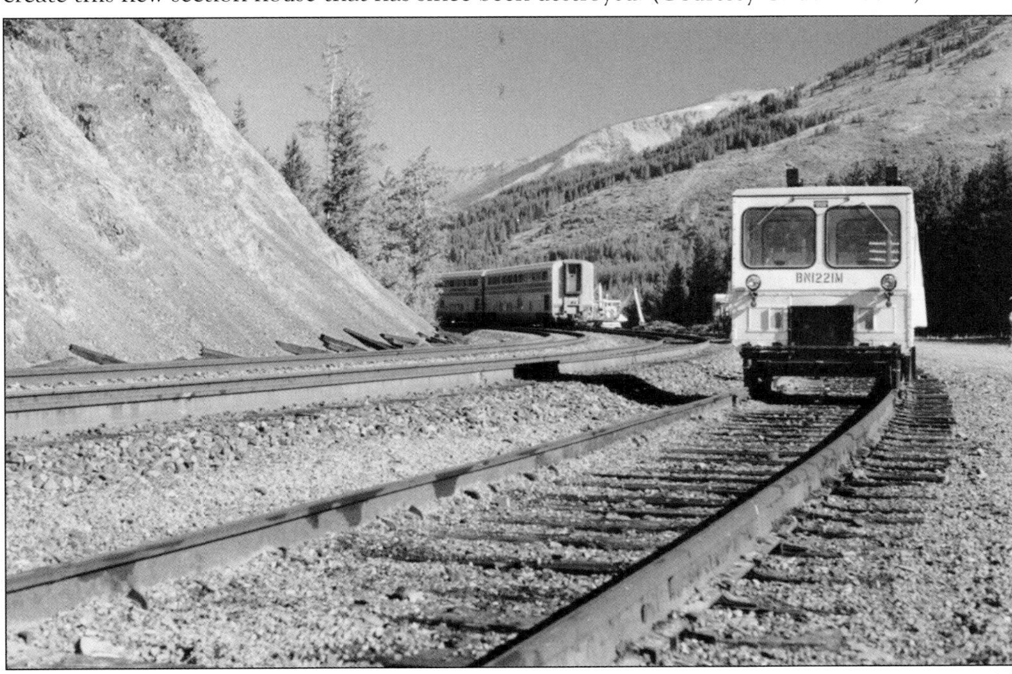

The southern portion of the Blacktail horseshoe curve is relatively level and provides a suitable place for sidings to store maintenance-of-way equipment. The tail end of the eastbound Amtrak *Empire Builder* passes a Burlington Northern "speeder" rail inspection car on the Blacktail siding. (Author's collection.)

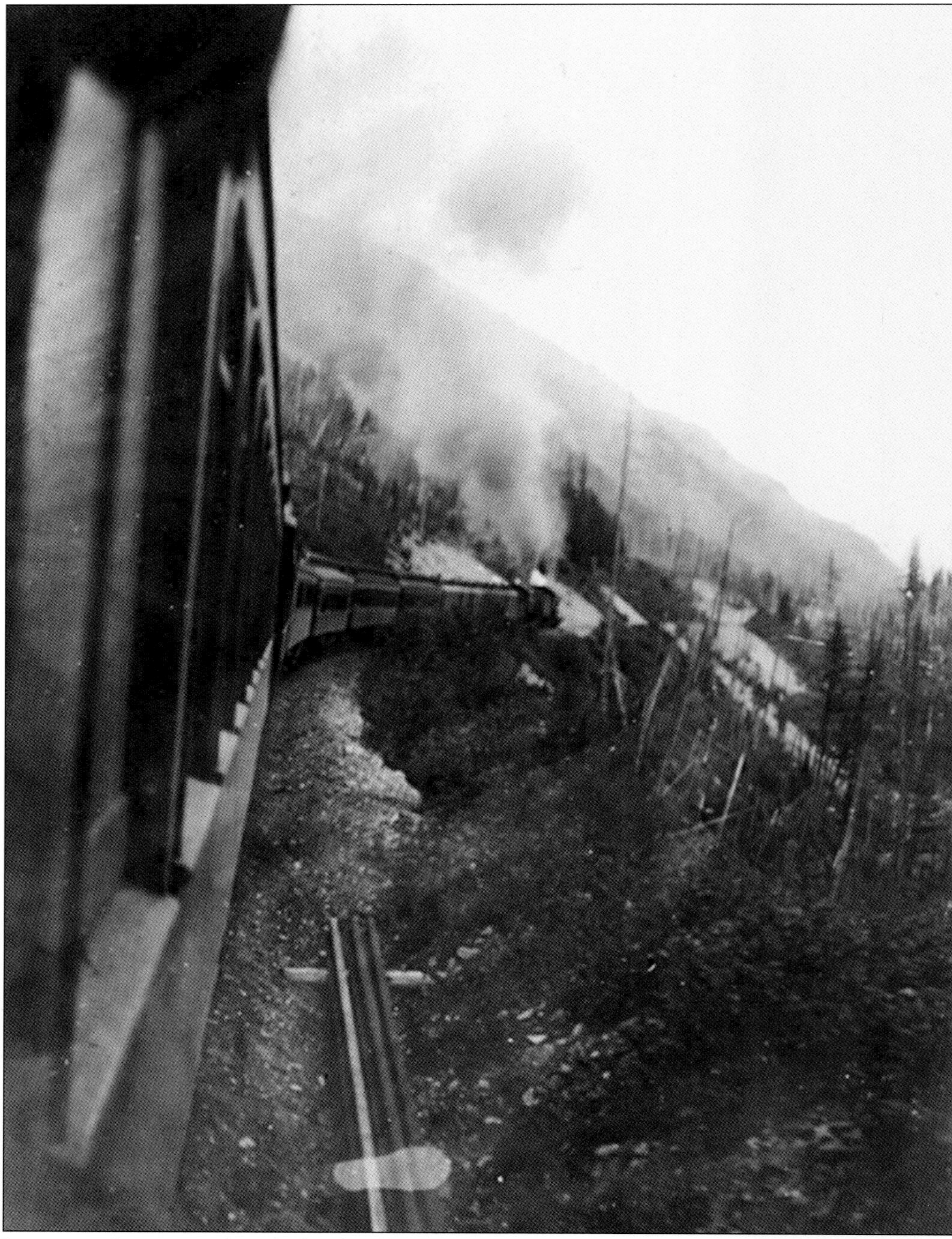

In an area known as the Blacktail Hills, Skyland was a short-lived siding between Fielding and Summit at about Milepost No. 1154 near what would later be named Marias. The area was named in commemoration of Maria Wood, a cousin of Capt. Meriwether Lewis of Lewis and Clark fame. The expedition never actually visited what is known today as Marias Pass, but came as close as Camp Disappointment, about 12 miles northeast of Browning, Montana. This photograph from the vestibule of the eastbound *Glacier Park Limited* is quite unique as the train operated only in the summer from 1924 to 1929, and the image is clear despite the rocking of the moving train heading upgrade between Blacktail and Summit near Skyland. (Author's collection.)

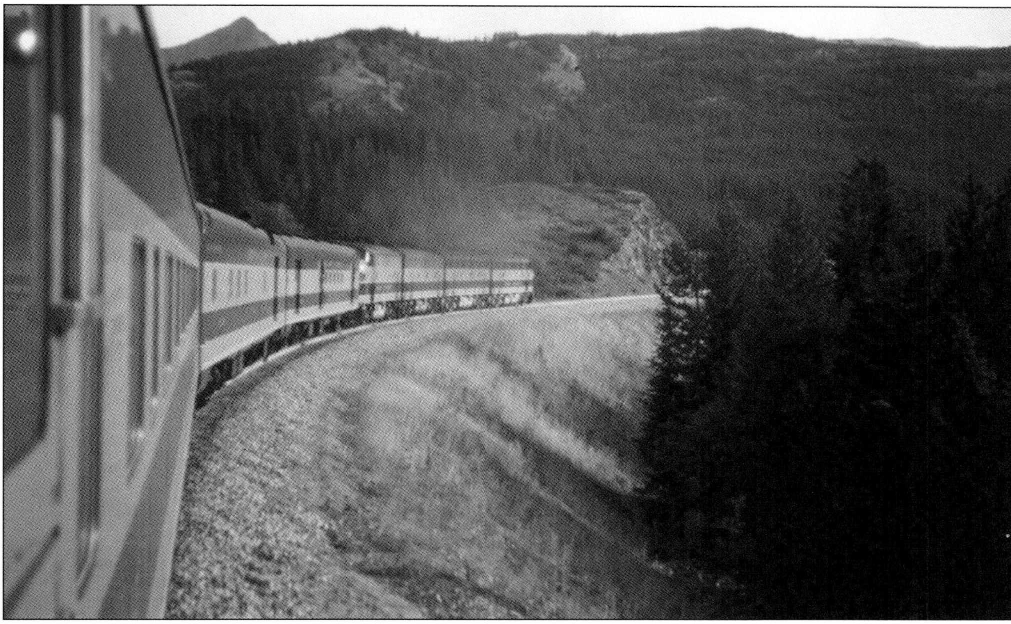

The mid-century *Empire Builder* normally operated with four EMD F-7 locomotives—one A unit with a crew cab, two B cab-less locomotives, and another A crew cab, making an A-B-B-A four-unit arrangement. Leaning out of the right side of the train, the photographer recorded the front-end power in the tight end of Blacktail Curve. (Courtesy Werkema collection, Great Northern Railway Historical Society.)

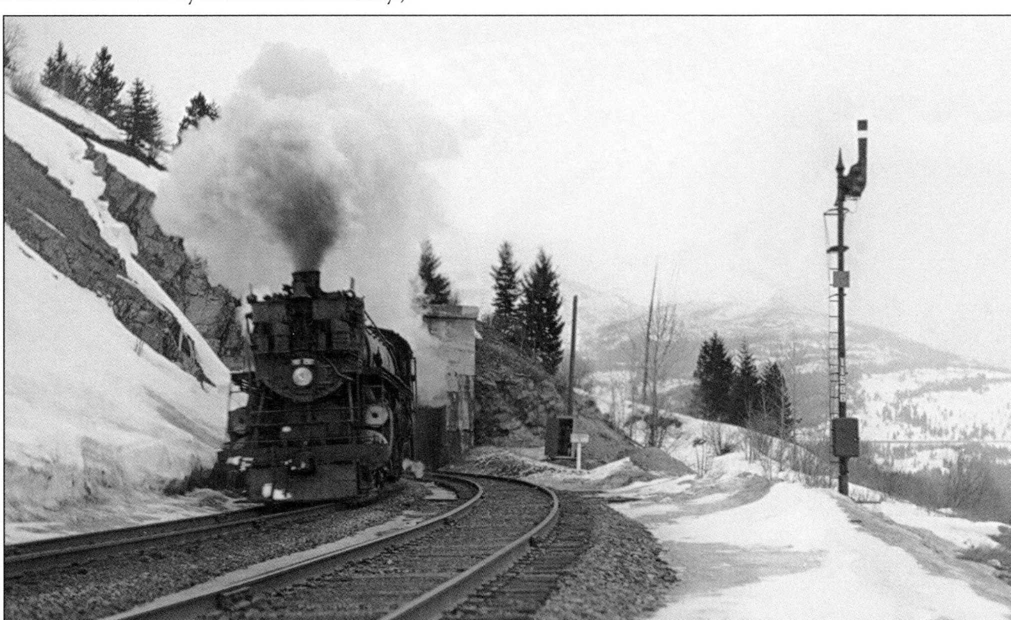

This is a classic image of mountain steam railroading; pictured is a 1940s-vintage westbound Great Northern passenger train led by a Class S 4-8-4 locomotive. It is exiting Windy Point Tunnel No. 1.5 at Milepost No. 1160.2 on a drab winter day. In 1936, S-2s were assigned to the Kalispell Division with engine Nos. 2586 through 2588; this arrangement remained through World War II. (Courtesy Ed Krona collection.)

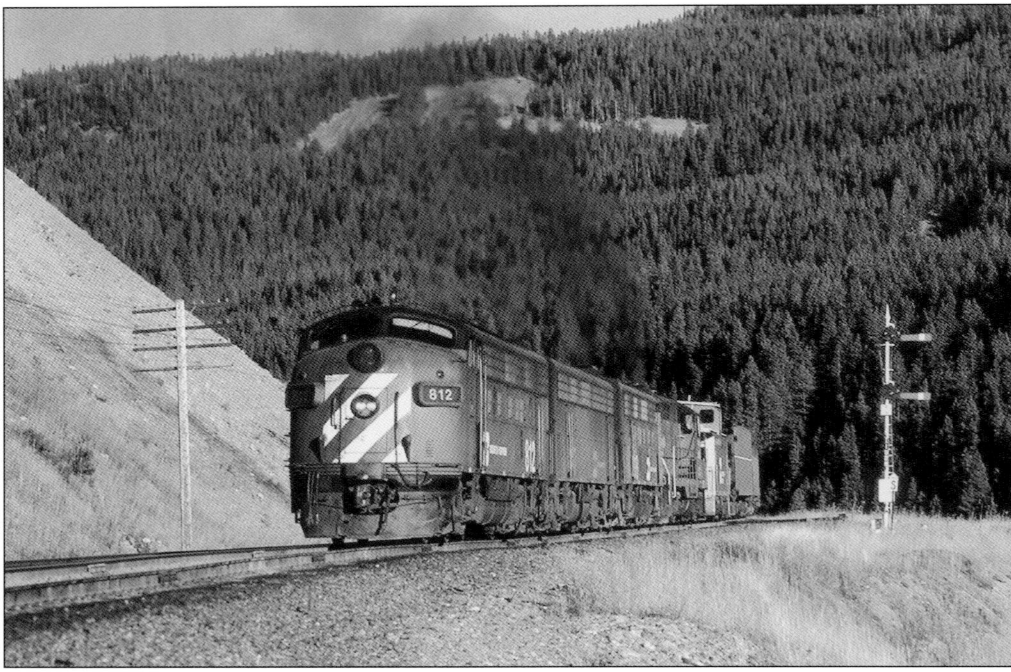

Here are two trains five years apart at the same place, Marias. Only a few miles from Summit, the original location named Skyland was used by the Great Northern until 1928, when the passing siding was removed. The Burlington Northern Railroad installed a Central Traffic Control (CTC) crossover in 1977 and labeled the location Marias. The image above from 1979 shows three F9s and a GP7 pushing an eastbound freight over the Continental Divide. Below, two EMD F45s and two SD40-2s slowly ascend the last four miles of the 1.8-percent grade to Summit in August 1983. (Above, author's collection; below, J. Lemke.)

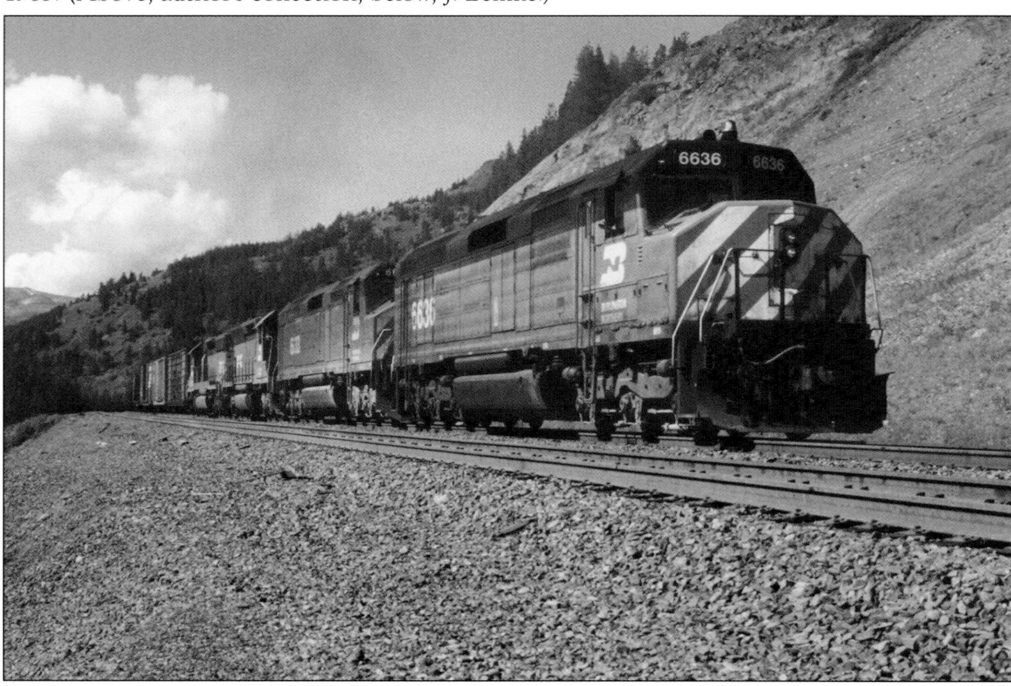

Seven

SUMMIT

TOP OF THE CONTINENTAL DIVIDE

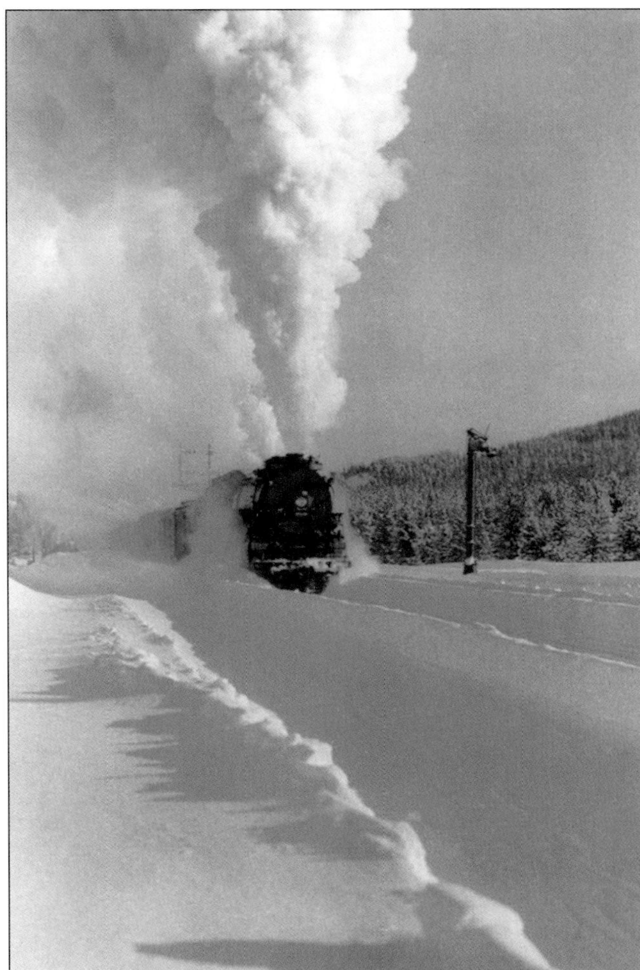

Jim Hill's confidence in John F. Stevens's ability as an engineer gave Great Northern the lowest Rocky Mountain railroad crossing in North America. Marias Pass is situated in a saddle between the icy arctic air of the plains and moisture from the coast, generating ideal winter blizzard and summer hurricane wind conditions. A Class P 4-8-2 speeds a westbound 1940s *Oriental Limited* through snowdrifts at Summit. (Courtesy Ed Krona collection.)

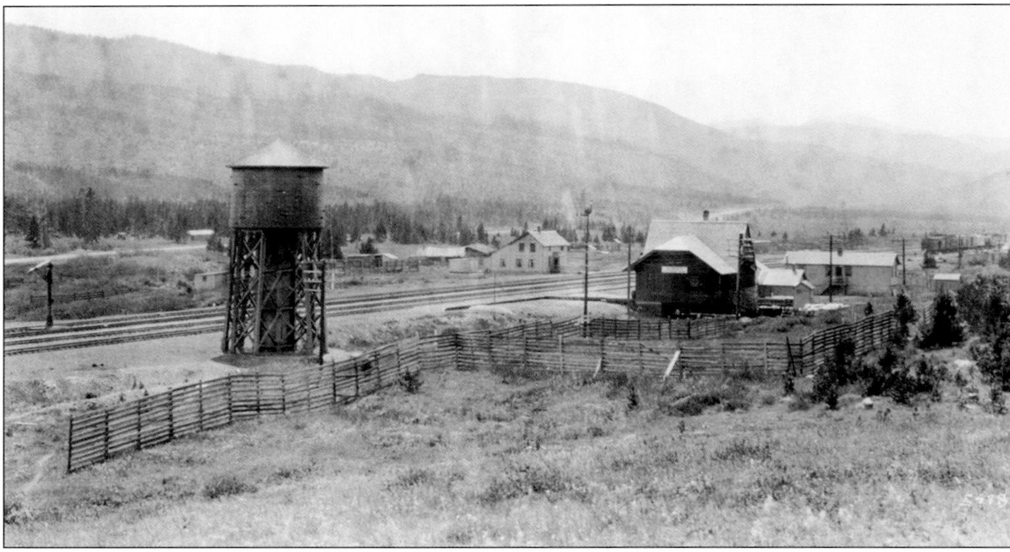

The Great Northern had a level area on the Continental Divide ideal for passing sidings. Originally, it also provided light locomotive repair with room for storage of maintenance-of-way equipment. The above image contains a wealth of details in an overview of the Summit facilities from the late 1920s. Note the 50,000-gallon water tank built in 1911, the chalet-styled Summit depot remodeled in 1929, employee bunkhouses in the background, and permanent snow fences protecting the station. A few hundred feet east of Glacier National Park, the Summit depot was the residence for the station agent and family, as evident from the children's bicycles in the June 1972 photograph below. (Above, photograph by Ferde Greene from the E.B. Gilliland collection; below, courtesy Chuck Hatler.)

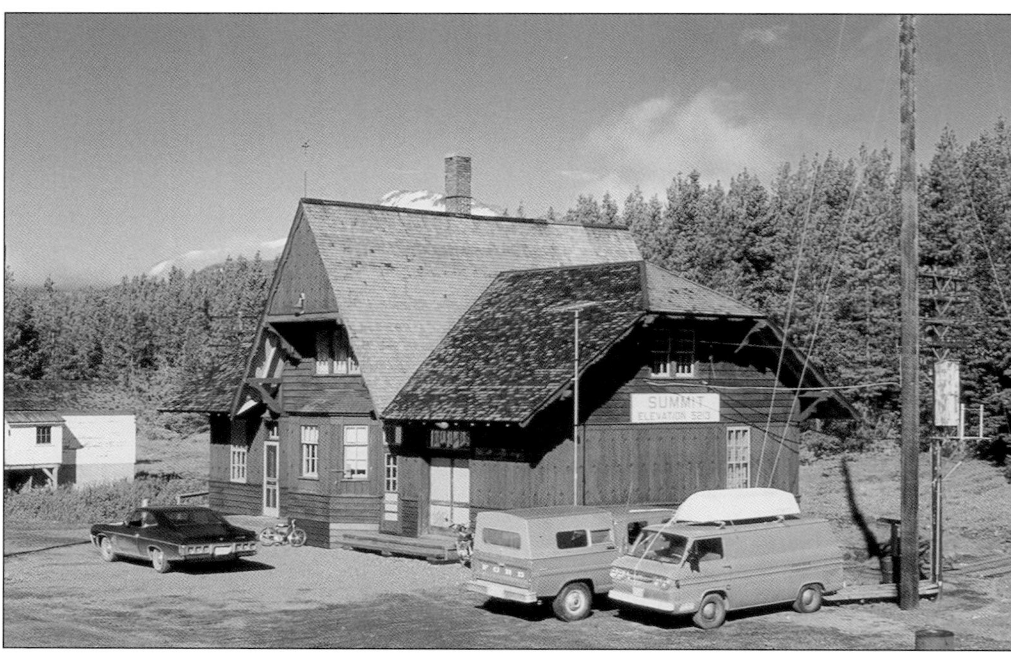

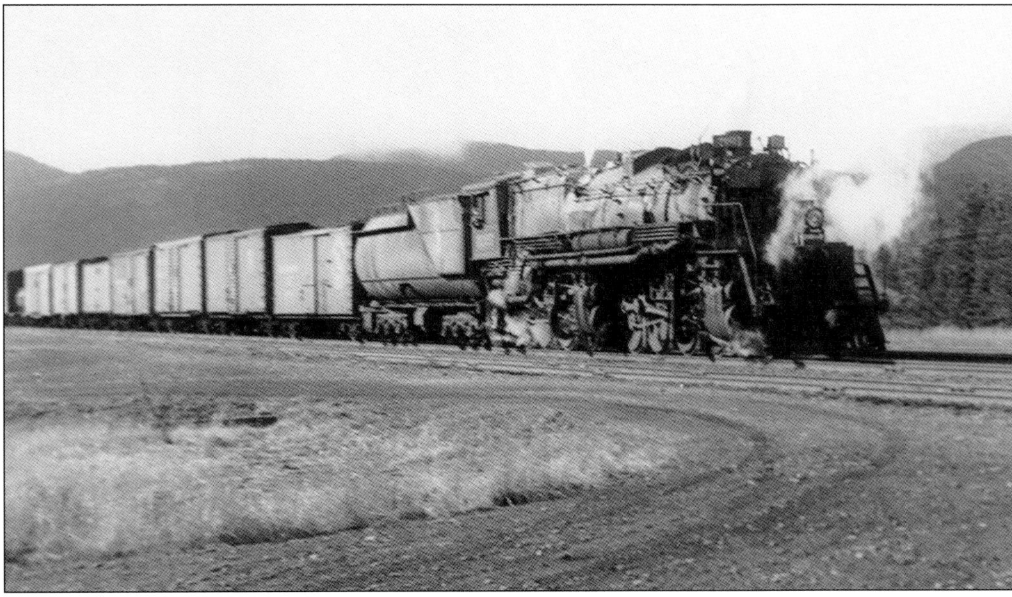

The Great Northern Class N 2-8-8-0 steam locomotives were capable of dragging about 4,000 tons of freight up a .07-percent grade without a helper. The two images on this page provide a glimpse of 1940s-vintage steam operation at Summit; above, N Class No. 2007 with an eastbound train awaits orders to advance downgrade to the division point at Blackfoot. At the east end of Summit yard, a westward train struggles up the final one-percent grade at the Continental Divide. After a brief stop to check brakes, it will continue at 25 miles per hour through tunnels and snowsheds, arriving at Essex an hour or so later. (Both, courtesy Ed Krona collection.)

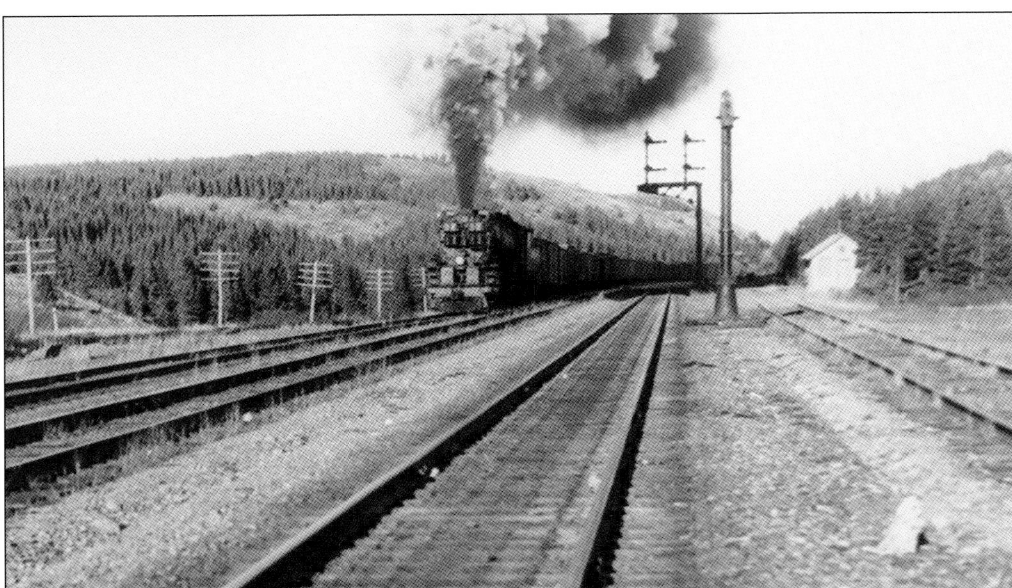

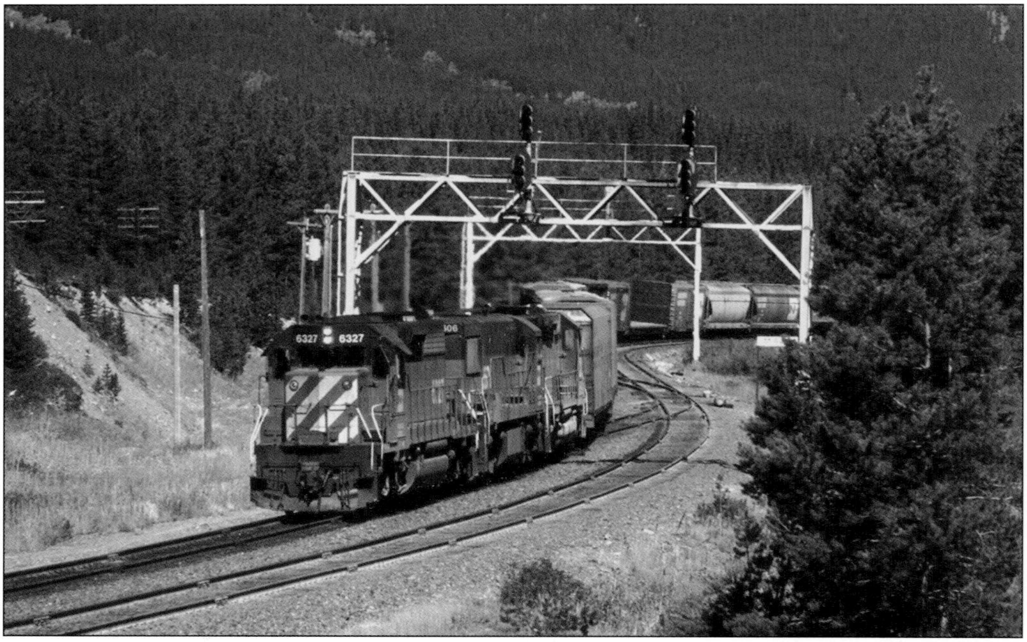

Centralized Traffic Control is designed to allow trains to meet and pass each other without interruption. In 1967, the Great Northern established CTC from Blacktail to Summit. The control bridges in these two photographs at Summit-Marias illustrate the flexibility of operating trains under CTC, as the double-crossover switch arrangement allows dispatchers to run one train around another without stopping and having crews realign the switches. The weather at the crest of the Continental Divide can shift from a pleasant day into violent storms in a matter of a few hours. (Above, photograph by Doug Harrop, author's collection; below, photograph by Keith Ardinger, author's collection.)

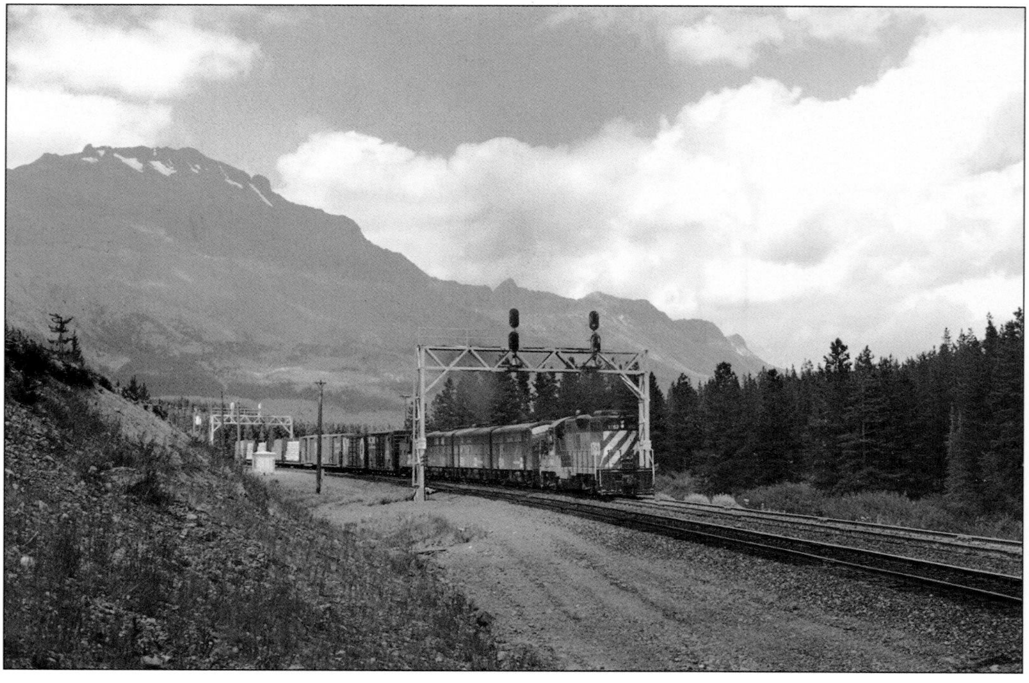

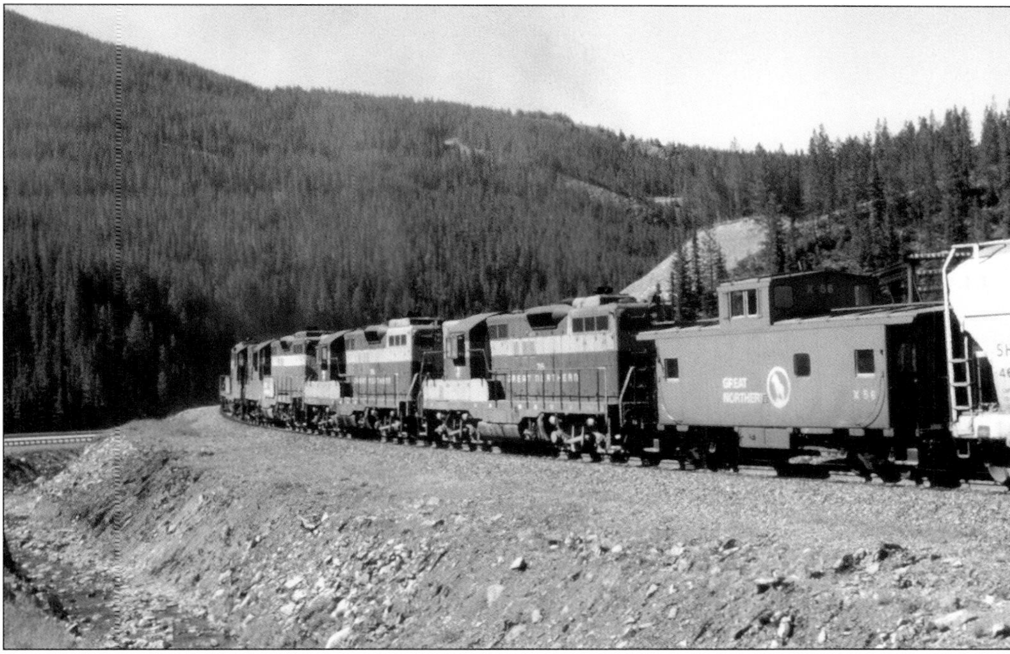

Taken a mile west of the Continental Divide, these two photographs illustrate the Great Northern motive power generally used as helpers in Marias Pass during the 1960s. The locomotives shown here are General Motors EMD GP7s and GP9s. Four GP9s added to a train would produce an additional 7,000 horsepower needed to haul more tonnage up the 30-mile mountain grade from Essex to Summit. Standing at this location from US Highway 2, two different views are possible; the photographer above was looking south into the Flathead National Forest; below, an eastbound train approaches Summit station on a March day beneath a glimpse of Summit Mountain in Glacier National Park. (Both, courtesy Cordell Newby collection, Great Northern Railway Historical Society.)

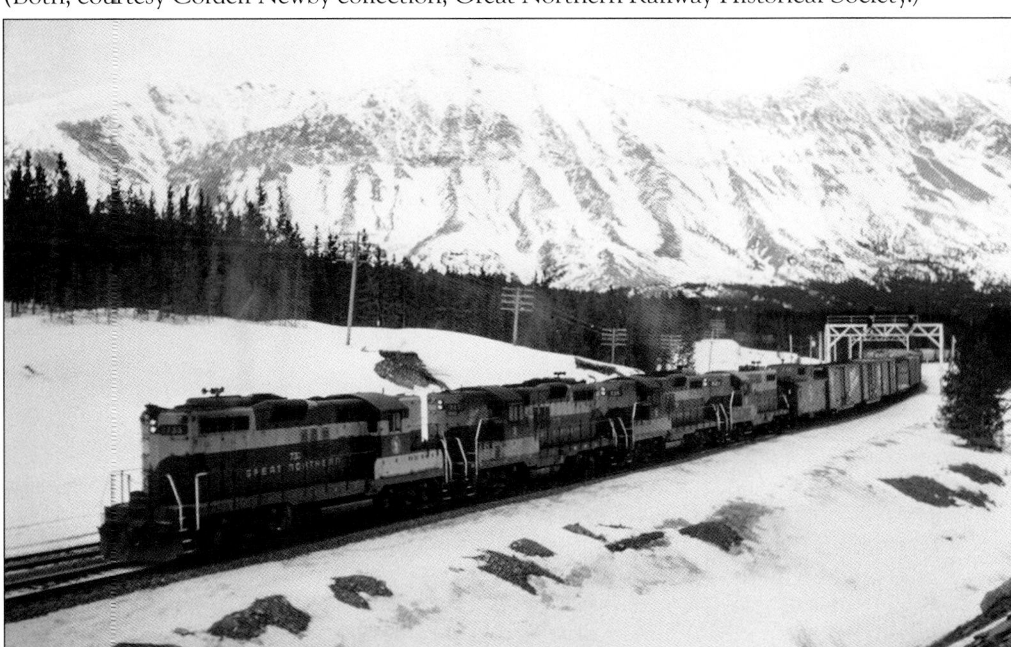

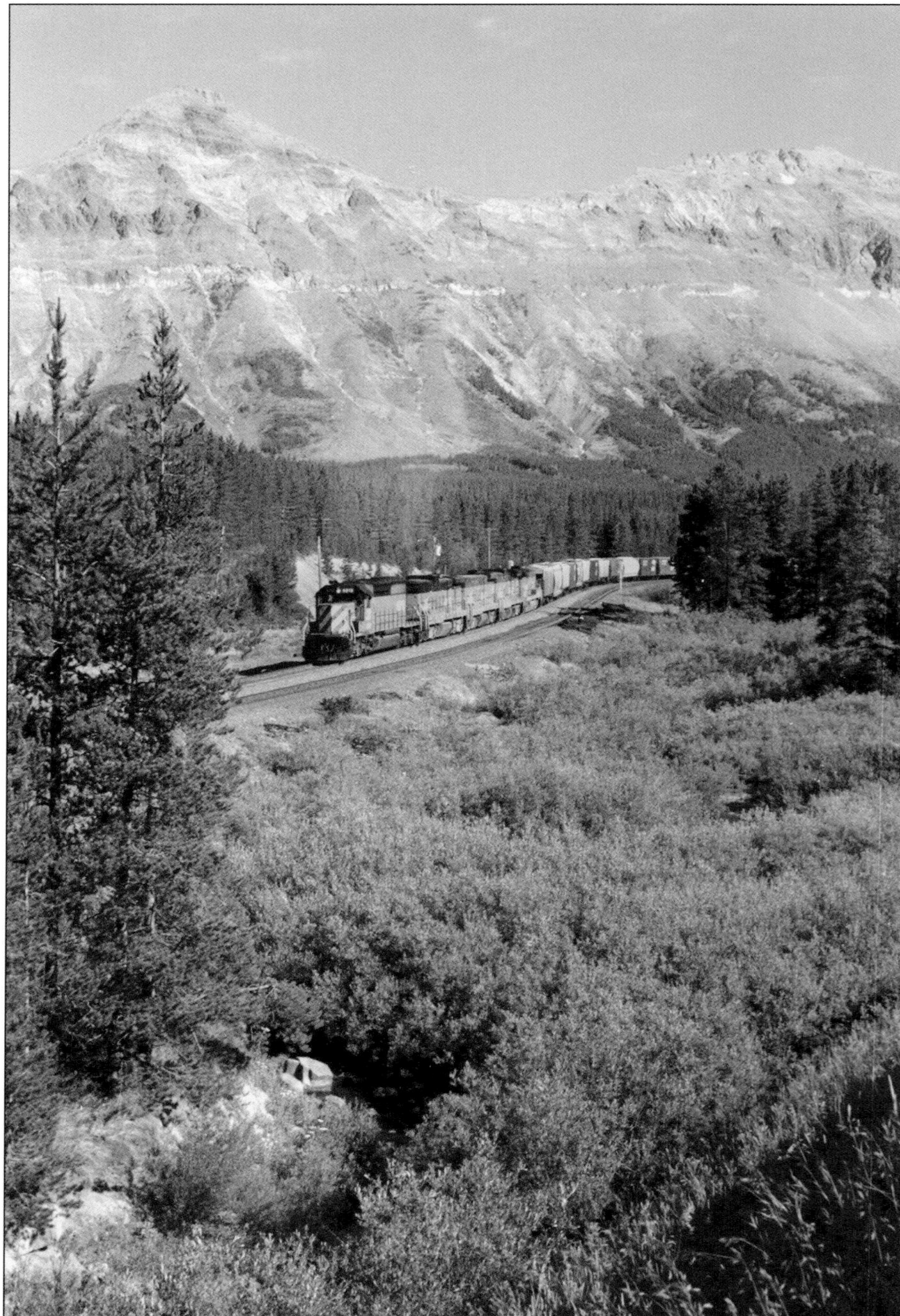

A westbound Burlington Northern SD40-2 and four General Electric B30-7As crest Marias Pass from the east on a warm July 1986 day as Summit Mountain soars nearly 9,000 feet into a clear blue Montana sky. Originating here at Summit, the 110-mile Glacier National Park section of the Continental Divide Trail winds through several rugged mountain passes in the United States before terminating in Canada's Waterton National Park in Alberta. The meadows in the foreground are the small beginnings of Bear Creek, considered the headwaters of the Flathead River drainage. (Author's collection.)

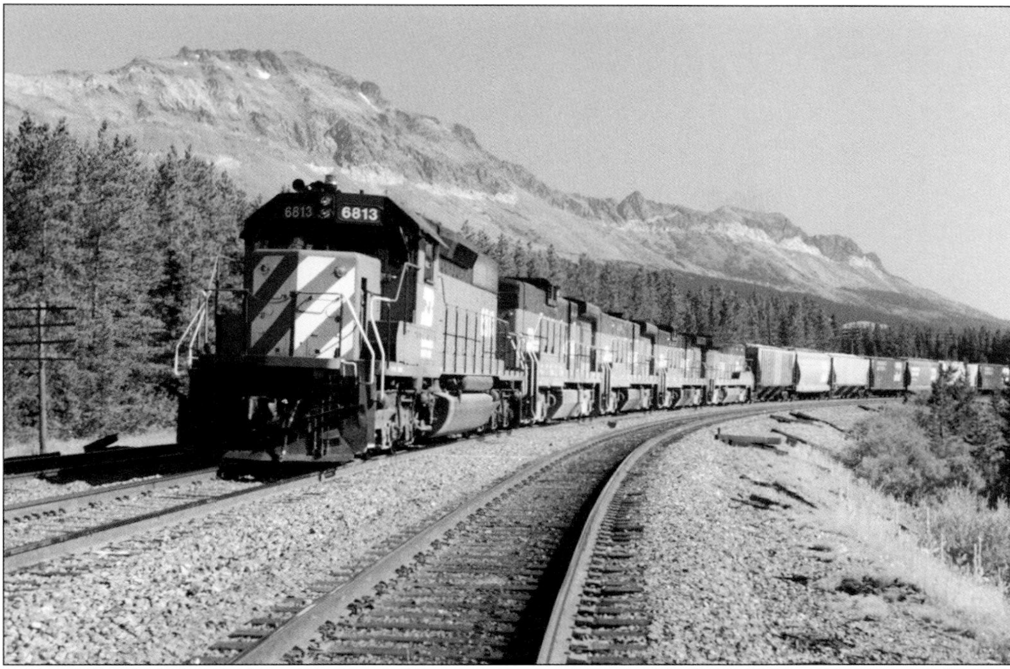

The topography at Summit is level at 5,213 feet for about a mile, creating a gap on the Continental Divide that allows trains to pause for inspection and to pass safely on flat ground. Burlington Northern SD40-2 6813 leads four cab-less General Electric B30-7As westbound at the west end of Summit yard; since there were only about 120 of these units, to have four of them in tandem was relatively uncommon. (Author's collection.)

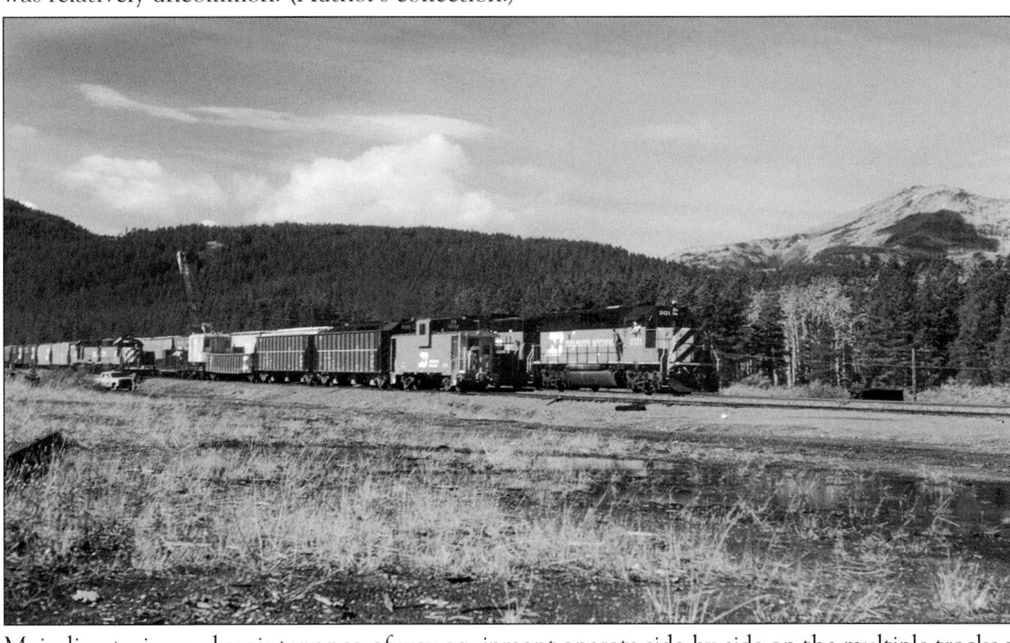

Main line trains and maintenance-of-way equipment operate side-by-side on the multiple tracks at Summit. This rail yard configuration gave dispatchers the flexibility to position trains wherever needed; here, an eastbound Burlington Northern priority freight passes a westbound work crew distributing ballast along the right-of-way. (Author's collection.)

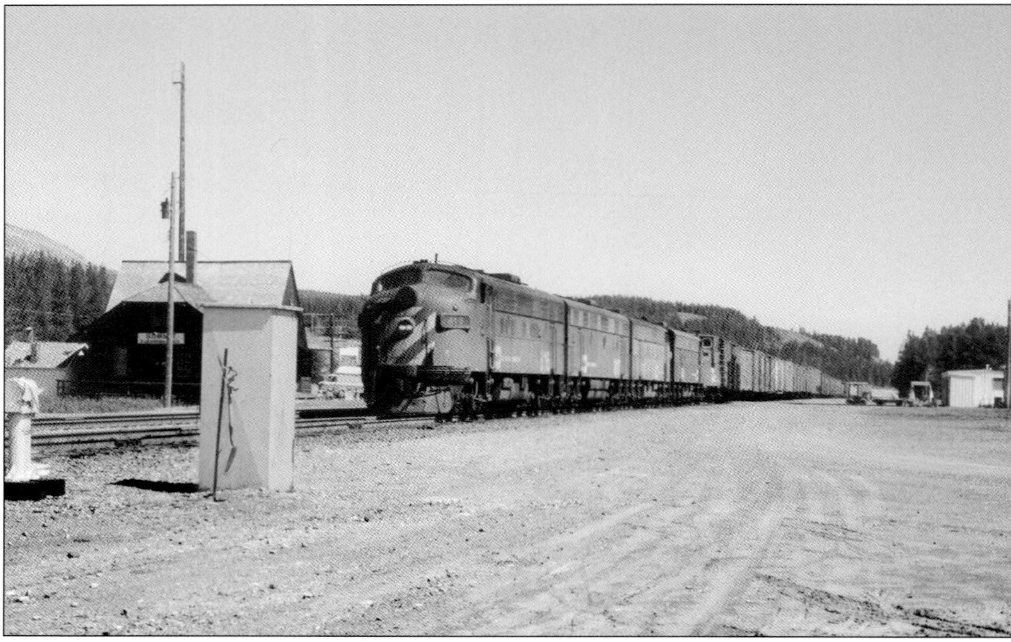

Shortly after the Burlington Northern Railroad merger in March 1970, EMD F units from across the rail system were utilized as standard helper power in the Rocky Mountains. Four F9s wait at Summit for permission to uncouple from this eastbound train and return downgrade to Essex. (Author's collection.)

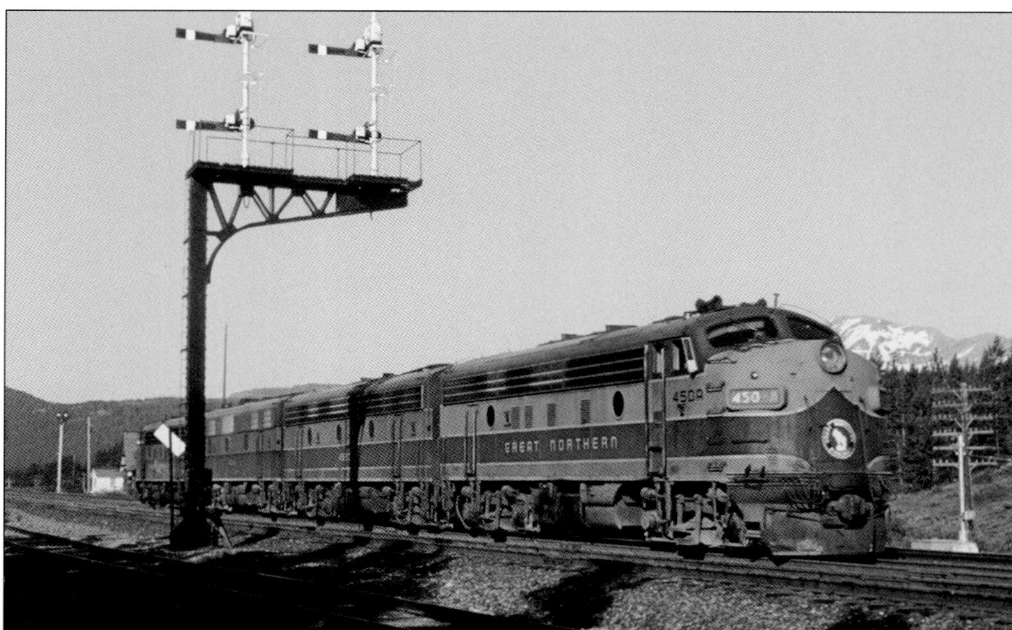

Four Great Northern F units pause beneath the double-track cantilever signal tower at Summit. The term F-unit refers to the locomotive model number; the F originally stood for "fourteen," as in 1,400 horsepower, not freight. The 1,500-horsepower 450-A was built in March 1950 and operated until August 1968, when it was traded to EMD in exchange for new second-generation locomotives. (Courtesy Jerry Quinn collection.)

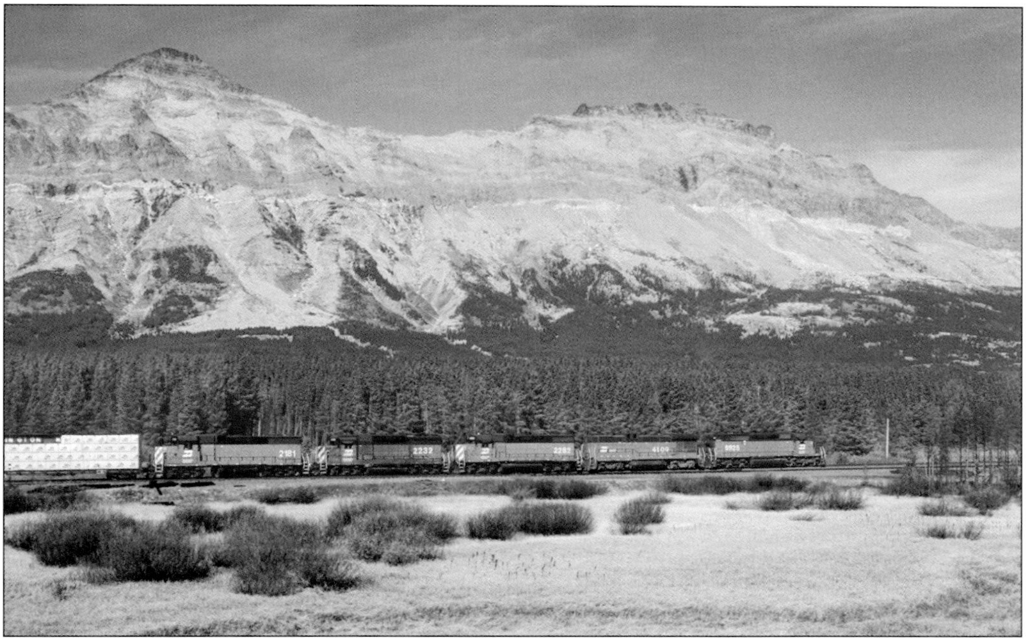

Little Dog Mountain (left) and Summit Mountain dwarf the five locomotives on this eastbound freight in the meadows at Summit. Out of sight just beyond the tracks is Three Bears Lake, built by the Great Northern for steam engine maintenance; this lake straddles the Continental Divide and permitted hybridization of the currently endangered westslope cutthroat with Yellowstone cutthroat trout from the Missouri River drainage. (Author's collection.)

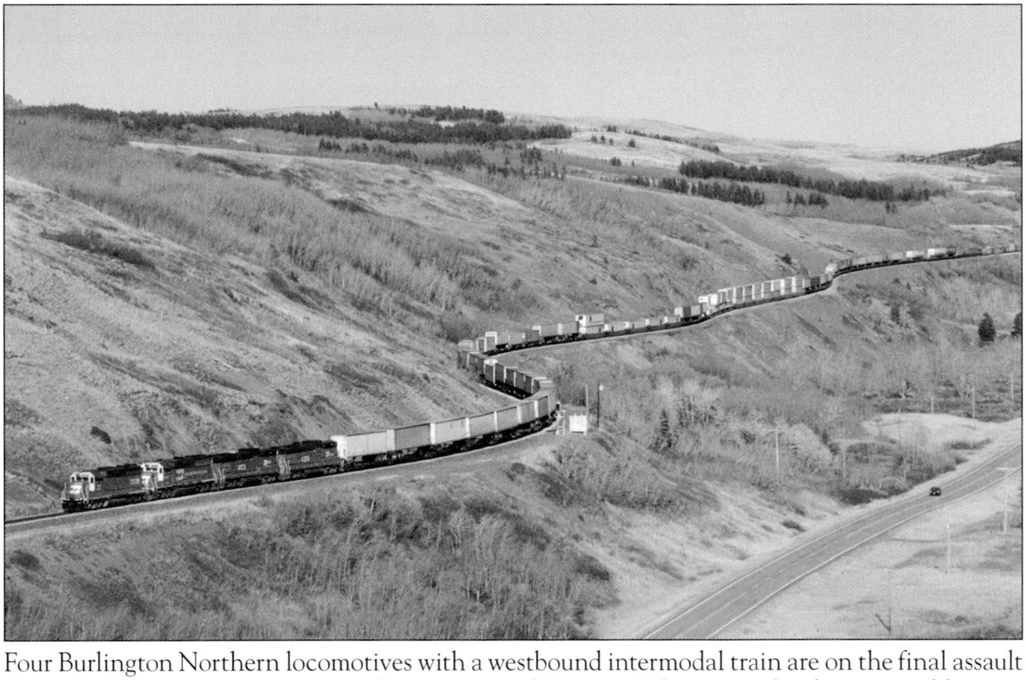

Four Burlington Northern locomotives with a westbound intermodal train are on the final assault through the aspen groves just a mile or so east of Summit. The prairie landscape quickly gives way to the predominately forested west side of Marias Pass on the crest of the Continental Divide. (Courtesy Jerry Quinn collection.)

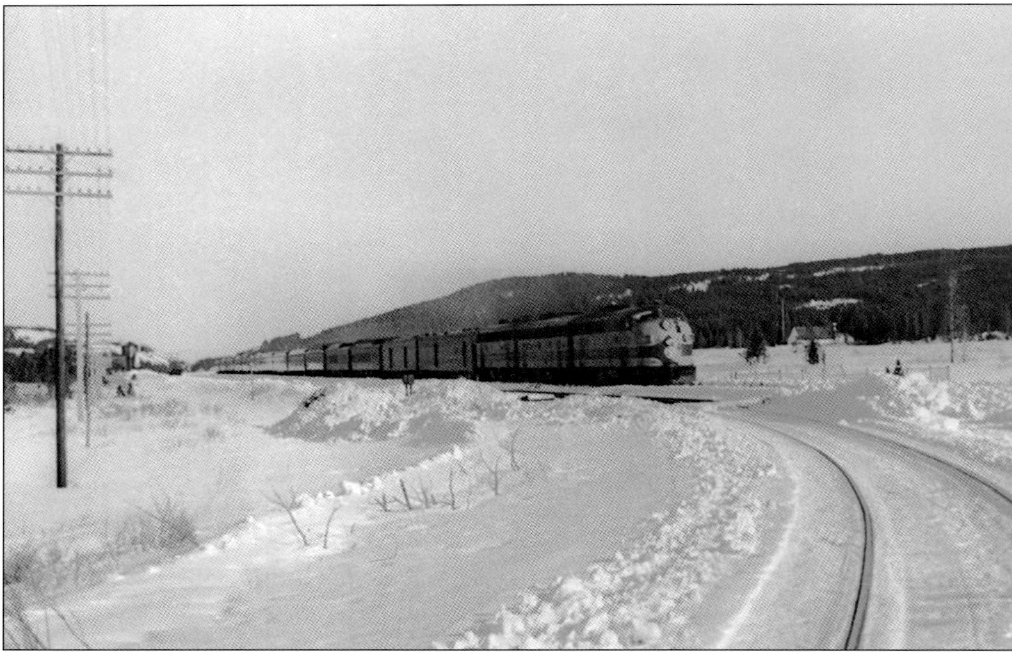

The Great Northern *Western Star*, westbound at about 9:00 a.m. on a cold winter morning, passes the balloon track at Summit. This was an oval track arrangement that allowed snowplows to be turned without having to be maneuvered through the traditional wye configuration where multiple switches could have been fouled by drifting snow. (Courtesy Ed Krona collection.)

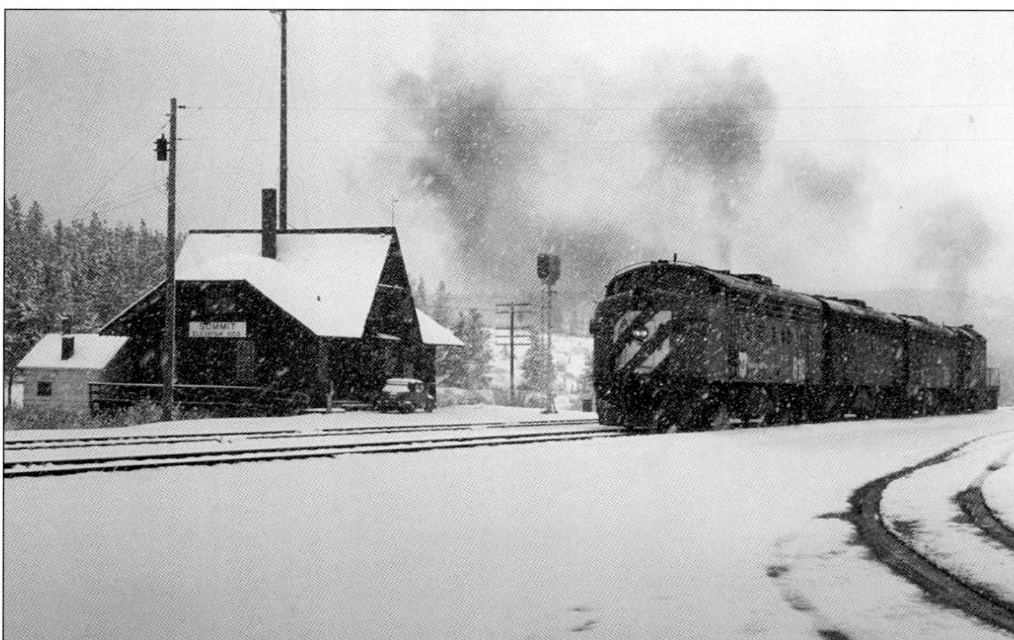

At an elevation of 5,213 feet, snow is a possibility at any time of the year. This scene of three Burlington Northern Fs and a GP9 was photographed in May 1976 in front of the Summit station. The Great Northern Summit depot was moved a mile or so west of the original location near US highway 2 in 1986, and in 2016 is a lodge and steakhouse. (Courtesy Jerry Quinn collection.)

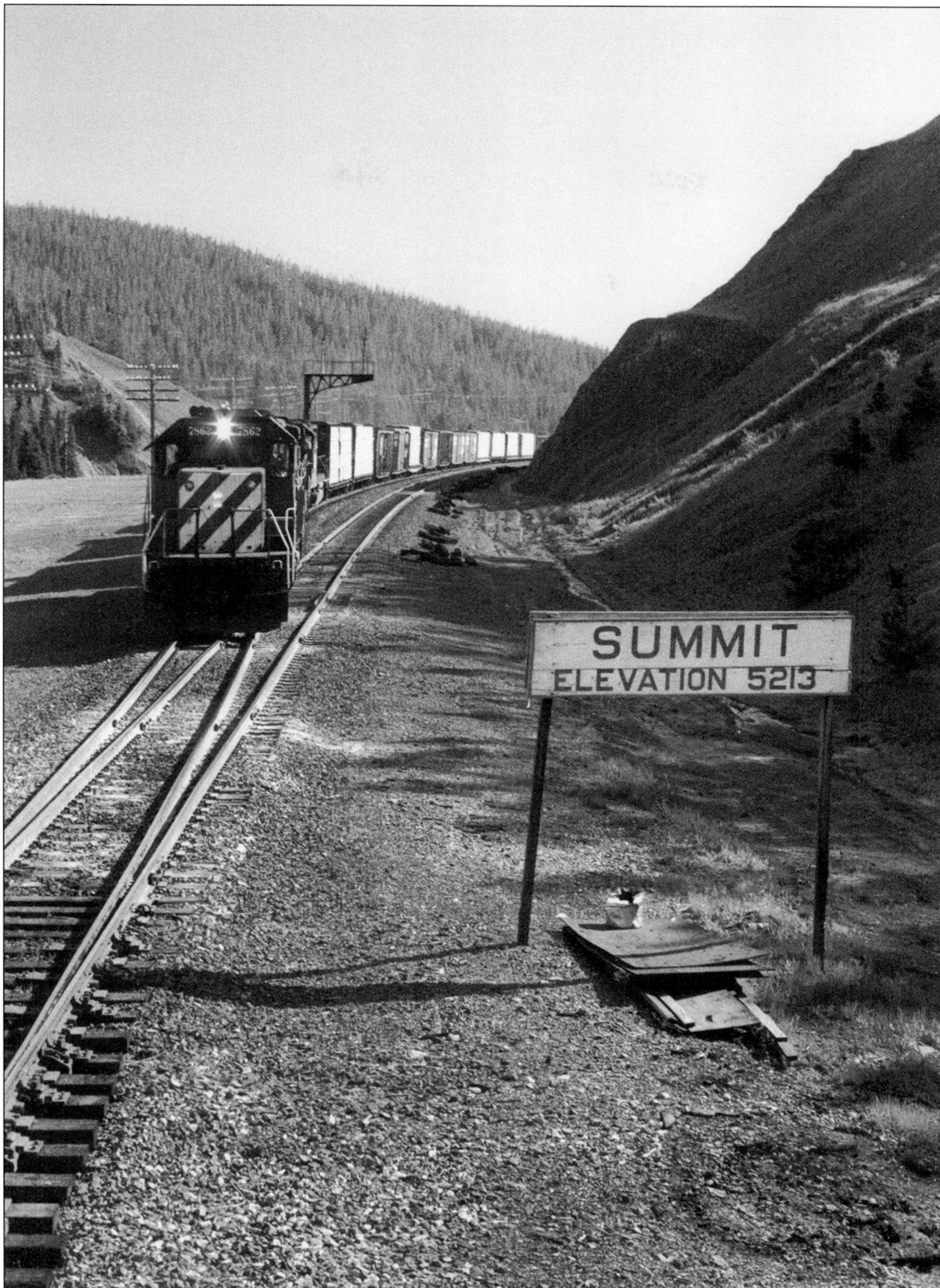

On a summer afternoon in 1986 at Milepost No. 1149.83, an eastbound Burlington Northern freight slowly enters single-track territory after leaving the double-track main line that began 15 miles west at Java; other than passing sidings, the entire route east through Montana is single track. The Summit location marker is the original depot sign, which was moved here when the station was relocated. (Author's collection.)

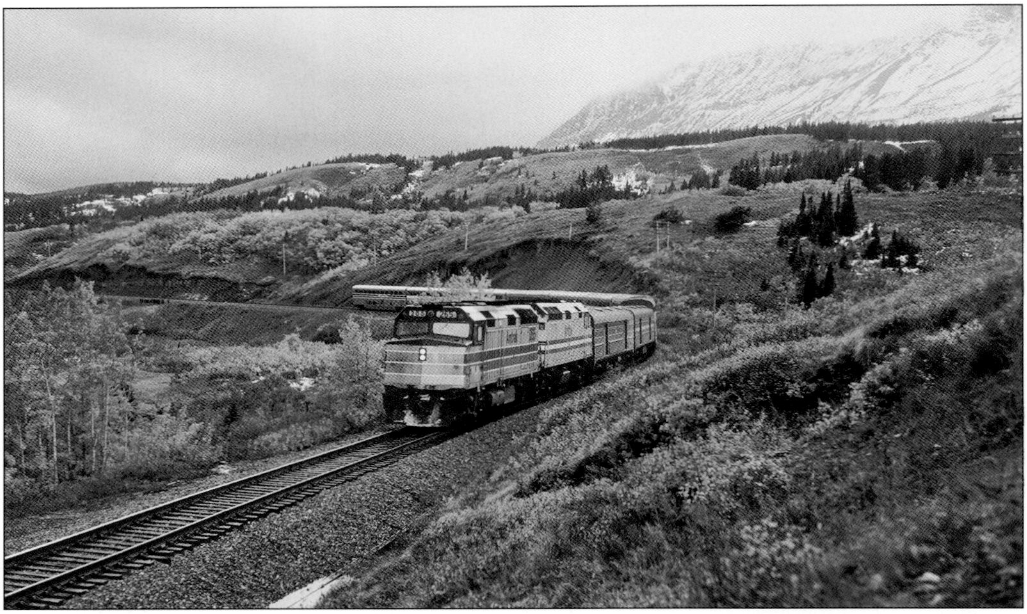

Early snows and heavy skies on Little Dog Mountain in Glacier Park hang over Amtrak 265 on the eastbound *Empire Builder* as aspen groves and stunted conifers succumb to open range on the Montana prairie. In 2016, former Amtrak 265 traversed similar terrain, providing passenger service on the 134-mile Tshiuetin Rail Transportation system, a Canadian regional railway through the wilderness of western Labrador and northeastern Quebec. (Author's collection.)

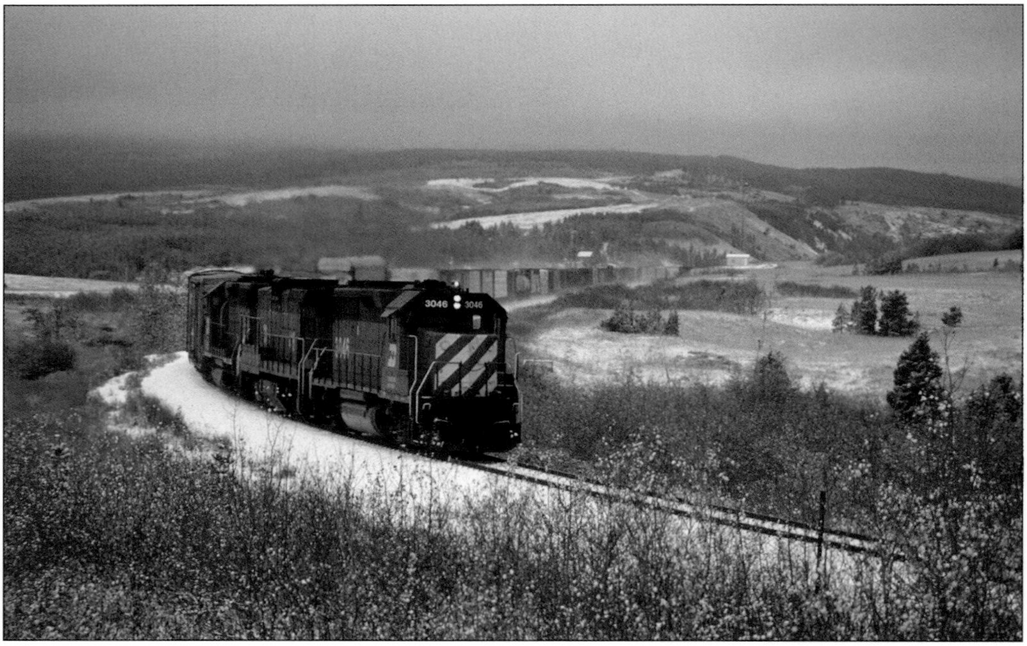

Two miles east of Summit is a slump in the terrain that creates the impression of reaching the Continental Divide crest, but in fact, it is a light grade for both eastbound and westbound trains. This spot is appropriately named "False Summit." In October 1990, Burlington Northern Extra 3046 East reaches the high point of False Summit near the former Great Northern station of Lubec/Rising Wolf. (Courtesy Jerry Quinn collection.)

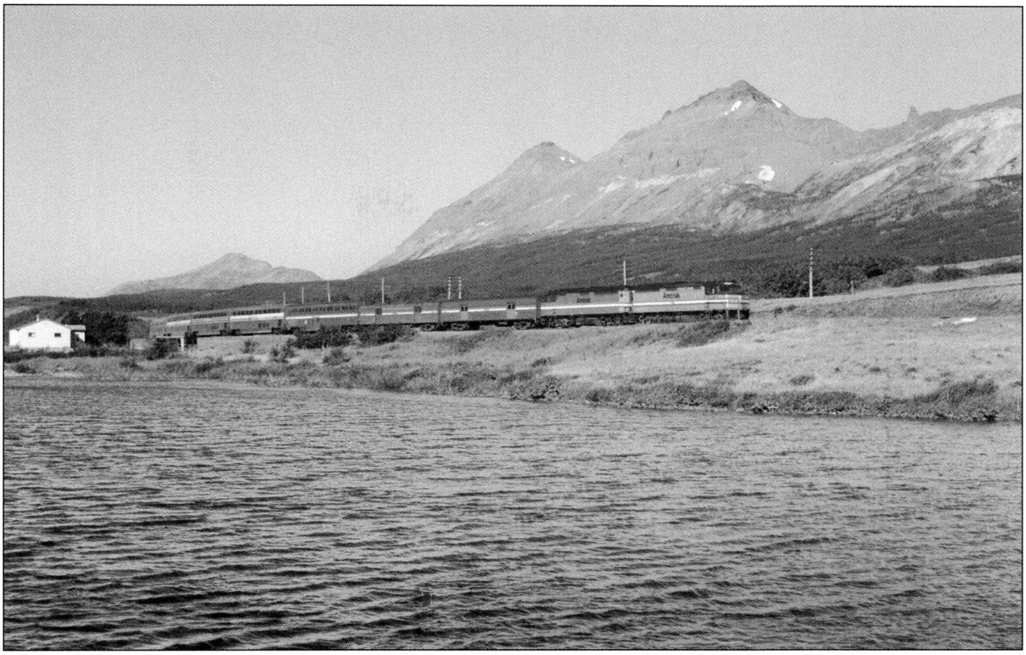

The slopes of Little Dog Mountain and Summit Mountain in Glacier National Park form an excellent backdrop for this 1987 eastbound Amtrak *Empire Builder*; in the foreground, the constant East Glacier wind ruffles the surface on one of the small unnamed ponds on the tableland surrounding False Summit. (Author's collection.)

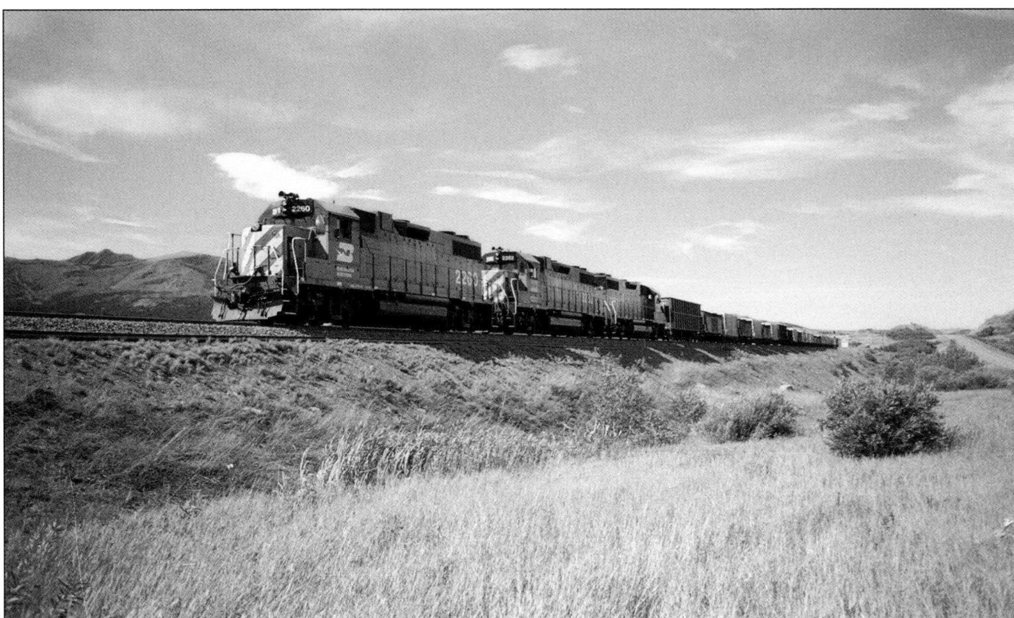

Most track maintenance is performed during summer months as weather permits. Three Burlington Northern GP38-2s with a 1986 rock train advance westbound toward Summit dumping ballast along the right-of-way at False Summit. In 1966, the Great Northern Railway relocated the rail line onto this fill, eliminating two miles of curvature and Snowshed No. 4A at Rising Wolf. (Author's collection.)

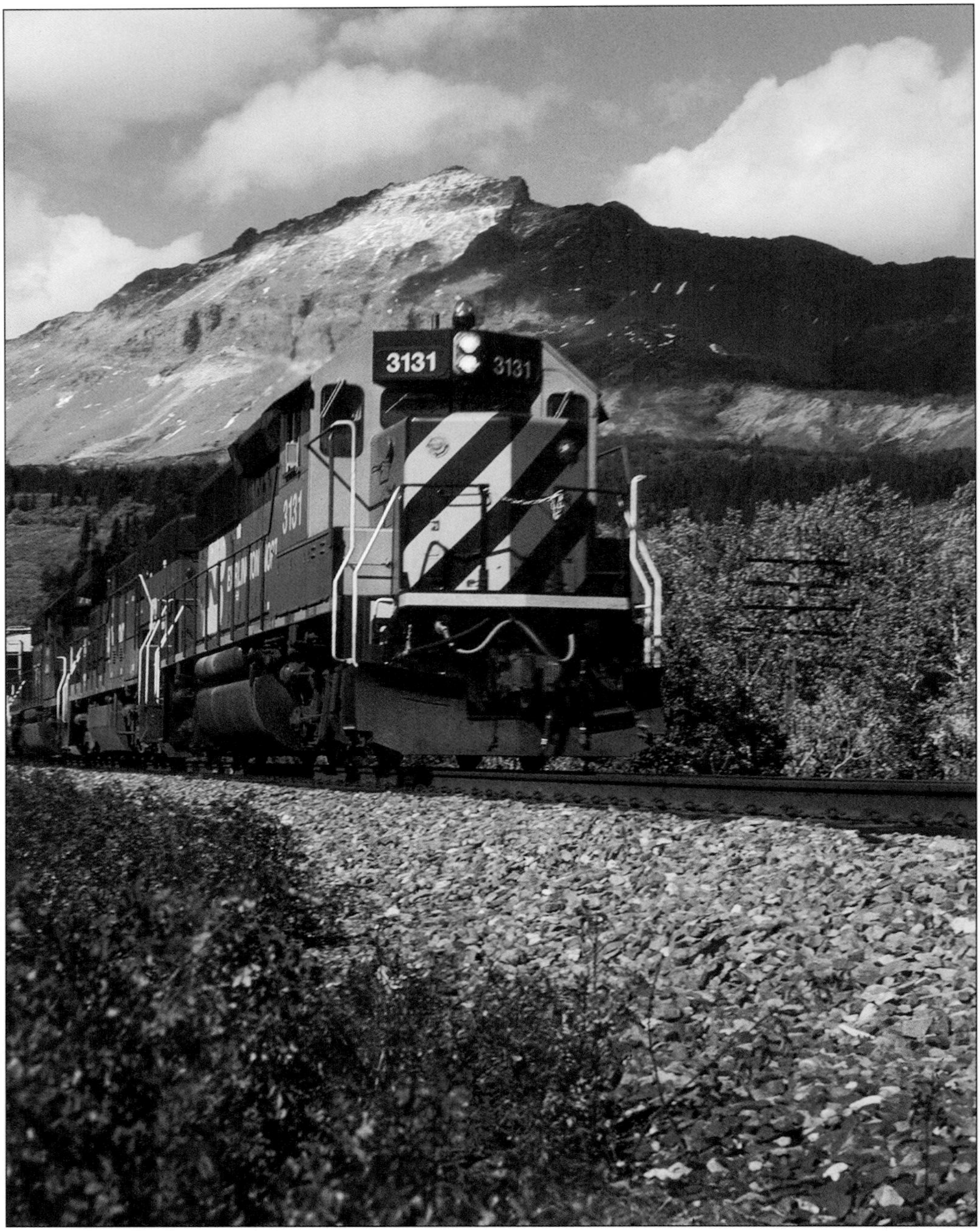

In 1985, Burlington Northern introduced the tiger-stripe paint scheme on 38 new EMD GP50s to improve forward visibility of the locomotives. By the time the GP50 debuted in 1980, railroads were much more interested in six-axle power because of their advantages. For instance, with the two extra axles, the locomotive's weight was more evenly distributed, which caused less wear on the rails and increased traction. These locomotives were some of the last four-axle General Purpose units purchased prior to the upsurge of double-stack traffic on the Burlington Northern and other North American railroads. In this July 1986 photograph, the snappy looking 3131 pulls an eastbound priority special between Summit and Bison under clear Glacier National Park skies. (Author's collection.)

Eight

WINTER

THE CHALLENGE OF FIGHTING SNOW

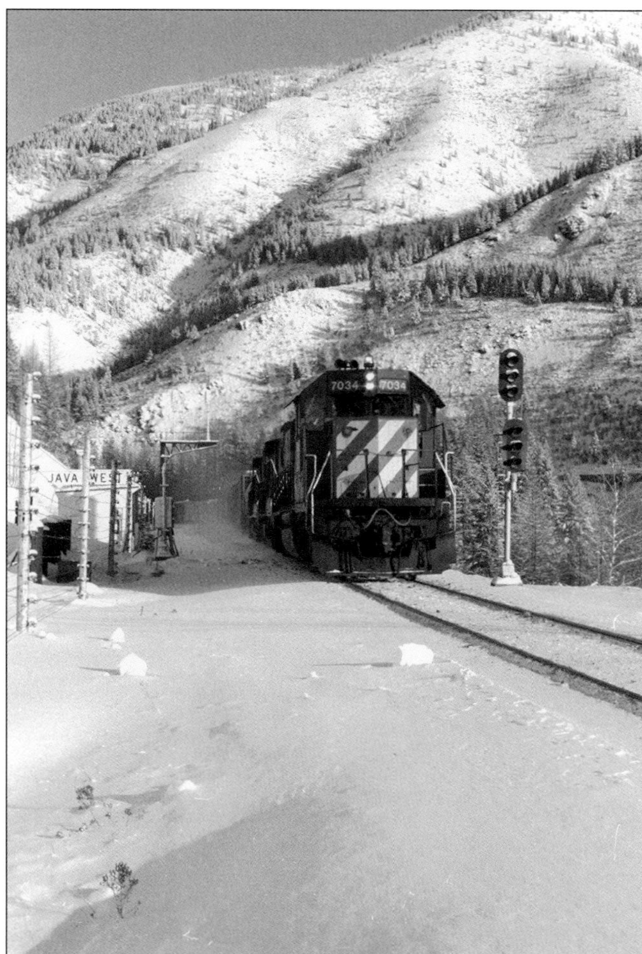

This 1986 photograph of Burlington Northern Extra 7034 East approaching the gauntlet at Java West is the picture-perfect portrait of winter railroading in Marias Pass, including clear Rocky Mountain skies, classic CTC block signals, functional slide fence wires, and a backdrop of Running Rabbit Mountain in Glacier National Park. (Author's collection.)

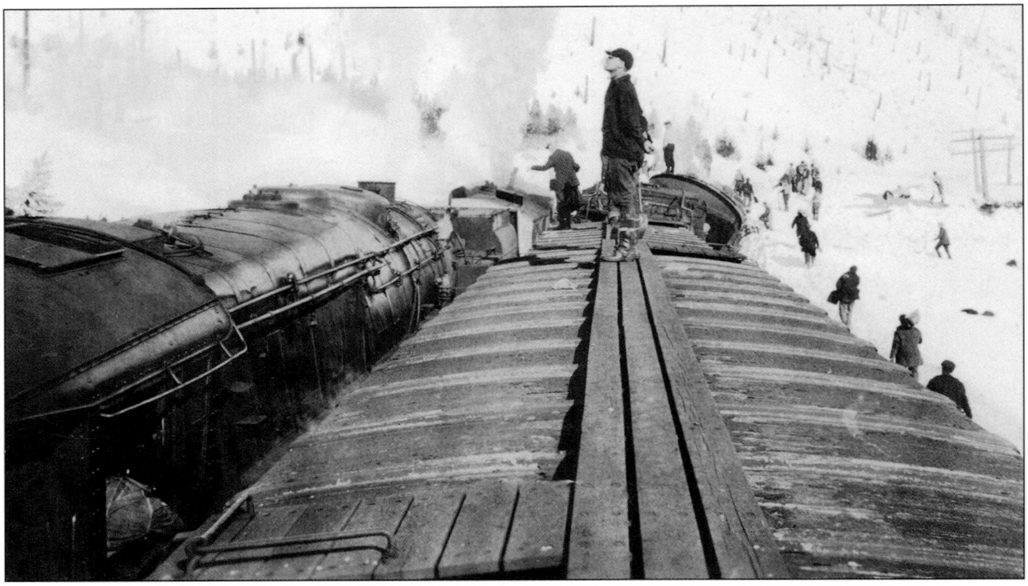

There are 11 snowsheds in Marias Pass. They were built to shelter the double-track main line from avalanches originating on the south slopes of Running Rabbit Mountain and Snowslip Mountain along the southern boundary of Glacier National Park. Between the snowsheds are sites of infrequent slides named Elk, No Name, Infinity, and Jake's. Here, at Jake's in the 1930s, a sentinel surveys the hillside, ready to warn of any imminent danger. (Author's collection.)

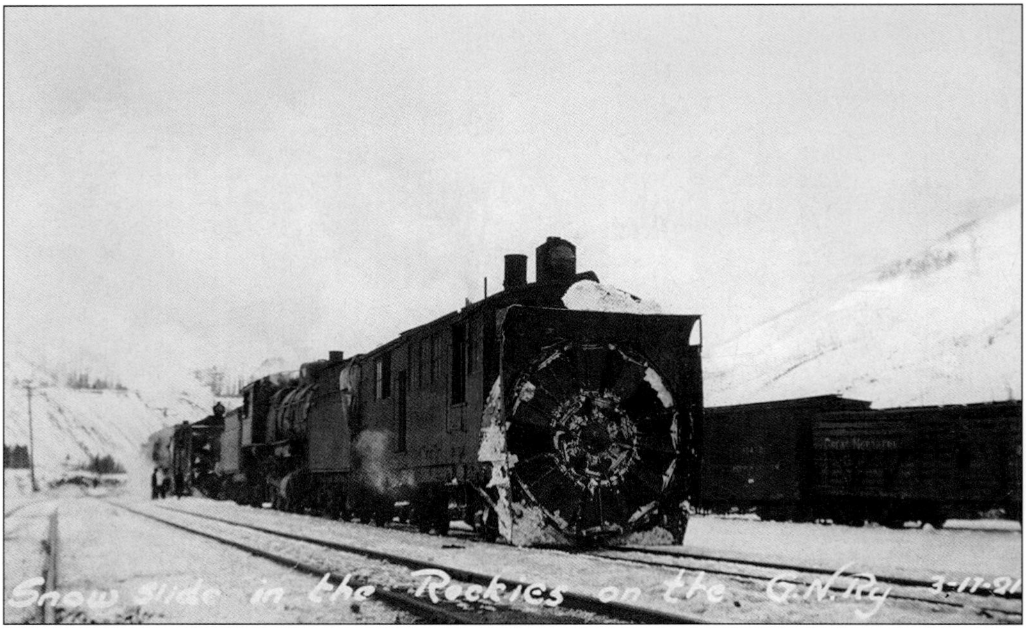

In March 1921, two Great Northern steam-powered rotary snowplows at Java await orders to clear any recent snowslides on the hill. Late-winter weather produces ideal conditions for dangerous slab avalanches in Marias Pass; after a full season of snowfall, warm rains crystallize the top layer of snow, producing a heavy, dense layer that slides easily down the slopes of Bear Creek canyon. (Author's collection.)

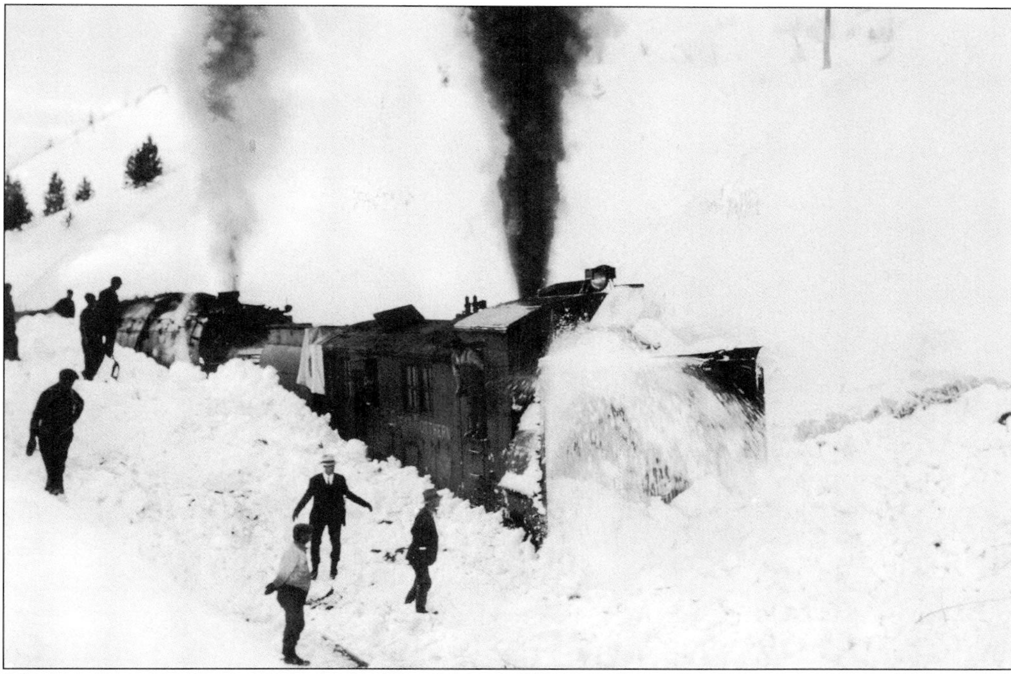

The rotary snowplow was developed in the mid-1880s; these early plows were not self-propelled, so a massive 2-8-8-2 Class R-2 steam locomotive was needed as a pusher. The large circular set of blades on the front end rotate and funnel the snow to either side of the tracks. No doubt the gentleman in the white shirt and tie is a senior railroad official inspecting the clearing of this slide during the 1930s. (Author's collection.)

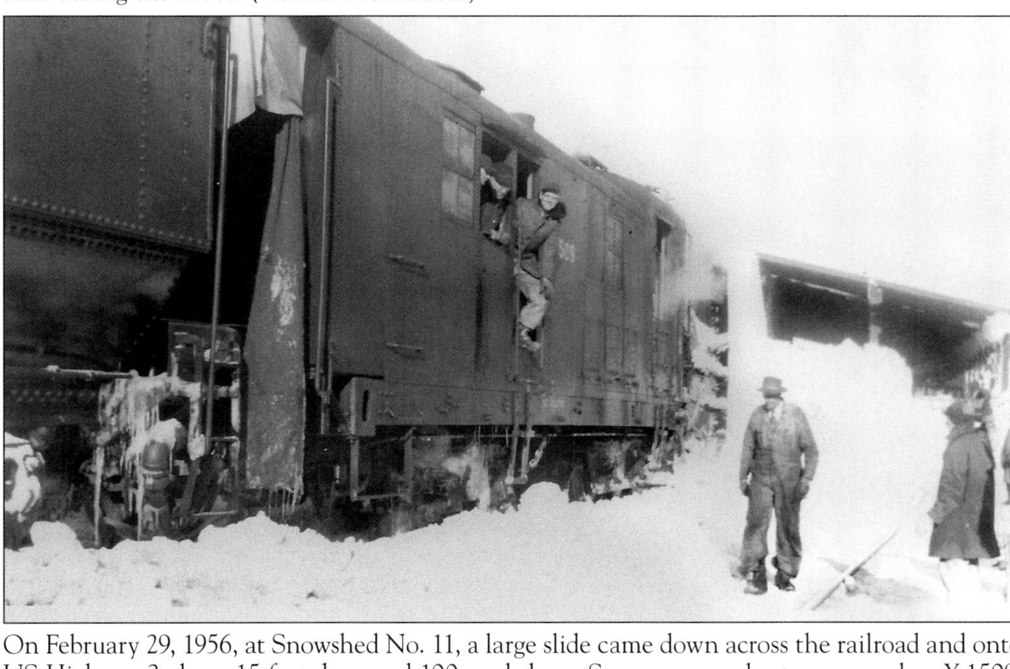

On February 29, 1956, at Snowshed No. 11, a large slide came down across the railroad and onto US Highway 2 about 15 feet deep and 100 yards long. Steam-powered rotary snowplow X-1509, built for the Great Northern Railway in January 1925 by Cooke Locomotive Work, was sent out from Essex to clear the tracks. (Elmer Absalonson photograph, courtesy Harold Absalonson.)

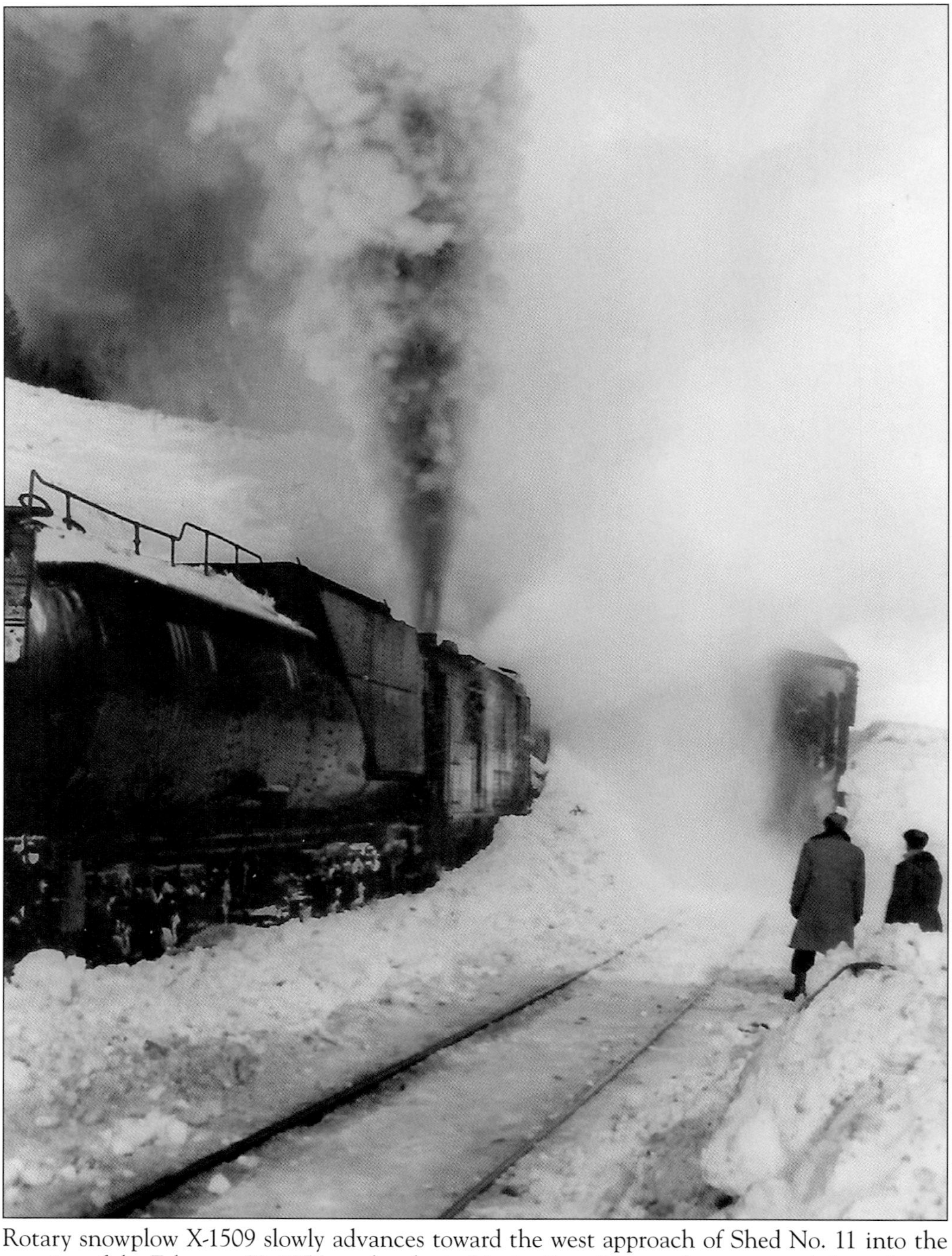

Rotary snowplow X-1509 slowly advances toward the west approach of Shed No. 11 into the remains of the February 29, 1956, avalanche in Marias Pass. Rotary plows were only brought out when absolutely needed, as they were expensive to operate for they were steam driven and required not only a full crew to keep them operating but also a spotting crew. This would be the last run for this steam-powered snowplow; it was rebuilt by the Great Northern and converted to electric power in 1960, and by 2017, after extensive rebuilding with diesel power, the nearly 100-year-old X-1509 (now 972555) is still operable on the Burlington Northern Santa Fe. (Elmer Absalonson photograph, courtesy Harold Absalonson.)

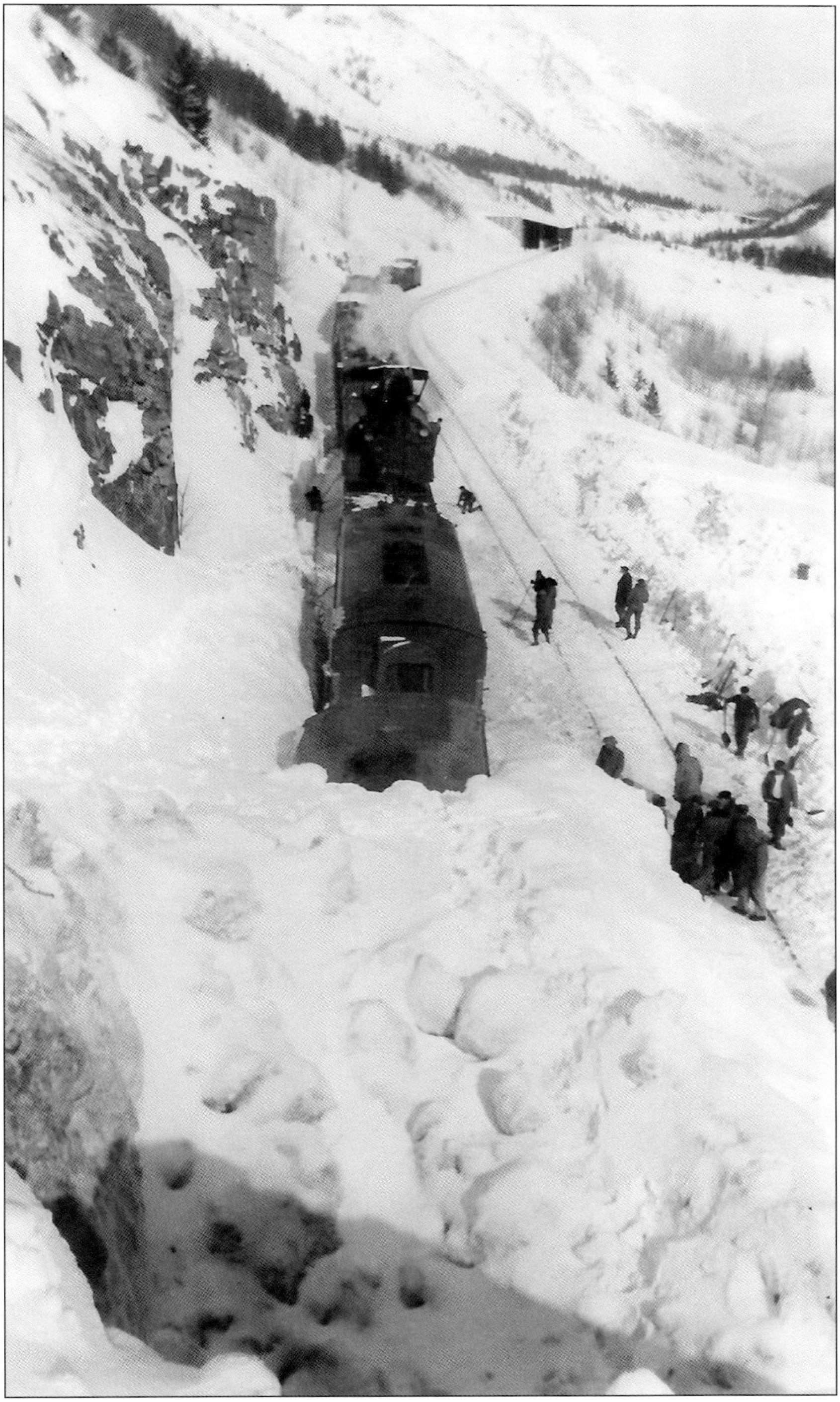

The extent of the February 29, 1956, snowslide is evident in this photograph taken from atop Shed No. 11 looking east. The avalanche covered both main line tracks, which prevented the steam derrick from Whitefish from assisting in cleanup. A crane from Lines East at Havre is attempting to free one of the two F units struck by the slide on a bright early March day. (Elmer Absalonson photograph, courtesy Harold Absalonson.)

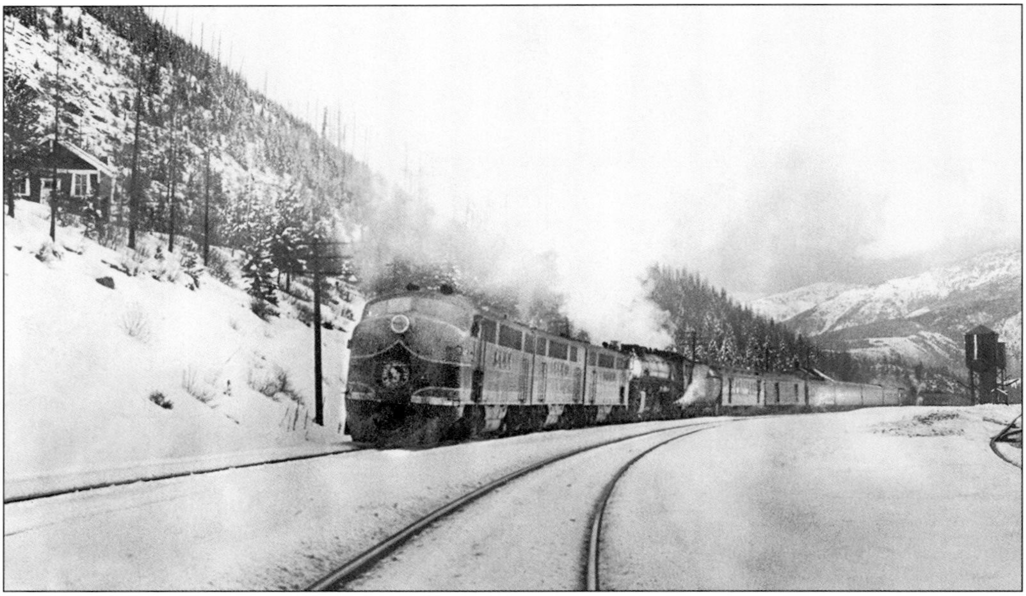

In October 1941, the Great Northern Railway purchased its only three-unit permanently connected FT locomotive, the 5900A. On a dreary winter afternoon, Train No. 1, the eastbound *Empire Builder*, has the 5900 assisting a 4-8-4 S Class northern upgrade after a brief stop at Walton. The passenger train is 12 cars long, which was more than one S-2 could handle in Marias Pass. (Courtesy Ed Krona collection.)

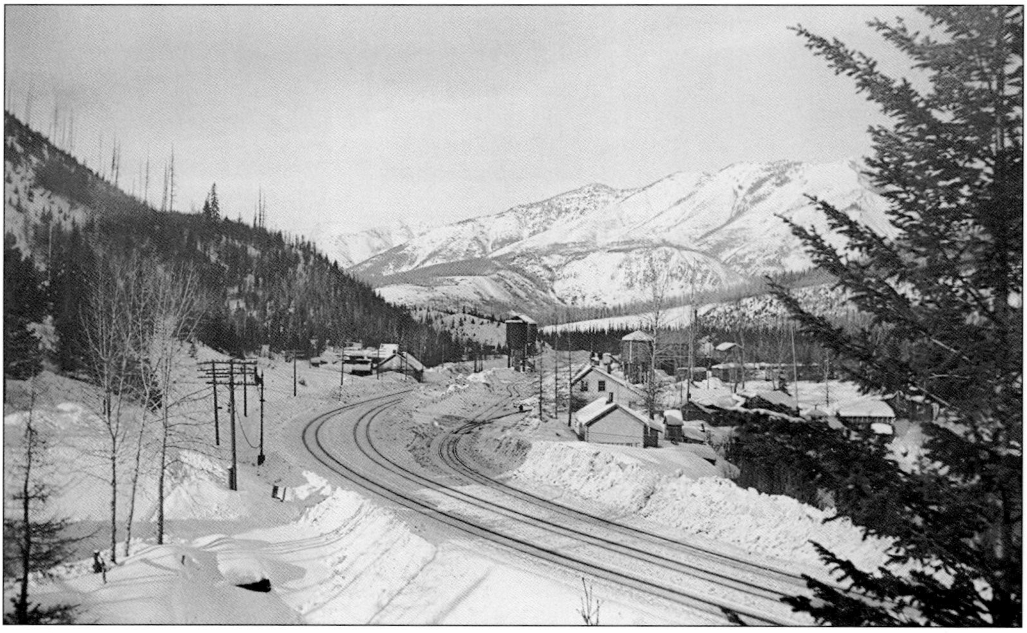

Looking north into Glacier National Park–Walton (Essex was renamed Walton from February 7, 1926, to January 15, 1947), this photograph is surprisingly devoid of trains or maintenance-of-way equipment. This scene was captured between 1935, when the last beanery burned, and 1939, when construction of the Izaak Walton started. (Courtesy Ed Krona collection.)

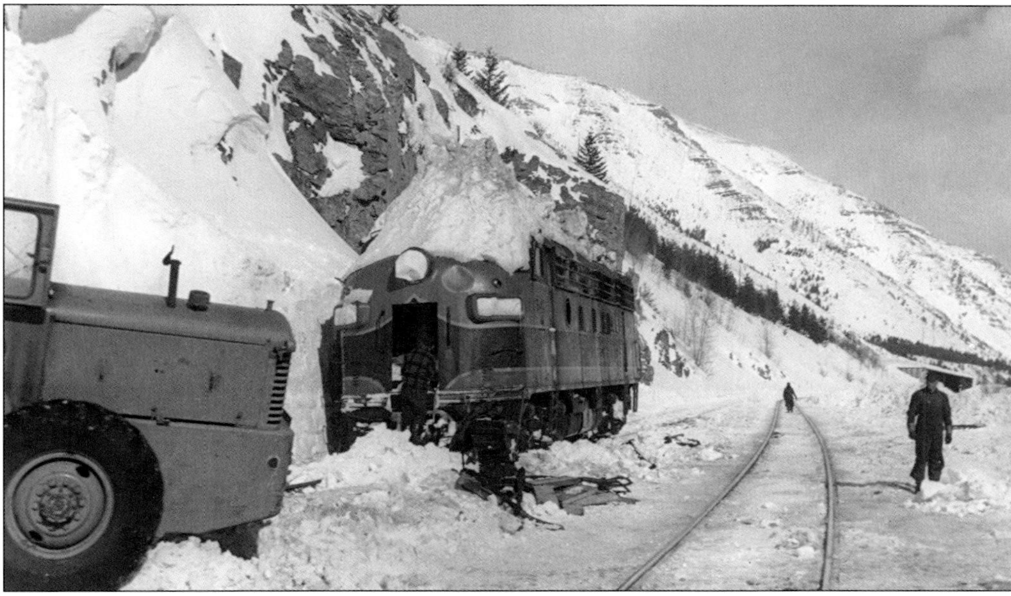

The Glacier National Park ranger station at Walton recorded the following account of the February 29, 1956, avalanche: "The engine slammed into a snowslide that had taken off the west end of the shed. Snow broke the window of the cab and pinned engineer Marvin Kaber; fellow crewmen worked with their hands and boards for an hour, it was reported he was not injured. The engine was apparently not derailed." (Courtesy Ed Krona collection.)

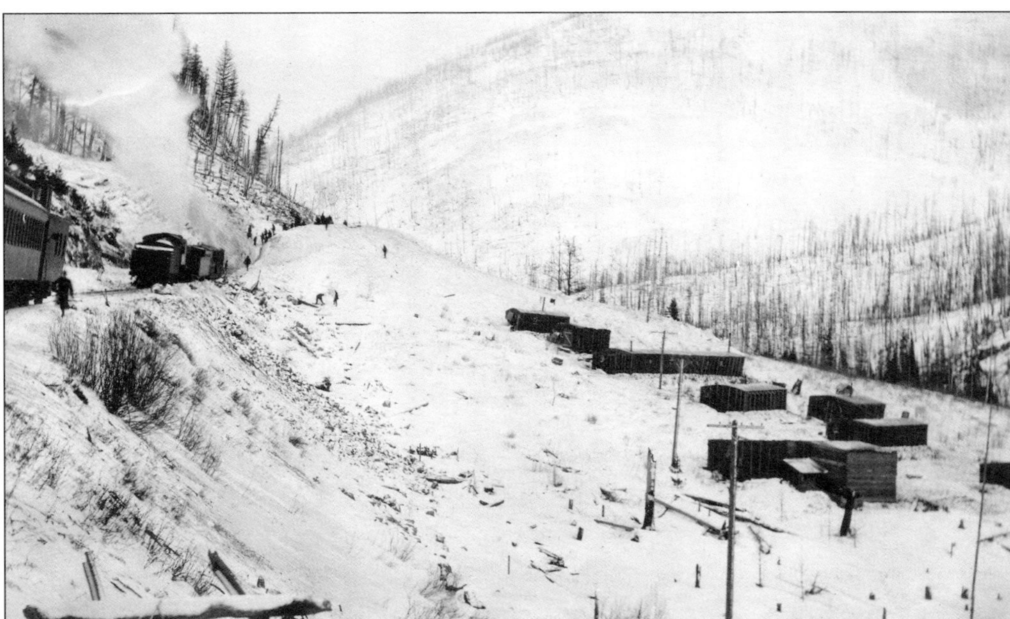

Sometime before 1910, when the double-track main line was completed from Java to Summit, crews cleared, shovel-by-shovel, a massive avalanche at Highgate. Protecting the tracks from snowslides in snowsheds required a systematic approach, and in 1919, Snowshed No. 7-A was constructed at this location to prevent this type of event in the future. (Author's collection.)

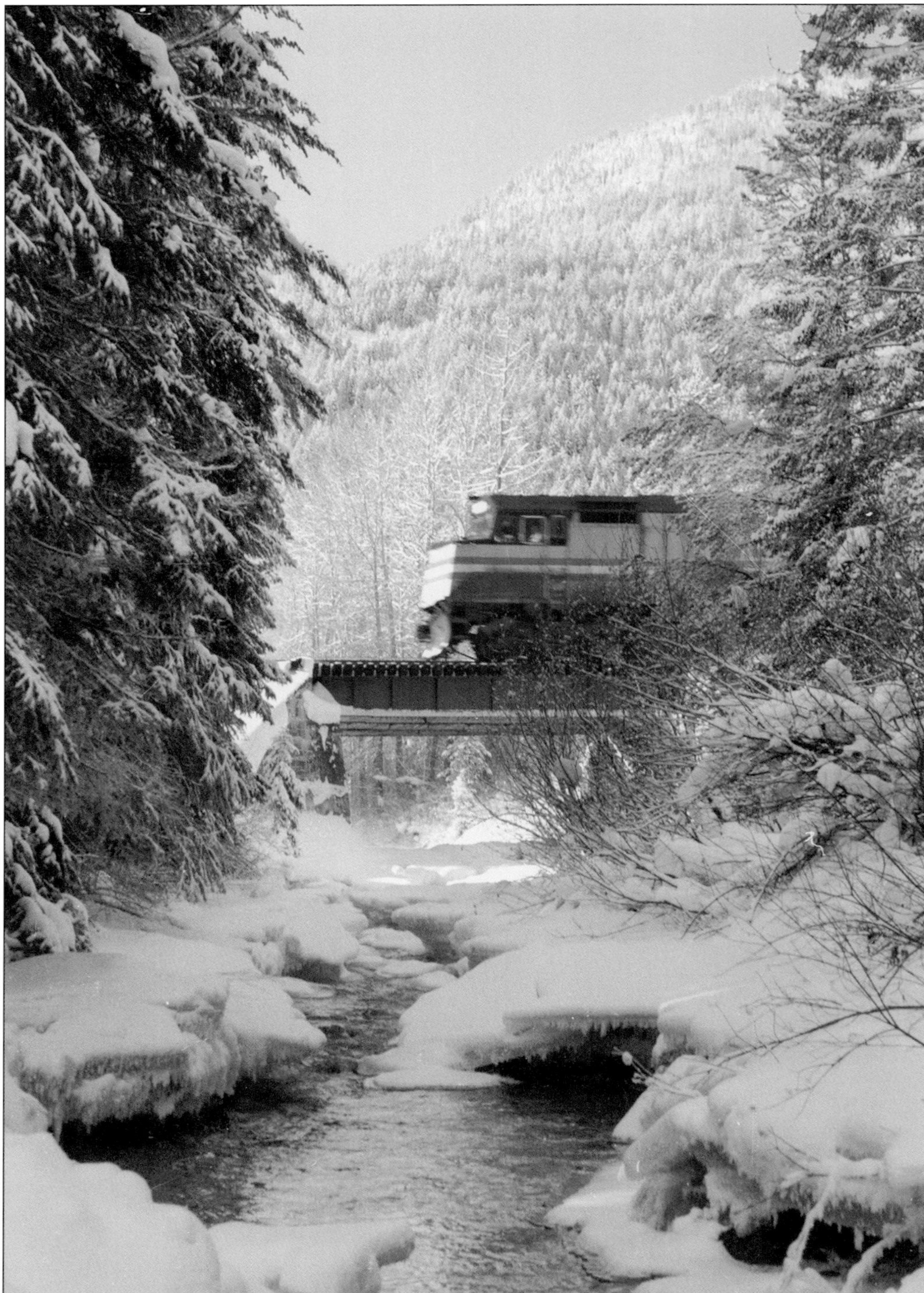

The Amtrak schedule of 1986 had the eastbound *Empire Builder* normally passing through Essex at about 9:00 a.m., but on this bitterly cold day, Train No. 8 was running nearly seven hours late. This Christmas-card setting is located about one mile north of Essex at Dickey Creek. (Author's collection.)

Nine

THE 1964 FLOOD

MARIAS PASS DISASTER

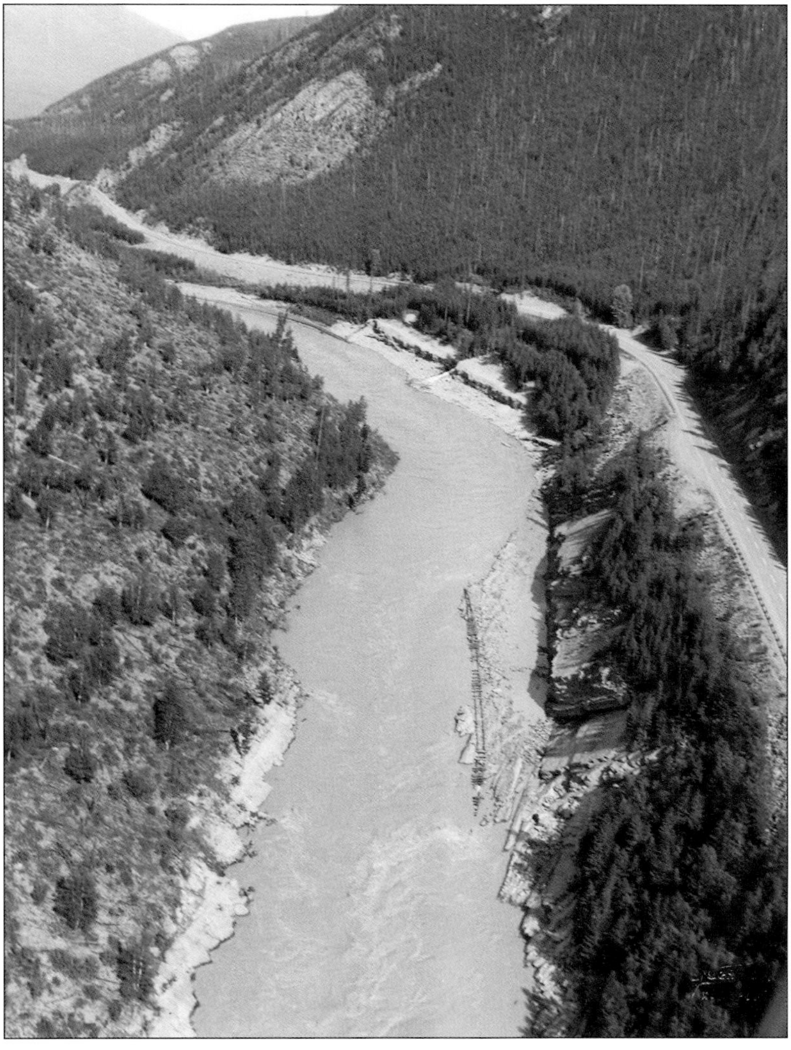

During the second week of June 1964, the worst natural disaster in Montana's recorded history descended on the state in a severe storm that dumped an unprecedented amount of rain between June 7 and 8. Glacier National Park reported 10 inches of rainfall in a 24-hour period. The photographs in this chapter are attributed to Mel Ruder of the *Hungry Horse News*, of Columbia Falls, Montana, courtesy of the Ed Krona collection. Pictured is an aerial view looking east from Tunnel No. 3.8 in Middle Fork Canyon.

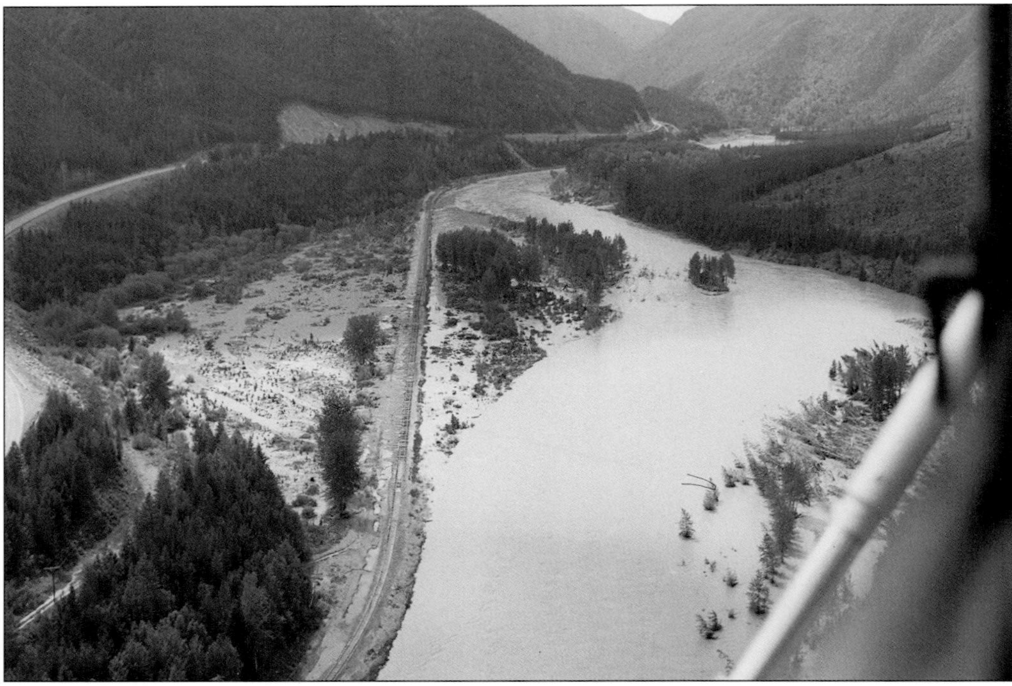

The Nyack area is relatively flat, allowing the river banks to widen out without much physical damage to the right-of-way, as can be seen in this view from above, looking west toward Belton at the confluence of Ouzel and Harrison Creek near the old Silvertip-Doody railroad siding.

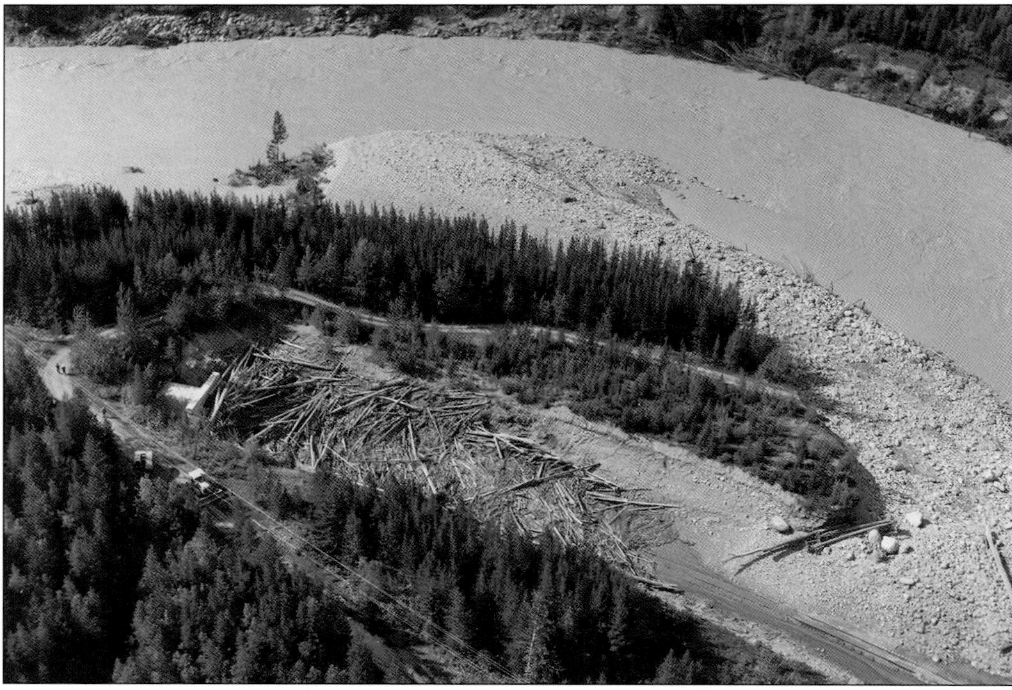

Looking down on the east portal of Tunnel No. 3.7 at Milepost No. 1191.2, this image clearly illustrates the damage to tunnels in the Middle Fork Canyon east of Belton; they were clogged with logs, ties, and other debris up to 26 feet above the rails.

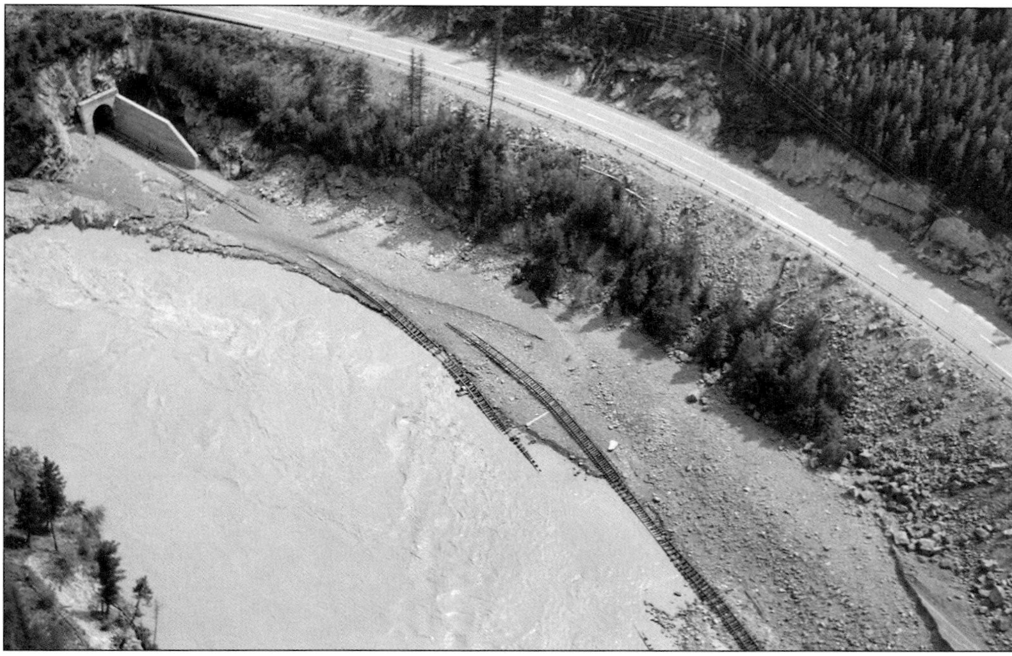

At the west portal of Tunnel No. 3.8 at Milepost No. 1192.5, the roadbed was scoured down to the bedrock. Remnants of the 1943 line relocation are now visible to the left of the tunnel entrance. The railroad expected it would need about one million cubic yards of rock and earth fill to repair the damage to the right-of-way.

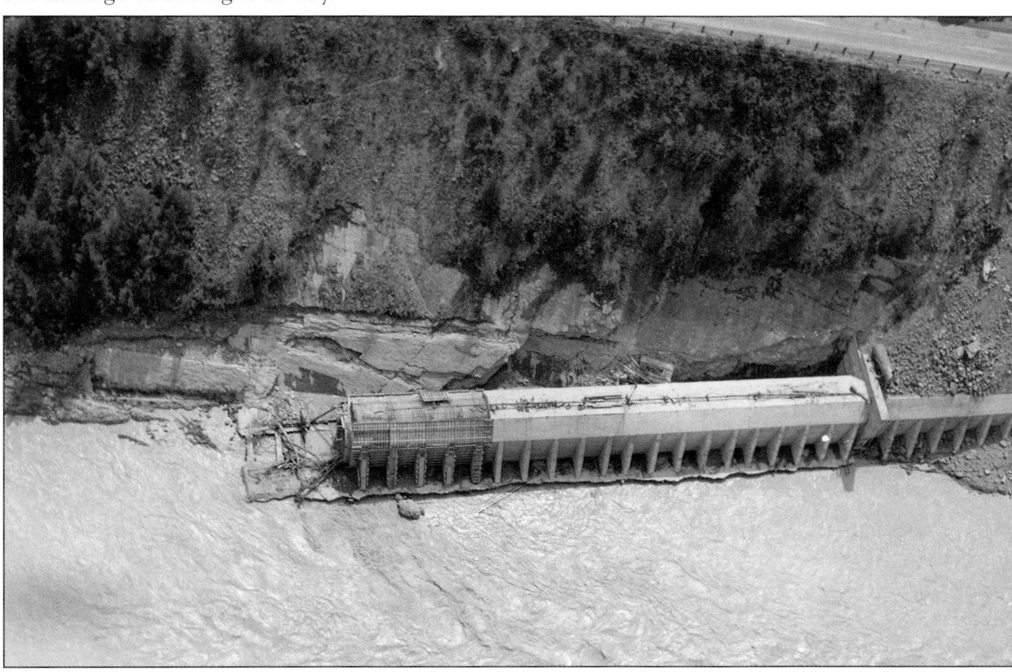

The 1956 extension to the east end of Tunnel No. 3.8 is totally exposed and cleaned down to bare concrete as if it had never been hidden under a mountain. Railroad engineers estimated it would take 17,000 cubic yards of crushed rock ballast and 100,000 yards of riprap to restore the roadbed to operational condition.

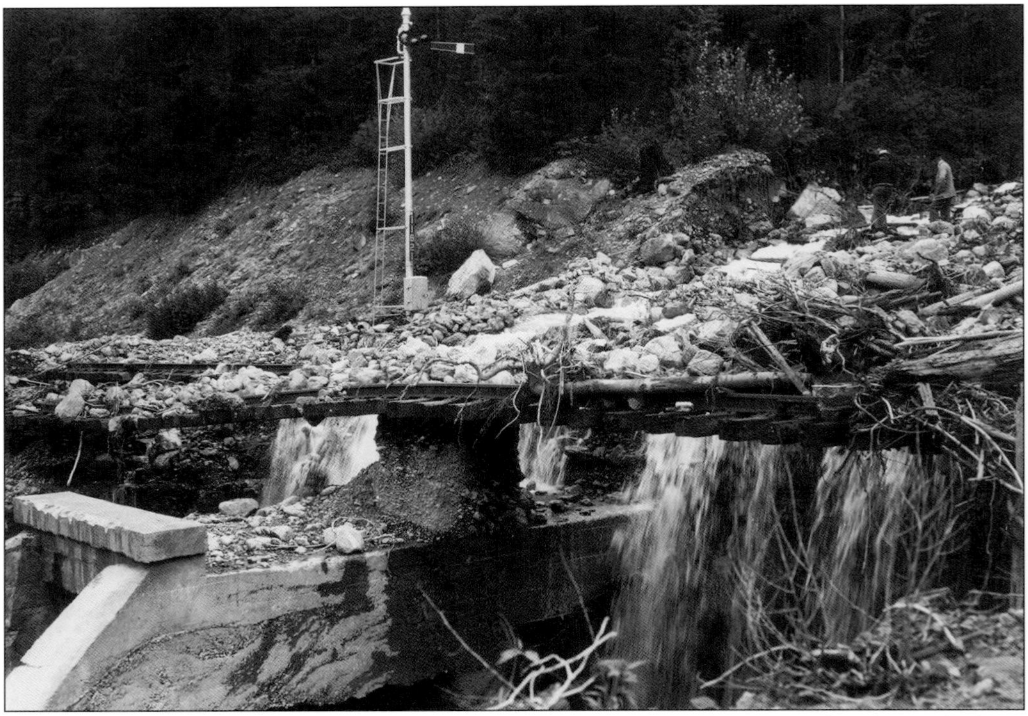

The semaphore at Milepost No. 1182.1 indicates an appropriate red stop signal at the washed-out bridge over Rescue Creek near Red Eagle. In this vicinity, about four miles of US Highway 2 was moved down from the hillside along Mount Penrose onto the current fill along the Middle Fork of the Flathead River.

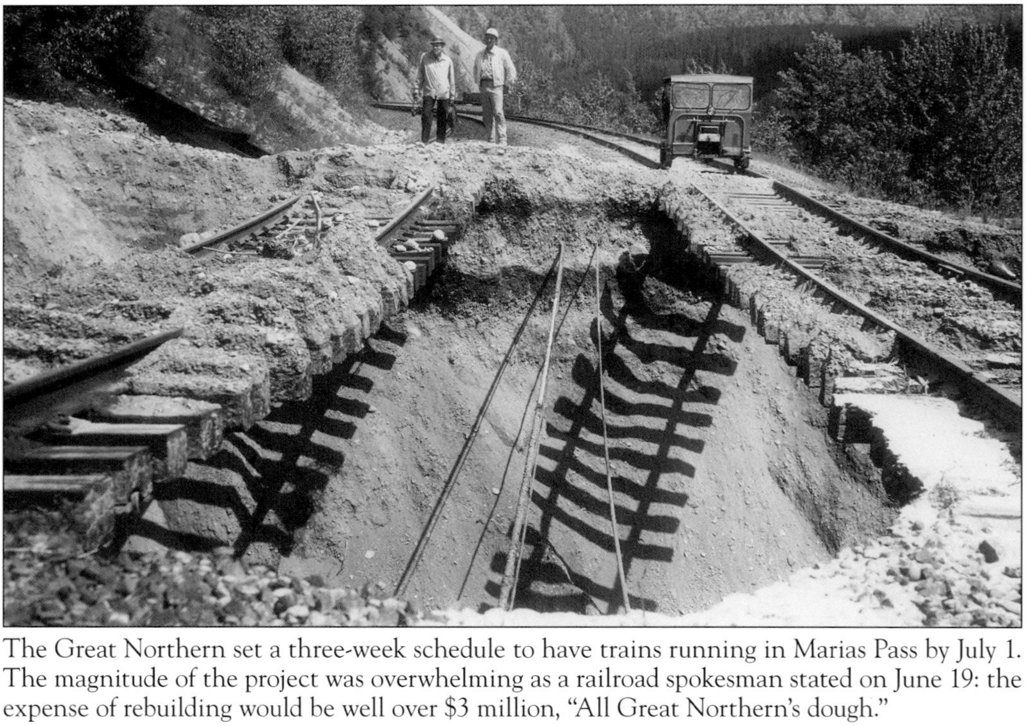

The Great Northern set a three-week schedule to have trains running in Marias Pass by July 1. The magnitude of the project was overwhelming as a railroad spokesman stated on June 19: the expense of rebuilding would be well over $3 million, "All Great Northern's dough."

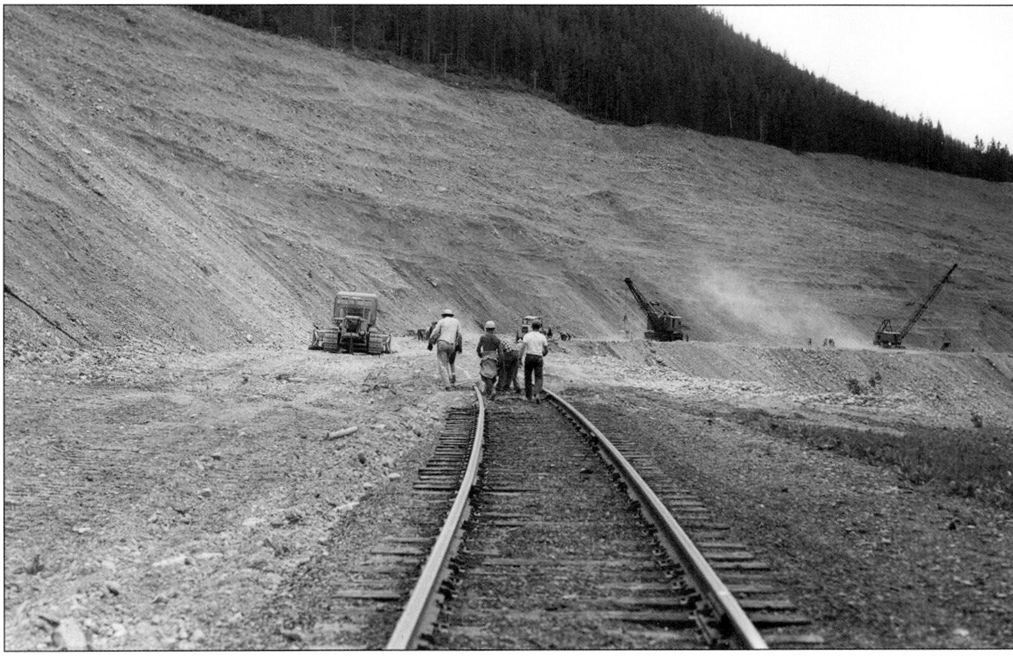

As much of the hillside slid into the Middle Fork of the Flathead River, the gauntlet between Sheep Creek Trestle and Nimrod required extensive repair. Equipment used in repairing the railroad included 30 bulldozers, four 1.5-yard shovels, eight 10-yard dump trucks, three 40-ton on-track combination cranes, and three work trains.

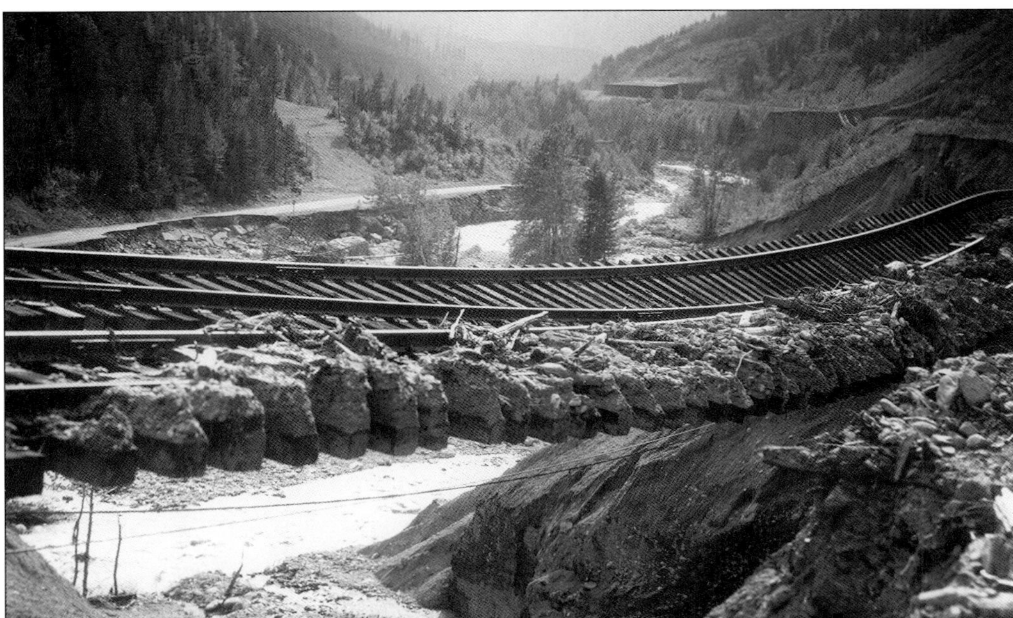

The four miles of track along Bear Creek in John Stevens Canyon between Snowsheds 11 and 8 sustained considerable damage, leaving the double track suspended in mid-air in many places. Looking west, Shed No. 10.7 in the background remained unharmed as the raging waters undermined the roadbed in many places at the site designated "1163" (the milepost number at that location).

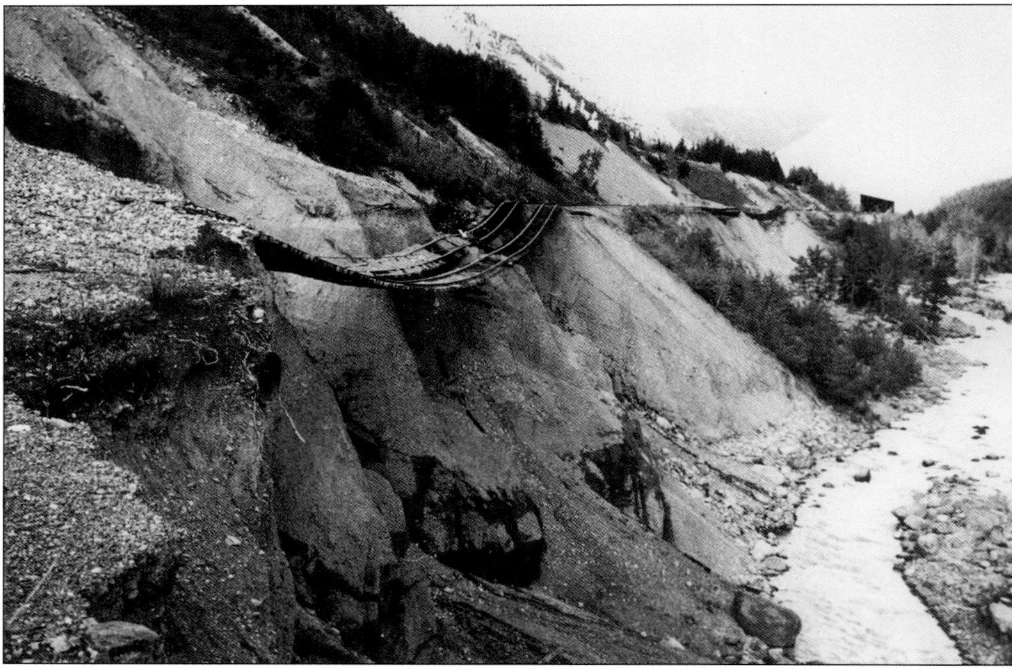

The view eastward from 1163 up the canyon toward Shed No. 10 conveys the appearance of a double-track suspension bridge high above the now calm Bear Creek. In addition to the 1964 flood, portions of the roadbed in Marias Pass were threatened by high water in 1974–1975.

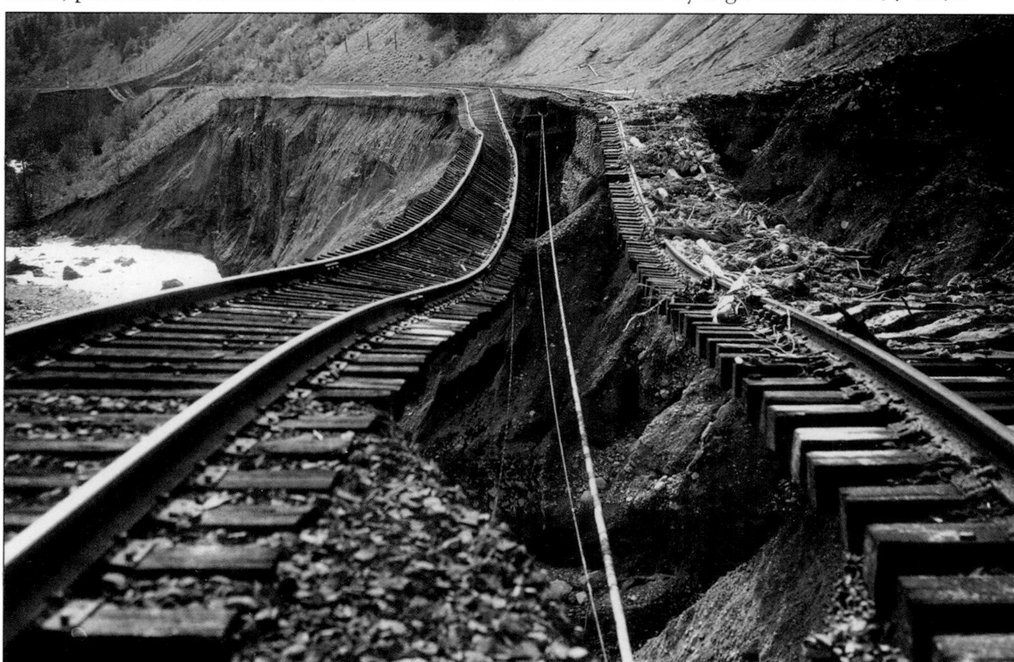

The south-facing slope of Running Rabbit Mountain in Glacier National Park at 1163 does not have a high incidence of dangerous snowslides; therefore, a snowshed was not needed at that site. However, the entire length of track between Sheds 10.7 and 10 is protected by a slide fence built primarily to warn crews of avalanches, but not necessarily flood washouts.

Ten

Then and Now
Changes through the Years

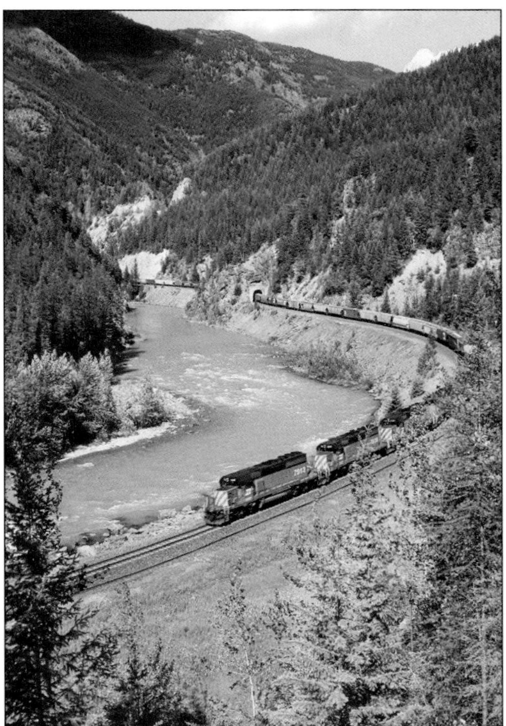

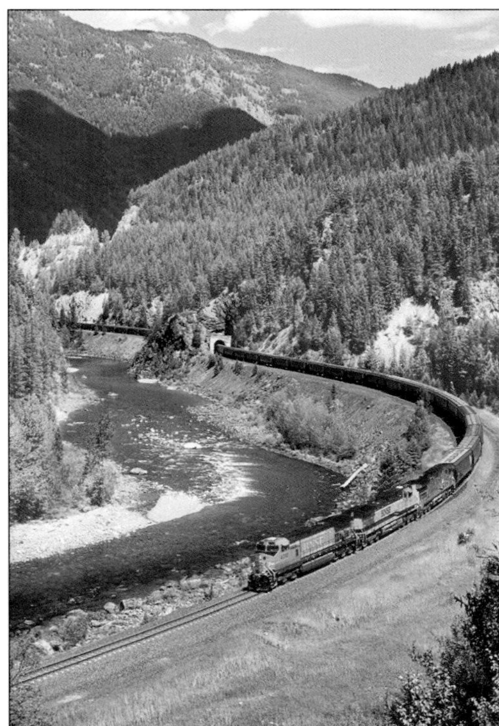

The Great Northern line in Marias Pass has changed throughout the years, but mountains and scenery remain unchanged. These two views of westbound trains near Belton were taken 30 years apart, in 1985 (left) and 2015. This location is nicknamed "Ken Good Curve." Ken Good was a Forest Service employee who cleared the area of brush for photographers until his death in a 2004 plane crash near Nyack Flats. (Both, author's collection.)

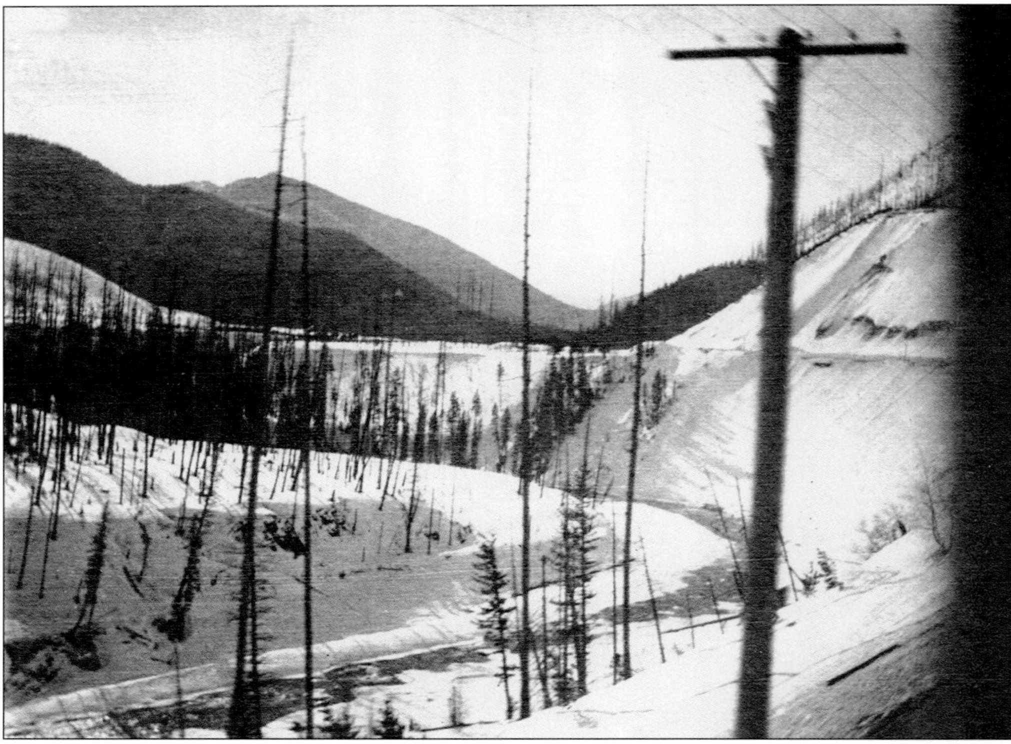

Photographs taken from moving trains around the turn of the 20th century were rare. The two images on this page are at the gauntlet near Nimrod/Java; both were taken from eastbound passenger trains. The photograph above is from about 1900, and the one below was captured 100 years later from the Amtrak *Empire Builder*. The Middle Fork of the Flathead River and Mount Furlong in the background have changed little in a century. (Both, author's collection.)

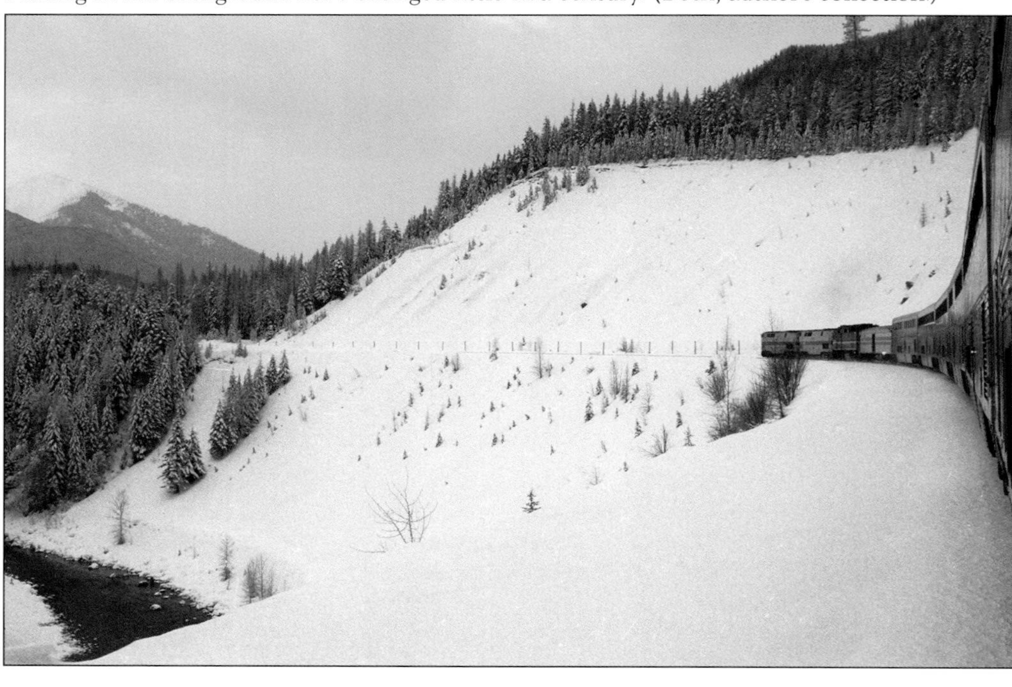

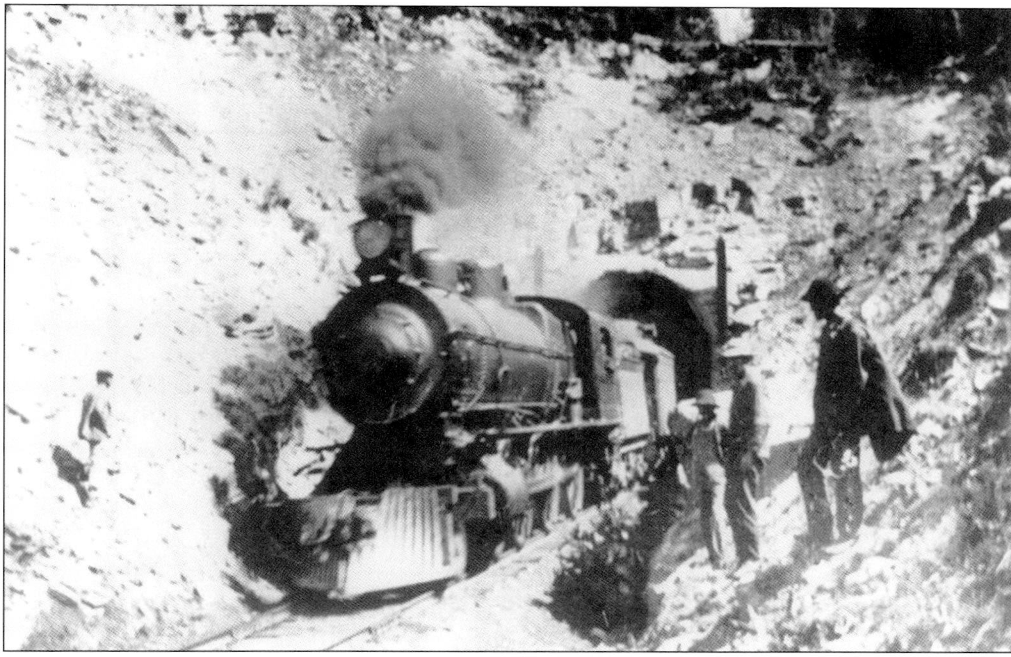

Haskell Pass was located 25 miles west of Kalispell on the original 1892 Great Northern survey. The choice of this pass versus the final Stillwater River–Kootenai River route is shrouded in mystery as there were two large wooden trestles, stiff grades, and the 1,400-foot Haskell Pass Tunnel making this route an operational debacle that was used for only 10 years. The image above shows one of the Great Northern Class F 2-8-0s exiting the tunnel with westbound Train No. 3 at noon in the late 1890s. Below, the west portal of the Haskell Pass tunnel is visible through the undergrowth in 2002. (Above, Doug Snackenberg collection; below, author's collection.)

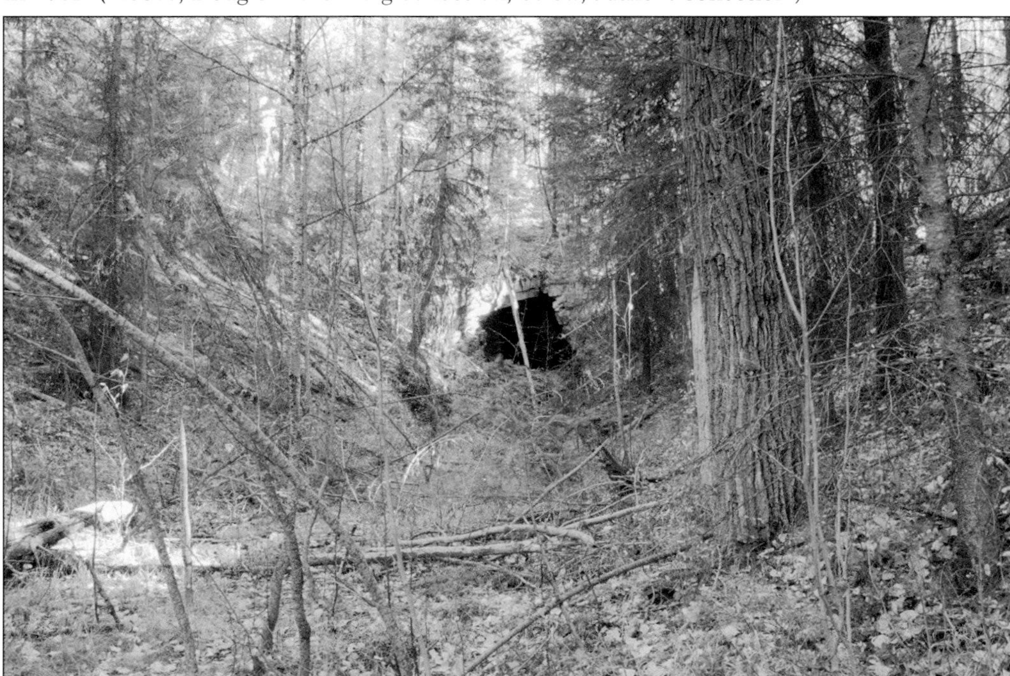

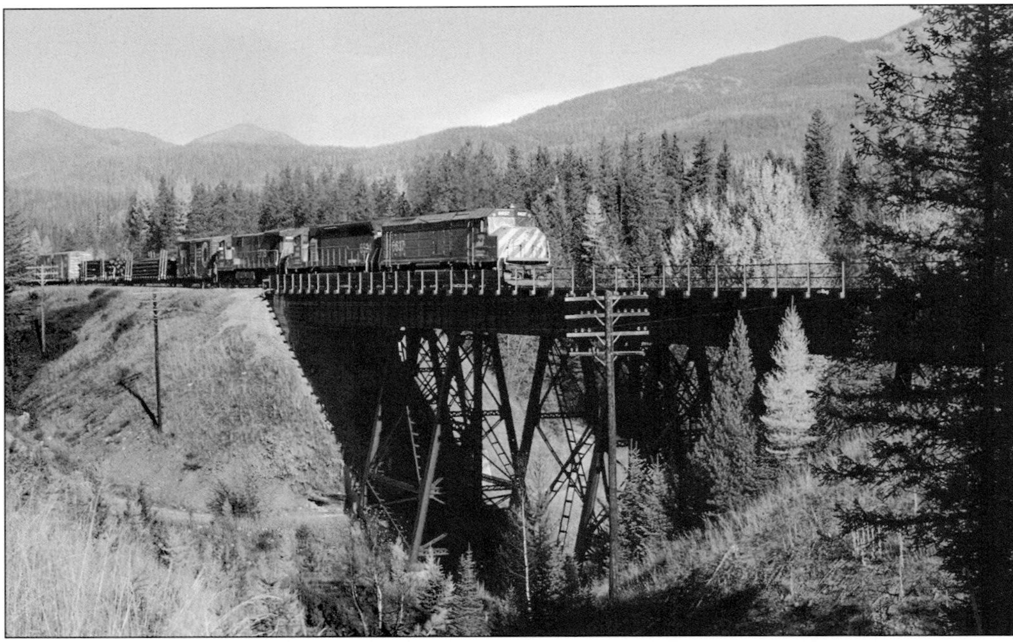

Trestles and bridges require considerable resources to maintain; to reduce cost and increase safety across ravines and gullies, trestles were often filled as capital was available. The steel girder trestle at Garry-Hidden Lake survived until 2000, when it was removed and Stanton Creek was diverted into a culvert. The Stanton Creek Trestle was a very photogenic location for both westbound and eastbound trains, with Threetops or Double Mountain in Glacier National Park as a backdrop. Above, Burlington Northern Extra 6637 East is headed toward Essex on October 20, 1974; in the photograph below, taken on April 21, 2011, seven Burlington Northern Santa Fe locomotives and two Essex helpers cross the fill where the former Stanton Creek trestle was located. (Above, courtesy Jerry Quinn collection; below, author's collection.)

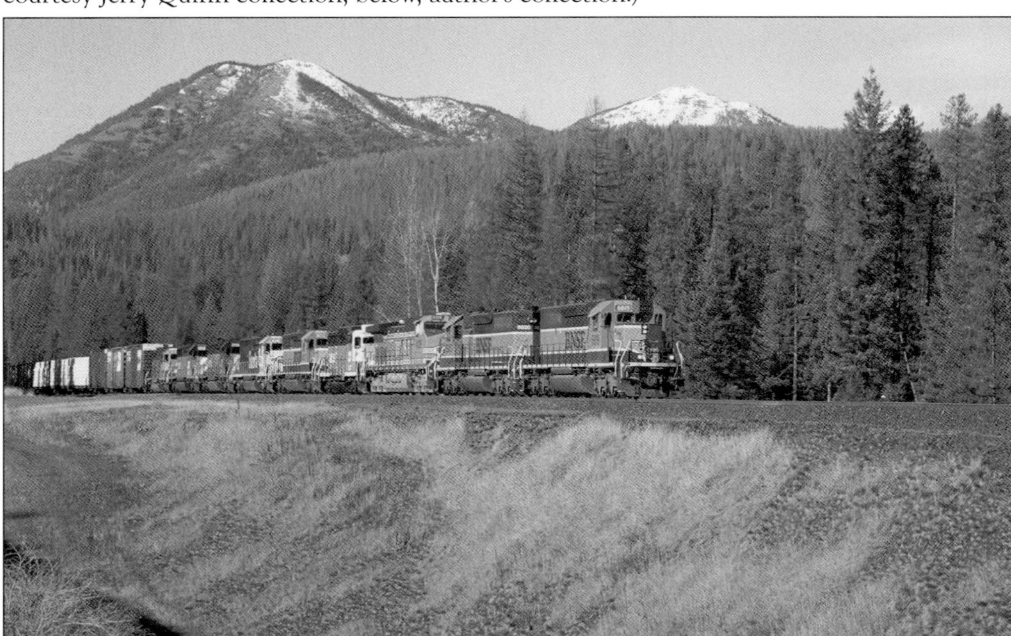

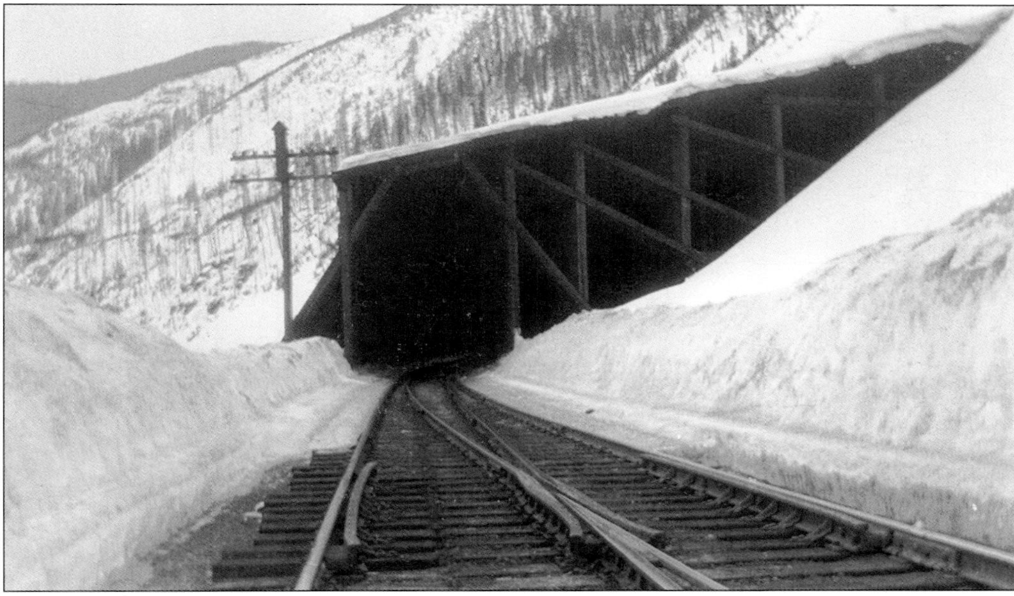

Snowshed No. 12, located one mile east of Essex, shelters the right-of-way from an area of infrequent avalanche activity on the slopes of Snowshed Mountain. The c. 1916 image above gives a good view of a gauntlet. The switch point in the center shows how the railroad achieved double-track capability without having to construct a second set rails. In the late 1920s, the snowshed was lengthened to 1,400 feet, the gauntlet was removed, and double track installed from Essex to Java/Nimrod West. Below, westbound 7055 exits Snowshed No. 12 on a below-zero morning in the winter of 1986. (Above, courtesy Ed Krona collection; below, author's collection.)

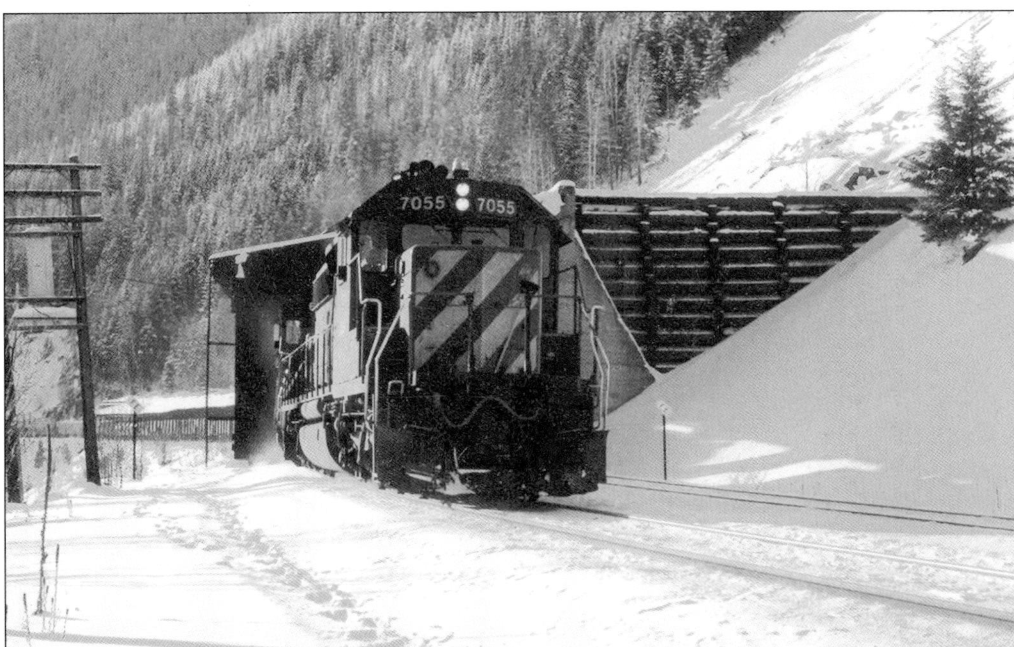

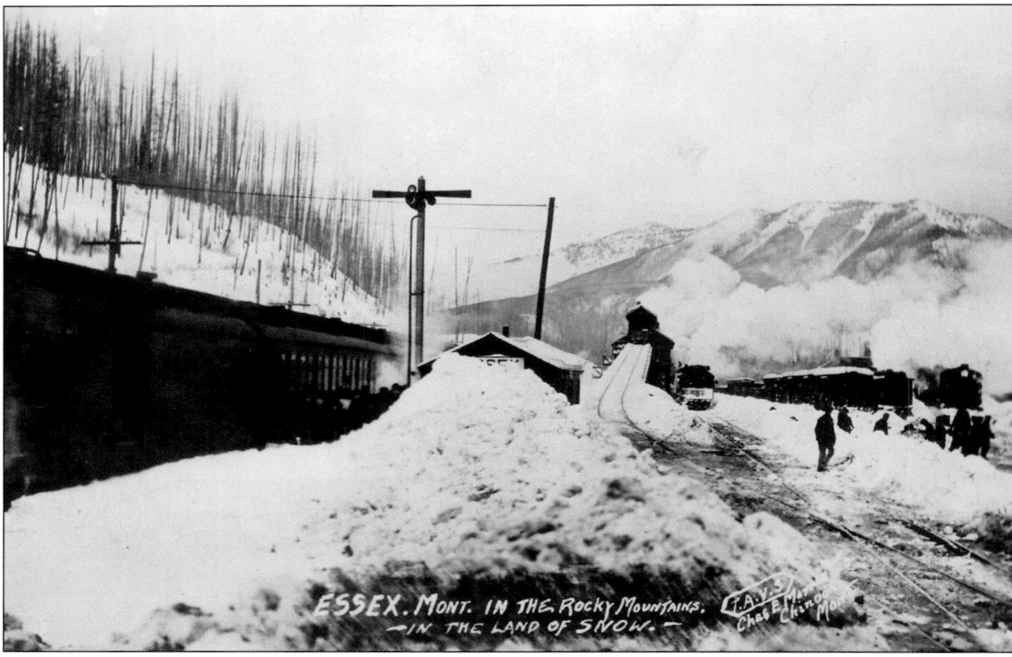

There are some interesting similarities in these two photographs taken from the same spot 78 years apart. The mountains of Glacier National Park in the background are the only shared features in both photographs, one from 1908 and the other in 1986. The facilities at Essex have changed as railroad technology advanced. The 12-by-34-foot station built in 1908 was moved from the center of the yard around 1920, to be replaced by the white 30-by-48-foot depot west of the mainline in 1927; the original coal chute from 1892 was retired in 1933; and a 50,000-gallon water tower was built on the location of the 1908 station. (Both, author's collection.)

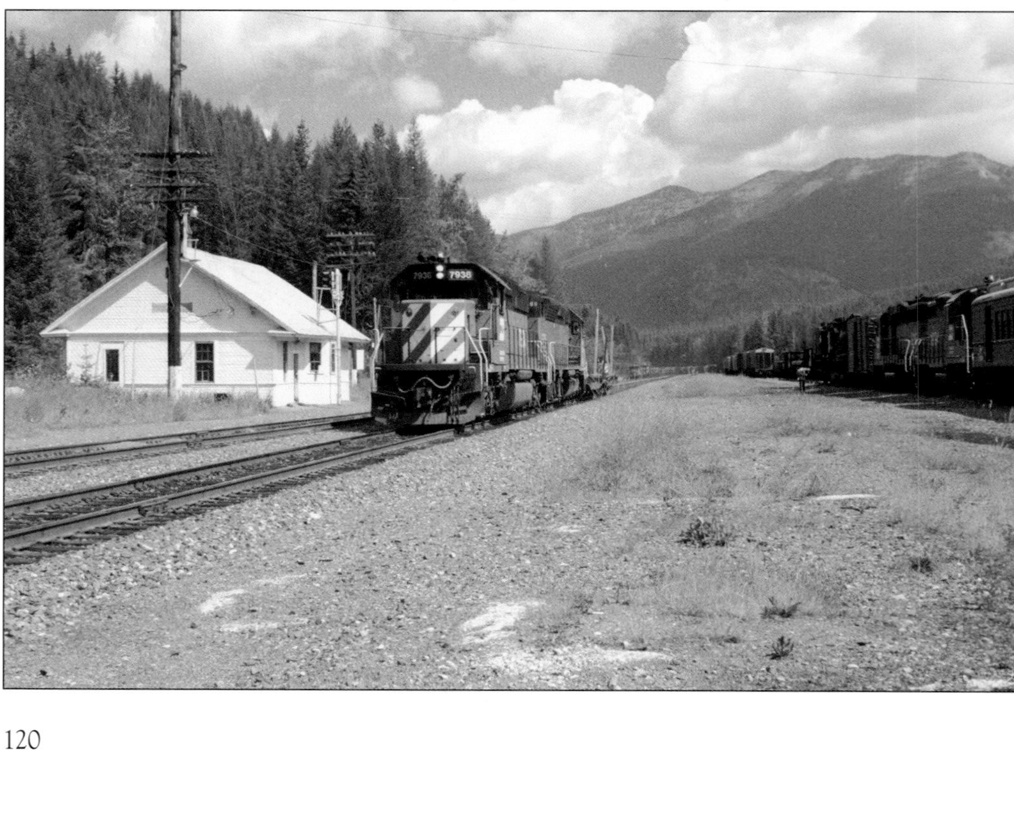

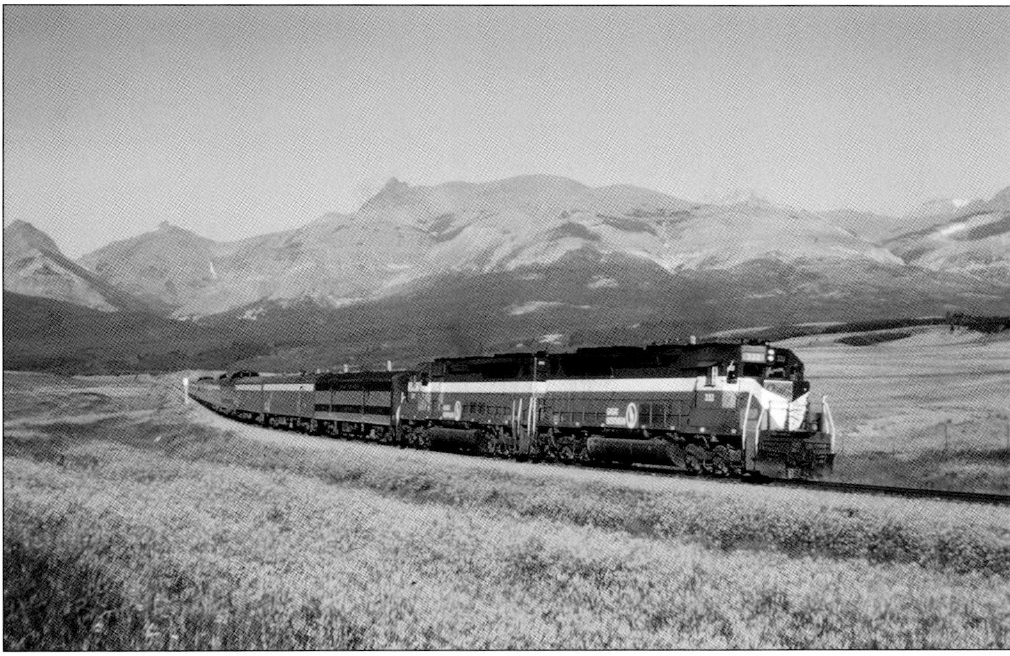

The northern portion of the Rocky Mountain Front in Montana stretches 150 miles from the Canadian border to Helena, and nowhere are the mountains more visible than on the approach to Glacier National Park from the east. These images show two trains 25 years apart heading east after crossing the Two Medicine Bridge at East Glacier. Above, in 1967, the Great Northern *Empire Builder* shows the transition from traditional Omaha Orange and Pullman Green to the new corporate Big Sky Blue colors, adopted in the late 1960s. In April 1992, snow lingers on the flanks of Mount Henry and Mount Ellsworth while three Burlington Northern SD40-2s and a General Electric U30 accelerate up the short grade toward Spotted Robe. (Both, courtesy Jerry Quinn collection.)

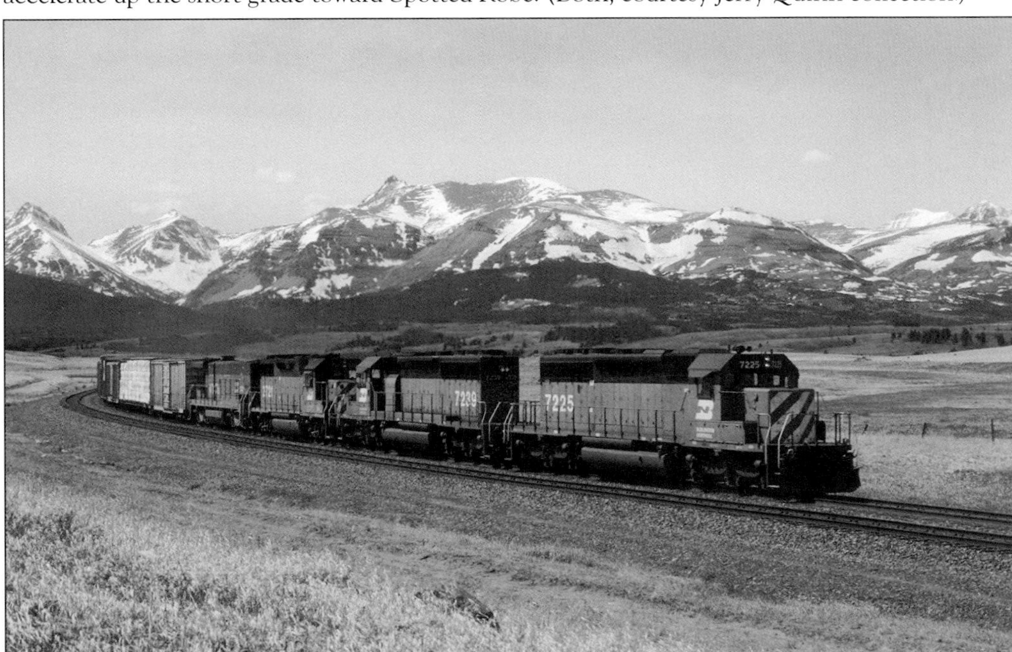

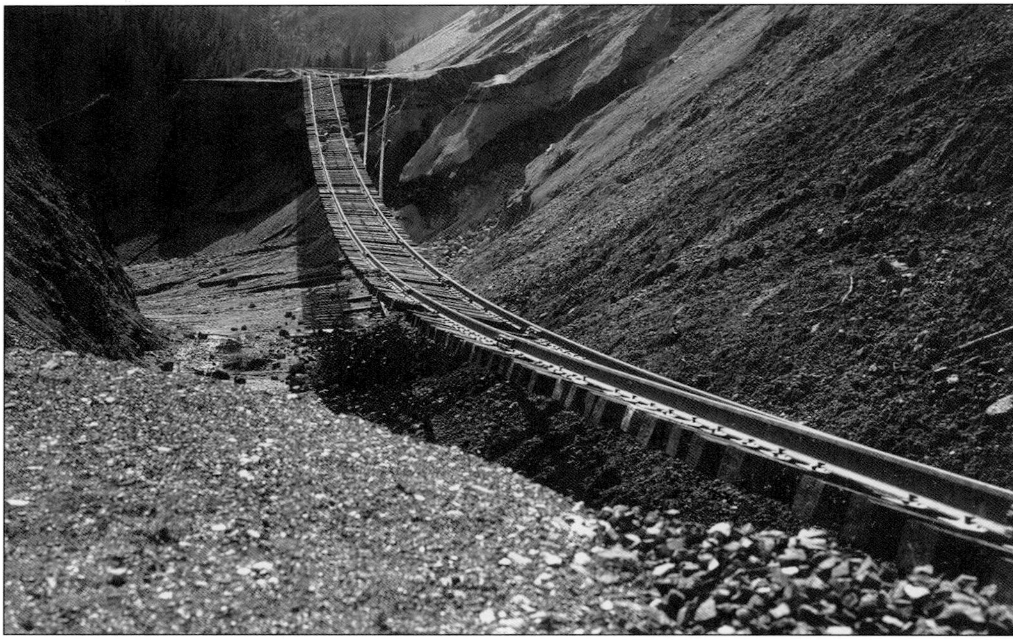

The June 1964 flood ravaged lower portions of Bear Creek with the accumulation of water from numerous streams and rapidly melting snow. Here at Marias, near Summit, the canyon is quite narrow, permitting a small volume of water to generate the same destructive power as witnessed downstream. The photograph above, attributed to Mel Ruder of the *Hungry Horse News*, reveals the extent of damage to the double-track main line near the Continental Divide. In the picture below, taken 20 years later in 1985, the trees are just beginning to grow up along the right-of-way as an eastbound Burlington Northern freight makes its final ascent to Summit. (Above, courtesy Ed Krona collection; below, author's collection.)

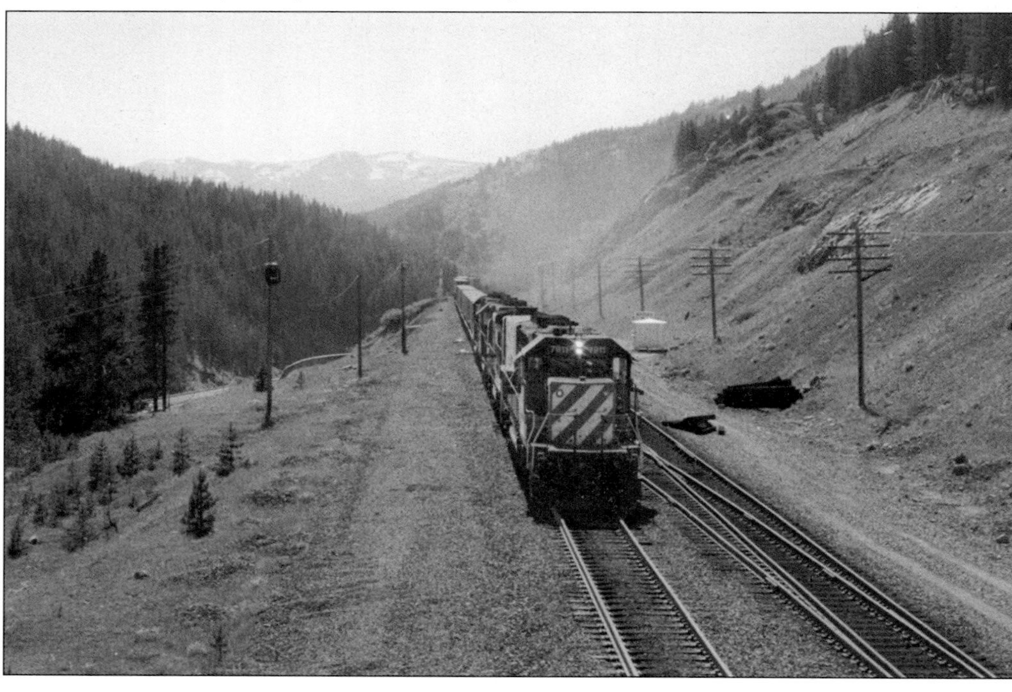

The rail line between Blacktail and Marias is out of the way for most railroad photographers, as the tracks are not visible from US Highway 2 and the locale is without any tunnels or snowsheds, giving the impression that the area is uninteresting. There are a few photogenic sites along the way however, like this one on the Autumn Creek trail. In the summer of 1986, the eastbound Amtrak *Empire Builder* at right passes under a rock outcropping in Glacier National Park; this scene is repeated below in 1999 with a Burlington Northern Santa Fe double-stack or S train, the current designation for BNSF Intermodal Double Stack Service. (Both, author's collection.)

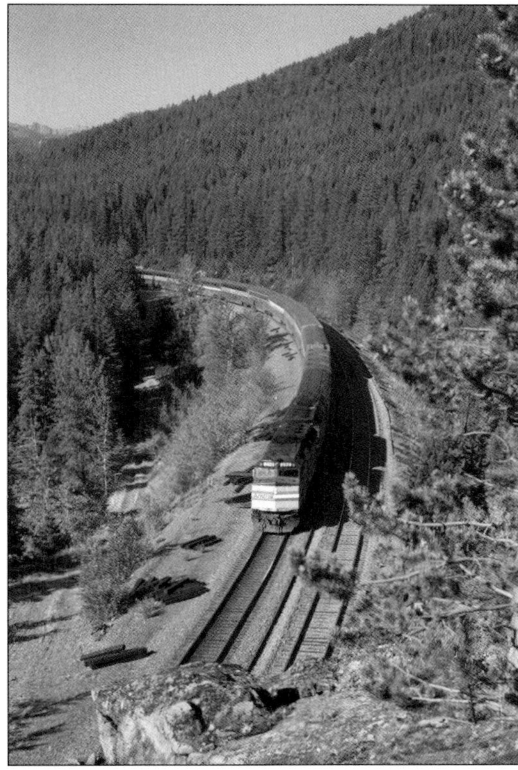

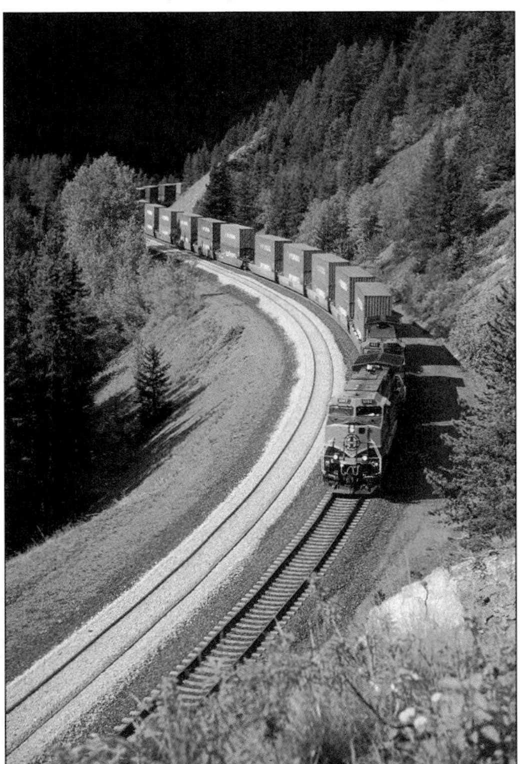

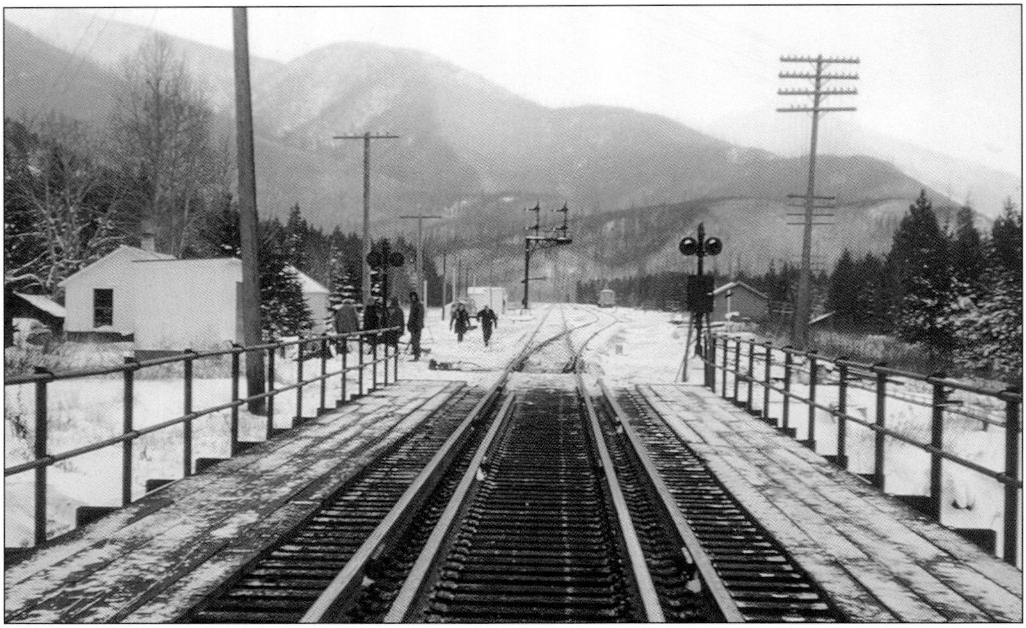

This location has a long and varied history. The original name Java was chosen in 1891, three years before the Great Northern Railway hammered the last spike at Scenic, Washington, on January 6, 1893. Java as a station was listed in the first *Kalispell Division Employee* of August 17, 1892. During the Glacier National Park promotion era, it was renamed Nimrod in 1926. The Burlington Northern restored the name Java in 1974, and in 1984–1985, it was replaced with the present nomenclature Java East and Java West. The image above features remnants of the gauntlet track removed in 1955; below, a westbound Burlington Northern Santa Fe General Electric C44-9W 1097 is passing the Java West sign in 1999. (Both, author's collection.)

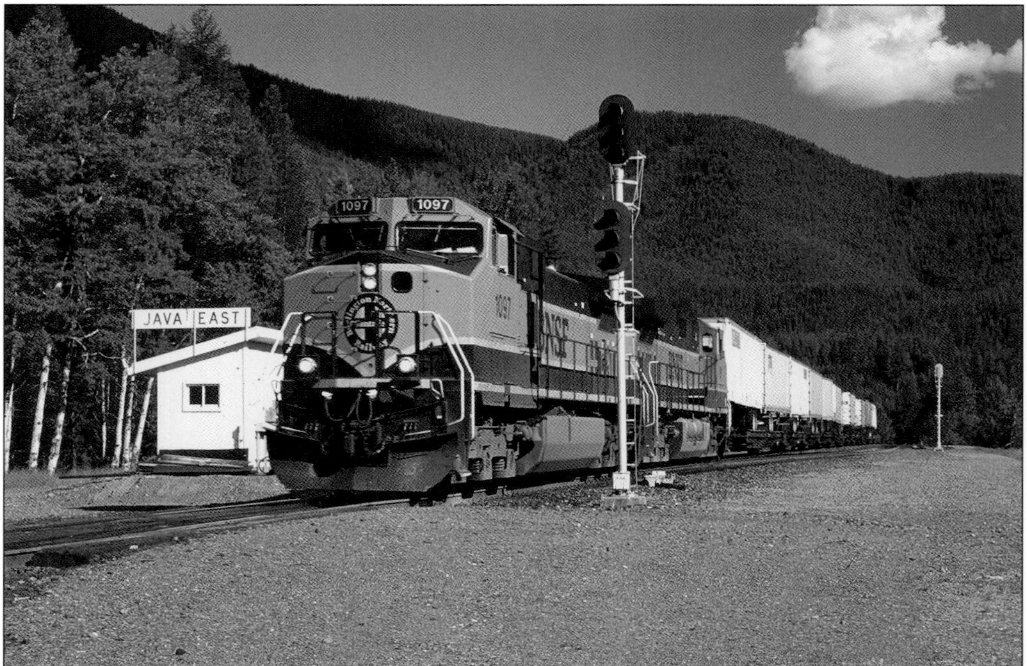

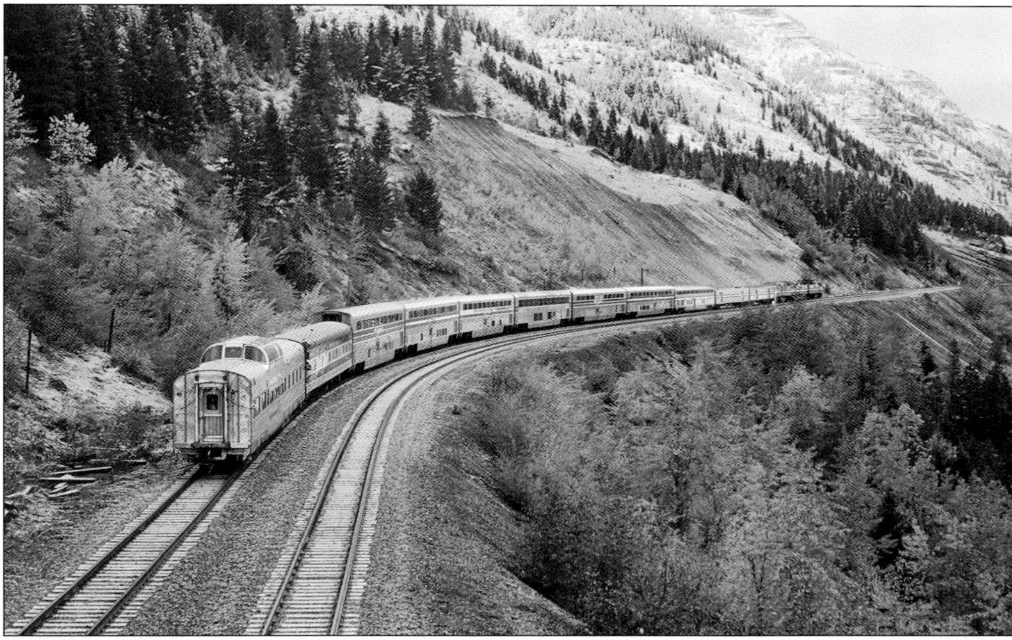

The Great Northern Railway line through Marias Pass parallels Glacier National Park's southern boundary for over 50 miles. When the railroad built through the pass in the 1890s, there was no special recognition for the area encompassing what is now a national park. The railroad and nature writers often composed new names or changed existing Native American names. The two trains on this page traverse the avalanche area known as 1163, between Snowsheds 10.7 and 10 on the lower slope of Running Rabbit Mountain, which is named for famed Siksika (Blackfoot) chief Running Rabbit from the 1890s. Above, two private cars trail behind the eastbound Amtrak *Empire Builder* on an early 1986 winter morning, and below, an empty coal train approaches Snowshed No. 10 in the 1990s. (Both, author's collection.)

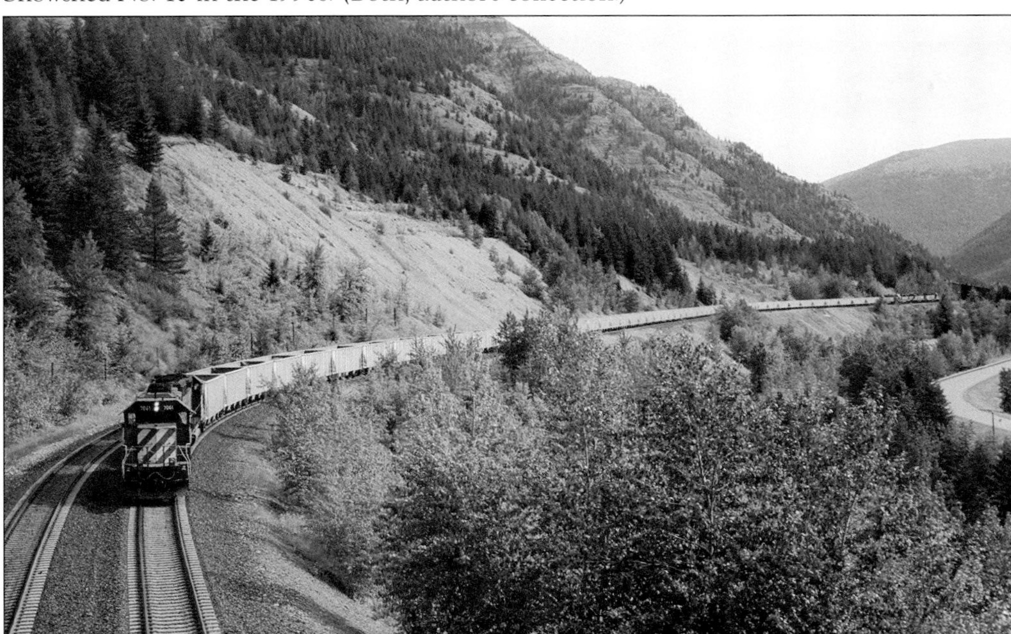

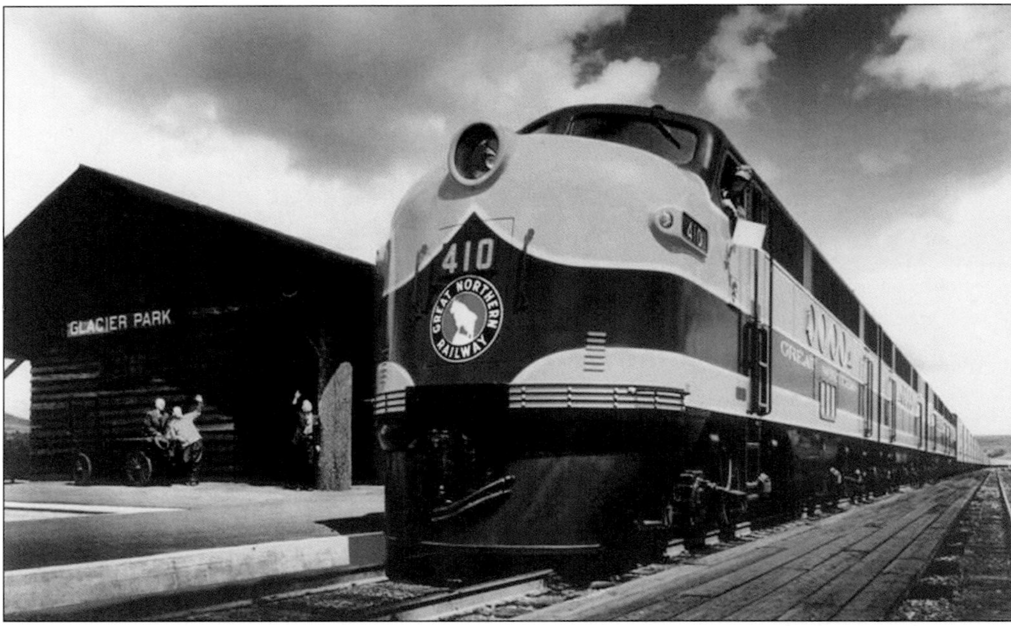

The station at Glacier Park has been a hub for park tourists since the depot was built in 1926. Historian William Farr said, "A popular Great Northern theme used to attract tourists in the 1920s and 1930s was to intertwine Glacier Park and the Blackfeet. Eastern tourists streamed out West following the call of primitive adventure . . . Filing off the train, they discovered on the broad lawns in front of the Glacier Park Lodge a real tepee encampment and Indians decked out in their best finery and chanting a welcome." The image above is a Great Northern photograph publicizing the new 1,350-horsepower FT locomotives operating in Marias Pass during World War II. Below, 50 years into the future in 1999, the Native American theme has softened, and the new SD70MAC 4,000-horsepower motive power waits patiently for the next assignment. (Both, author's collection.)

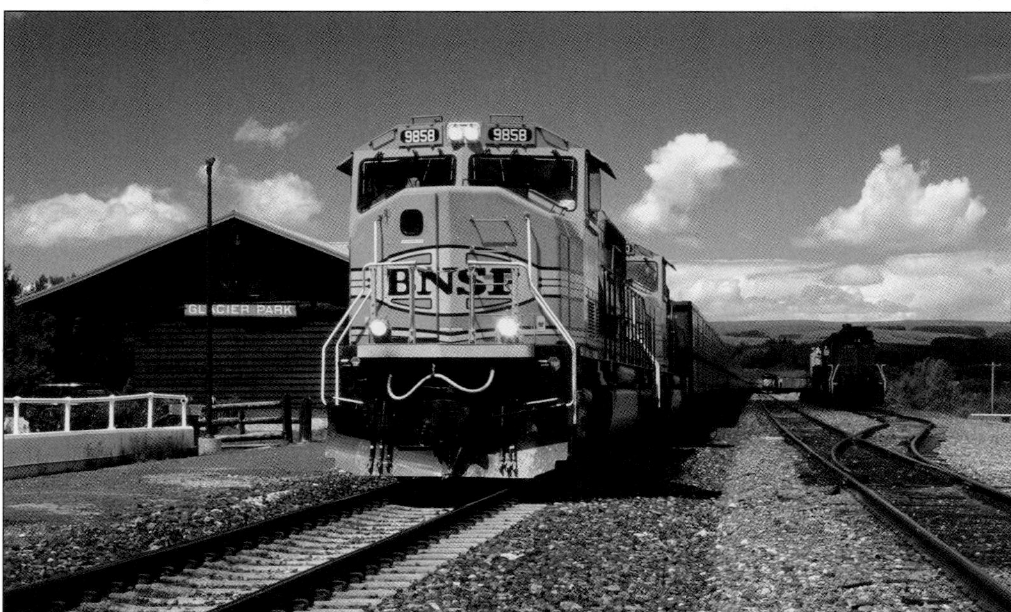

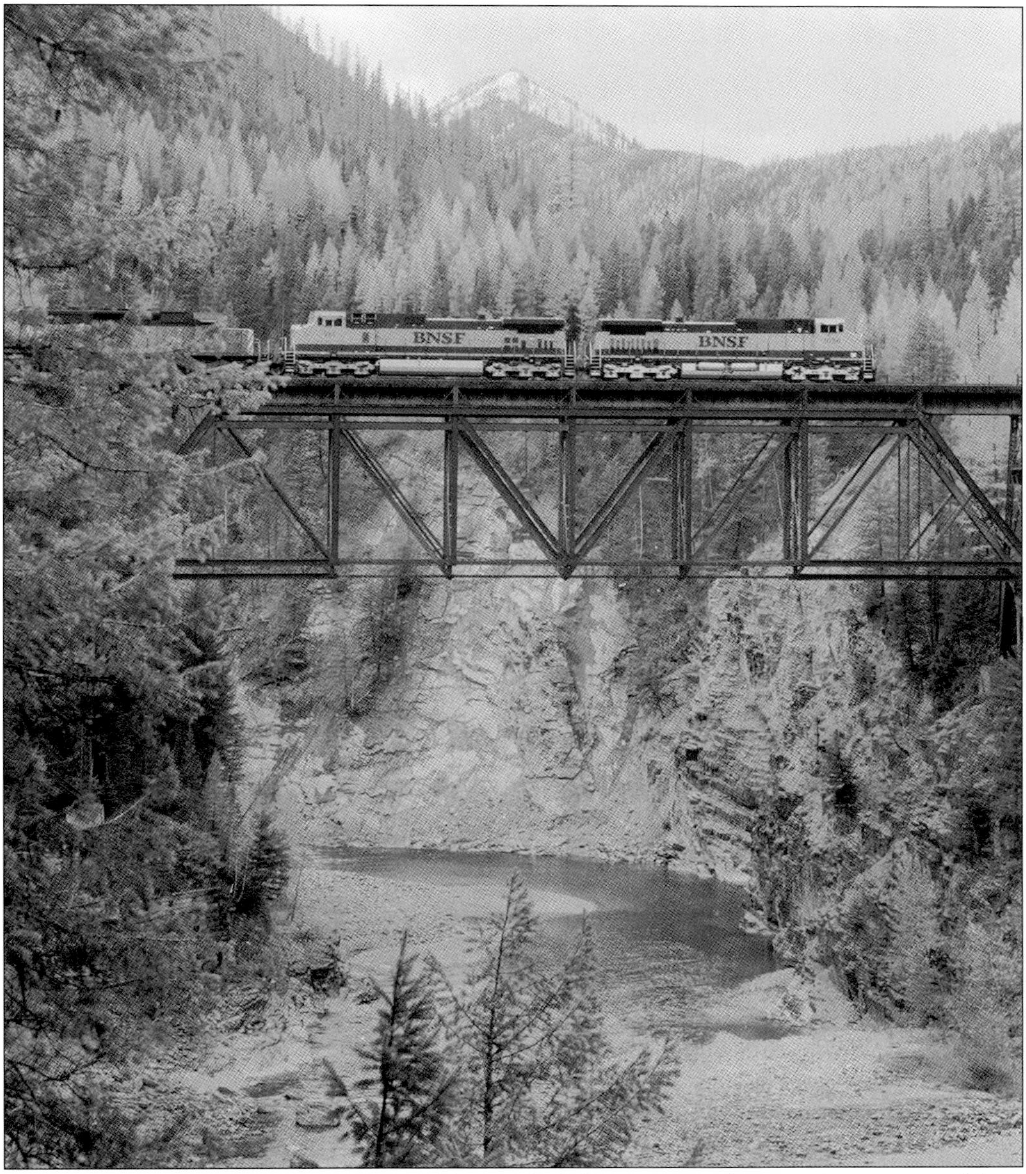

When James Jerome Hill, the "Empire Builder," pushed the Great Northern Railway westward from Pacific Junction, Montana, on August 1, 1890, he could not have imagined the impact his railroad would have on the economic and cultural development of the northern United States. Hill's goal of developing and expanding the resources of Montana, Idaho, and Washington depended on the discovery of a Rocky Mountain crossing lower in elevation and operationally superior to other transcontinental railways. Marias Pass allowed the Great Northern an opportunity to obtain and establish markets in agriculture, mining, and timber, while progressively upgrading infrastructure for increased safety and profit. Today, the Burlington Northern Santa Fe continues to improve profitability of rail traffic in Marias Pass, notably advancing from labor-intensive steam engines to energy-efficient General Electric C44-9W locomotives, as seen on the Java Trestle over the Middle Fork of the Flathead River. The Great Northern Railway's influence in Marias Pass will always reflect Jim Hill's vision—"Most men who have really lived have had, in some shape, their great adventure. This railway is mine." (Author's collection.)